Ask the Teacher :

A Practitioner's Guide to Teaching and Learning in the Diverse Classroom

Second Edition

Mark Ryan
Walden University

PEARSON

Boston | New York | San Francisco
Mexico City | Montreal | Toronto | London | Madrid | Munich | Paris
Hong Kong | Singapore | Tokyo | Cape Town | Sydney

Executive Editor and Publisher: *Stephen D. Dragin*
Series Editorial Assistant: *Katie Heimsoth*
Marketing Manager: *Weslie Sellinger*
Editorial Production Service: *Omegatype Typography, Inc.*
Composition Buyer: *Linda Cox*
Manufacturing Buyer: *Linda Morris*
Electronic Composition: *Omegatype Typography, Inc.*
Cover Administrator: *Linda Knowles*

For related titles and support materials, visit our online catalog at www.ablongman.com.

Between the time website information is gathered and then published, it is not unusual for some sites to have closed. Also, the transcription of URLs can result in typographical errors. The publisher would appreciate notification where these errors occur so that they may be corrected in subsequent editions.

ISBN-10: 0-205-52219-X
ISBN-13: 978-0-205-52219-4

Library of Congress Cataloging-in-Publication Data

Ryan, Mark
   Ask the teacher : a practitioner's guide to teaching and learning in the diverse classroom / Mark Ryan. — 2nd ed.
     p. cm.
   Includes index.
   ISBN-13: 978-0-205-52219-4 (pbk.)
   ISBN-10: 0-205-52219-X (pbk.)
   1. Teaching. 2. Multicultural education. I. Title.
   LB1025.3.R925   2008
   371.102—dc22

                              2007008468

Printed in the United States of America

10 9 8 7 6 5 4 3 2   11 10 09 08

All illustrations by Laura Berlin.

To a caring teacher—one who has been a model professional educator for over half a century.

*While encouraging her students
to empower themselves through music
and share their talents with others,
she continues to teach that
special harmony of heart, mind, and spirit.*

My mother, Jacqueline Jewel Ryan.

About
the Author

Mark Ryan has taught at all grade levels from elementary school classes to university seminars. He holds a Bachelor of Arts degree from the University of California at Santa Cruz, a Master of Education degree from the University of Puerto Rico at Rio Piedras, and a Doctorate in Higher and Adult Education from Arizona State University at Tempe. He was awarded the President's Distinguished Teaching Award at National University and has co-authored, with Dr. Peter Serdyukov, a book entitled *Writing Effective Lesson Plans: The 5-Star Approach.*

Contents

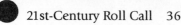

UNIT 2   Culture to Culture   35

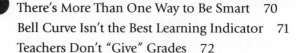

UNIT 3   The Why and How of Classroom Psychology   69

UNIT 4   Discipline: The Rules of the Road   103

unit 5 Testing: Getting It Right 131

unit 6 Curriculum: What to Teach 149

unit 7   Methodology: How to Teach   173

unIT 8 Learning to Read, Reading to Learn   201

unIT 9 Inclusion and Service: Yes, That Means Everyone   229

UNIT 10 Tools of the Trade   255

Preface

A*sk the Teacher* is fundamentally a work for the teacher candidate. In this foundations text, concise and coherent answers to questions about school and the learning process are gleaned from two distinct repositories of knowledge. The first is research-based learning theory, which articulates what we know about the associative nature of knowledge. The second is authentic professional classroom experience, which, over an extended period of time, allows for a fair assessment of a given learning theory's efficacy. Accordingly, it is the combination of learning theory and practical experience that provides a strong paradigm for formulating best practice, which in turn can produce the ultimate teaching goal: enhanced student academic achievement combined with social development.

An educational foundation text is at its very essence a work based on philosophical notions. An idea such as the notion of equal access for all students in a classroom, ever more culturally and linguistically diverse, is obviously value-laden. Values are crucial in both an individual and collective sense because they directly affect the quality of the professional practice. Professional principles embraced by the competent and caring teacher can be said to produce an ethic that drives practice.

Although the concept of educational foundations may exist as conceptually distinct from educational psychology, curriculum, methodology, educational technology or parent involvement, realistically the practitioner must understand how these components are linked in order to teach effectively.

This edition has eleven basic sections, but they exist only for the reader's convenience. From the first day of pedagogical study forward, questions about educational practice are inextricably connected to a multitude of elements that make up the eleven units.

By joining all of these elements in one book, the teacher candidate may begin to perceive the strong links among all of these critical rudimentary components. As new teachers will attest, one thing is certain from the first day of class forward; students will be asking questions from the opening minutes of class to the end of each school day concerning the entire gamut of an instructor's educational expertise.

It is clear that social change in the diverse classroom calls for an ever-increasing use of educational psychology in the areas of academic achievement and social development. Although school psychologists have an important role to play in this process, it is the classroom teacher who daily must come up with answers and down-to-earth solutions to both short-range and long-range challenges in the lives of students.

This text, then, is a practitioner's view of the kinds of educational procedures that have their roots in applied psychology. As a scientific field of study, psychology has a very special role to play in outlining a quality educational experience for all students. While psychology can point the way to effective educational theory and practice, it is the professional practitioner who must first avail himself or herself of the contemporary strategies psychology brings to modern challenges in classroom learning and social behavior. Only then can today's teacher incorporate those approaches into his or her instructional repertoire.

Formal compulsory education, once considered an "on campus" proposition, has now become conceptualized as a community issue. This has allowed teachers to also think in broader terms in working with families and other community resources to best serve their students' academic and social needs.

Psychology is one discipline identified with fluid care across school and community environments. The rich scientific base of applied psychology in education must be explored and understood if innovative change is to occur. As an empirical enterprise, psychology is uniquely suited to create, implement, and evaluate instructional, methodological, and assessment models to best serve the needs of a society with ever greater demands on the services schools are asked to provide.

Students, primarily through an informed teacher, can gain access to the most modern, empirically sound classroom practices. The practitioner's knowledge of applied psychology becomes the pathway to a new school model for a diverse society.

After a teacher has decided on a philosophical approach to education, used research-based applied psychology in the classroom, and presented an enriched core curriculum to all students, he or she must decide on a variety of methodological procedures and technological tools. In doing this, the practitioner can now foster an environment through methodological approaches appropriate to each student's learning style. Correspondingly, students can then approach distinct classroom challenges such as the opportunity to speak a second language, complete a mathematics problem, or collaborate on a cooperative team. Each of these diverse developmental tasks may require the instructor to present the material in a variety of ways, so that all may learn.

This, of course, reveals the complex nature of the learning process, a process that requires not only different methodological approaches but also different learning tools. One of those tools is the computer. Teaching and learning have undergone profound changes due to the use of computer technology. Shifts include a move from whole-class lessons to small-group instruction, from lecture and recitation to coaching, and from assessments centered on test performance to assessments based on projects and sustained effort.

In short, computer technology has changed teaching methodology in a profound sense. As we move to a more cooperative classroom where verbal thinking gives way to the integration of visual and verbal thinking, the "how to" questions become extremely relevant. Efforts the technologically literate teacher puts into contextualizing and modeling the core curriculum are at the heart of an informed methodological approach.

A century ago, John Dewey understood that how students are taught is as important as what they are taught. In the diverse classroom, methodological paradigms that accept the notion that effort produces ability are key to reaching the ultimate goal of enhanced student achievement and social growth for all students.

A child's self-understanding is constructed from experiences made up of his or her interactions with others. The most significant others in the life of a child are parents and immediate family members. As a child grows through adolescence and attends kindergarten through high school, he or she will only spend 9 percent of that time in a formalized school setting. The other 91 percent of the time is spent outside the school walls.

As every practitioner in the field of learning knows, education is always taking place. It is also clear to every enlightened educator that a child's first and most important teachers are the youngster's parents. Enlisting the parents in helping to provide a quality education should be a priority of every professional educator in elementary through secondary school. When parents and teachers work in harmony, both gain confidence in their modeling and teaching roles, leading to enhanced student achievement. Parents and teachers working as a team can foster awareness in children that schoolwork is valued. Thus, daily learning activities are seen as meaningful and rewarding.

Of course, sometimes the option of working with a parent does not exist. Many times a professional educator must work with a grandfather, grandmother, older brother, or older sister. Whoever the caring person is, the effect should be positive. This is due to the fact that all share a common bond, all care about the child in question, and all are genuinely dedicated to helping that youngster become successful. There can be no doubt that family involvement (i.e., guardians, grandparents, brothers, and sisters) in a child's education is vital for his or her academic success. The initial emphasis as well as the sustaining impetus in developing learners with high expectations, an expanding literacy, and a love for lifelong learning, occurs in the home.

The root of every professional educator's answer to the various classroom questions should emanate from a philosophical core. Being able to articulate consistent and caring answers is the quintessential task of a teacher. The answers given by a professional educator ought to demonstrate both expertise and enthusiasm for the subject matter. Hence, expert knowledge and a passion for learning are the very warp and woof of professional advice.

A straightforward answer to the teacher's quandary of, "How best can I serve these students?" in today's ever more diverse classroom can be confidently approached when based on a recognized competent and caring premise. Thus, formulating a philosophical core is of ultimate importance because it gives the professional educator a compass focused on the North Star of an enlightened foundation for professional practice.

ACKNOWLEDGMENTS

The author of any book has a lot of people to thank. At the top of the list is the late Dr. Roger Axford, my mentor at Arizona State University, who always encouraged me, as a graduate student, to seek the truth and write with conviction. The initial construction of the Q&A format for newspaper and radio distribution is due to the efforts of two wonderful editors, Jacqueline Ryan-Rojas and Melanie Rodriguez. Paul Gibbs Ryan has provided, through the years, critical promotion and design strategy.

I also wish to extend my gratitude to the many practitioners who helped during the preparation of this edition. I owe a great debt of appreciation to my colleagues from around the country who gave expert advice on each of the twelve sections of the book, particularly: Dr. Lauren Birney, Professor Carolyn Brannon, Dr. Jacque Caesar, Professor Anita Canul, Professor Eloise Cole, Dr. Prem S. Dean, Professor Lisa Haydt, Dr. Jack Housden, Professor James Hutcherson, Professor Gary Jimenez, Dr. Paul Johnson, Professor Celia Kelly, Dr. Katie Klinger, Professor Lance Larson, Dr. Lorraine Leavitt, Dr. Idrenne Lim-Alparaque, Professor John Luster, Professor Lois Lytle, Professor Carol Matthews, Dr. James Mbuva, Professor Patrick McElhaney, Dr. James Mitchell, Dr. Gwen Parry-Stowers, Professor Theresa Punzalan, Professor Kathlyn Roberts, Dr. Manuel R. Roman Jr., Professor Luz M. Salazar, Dr. Barbara Salice, Professor Rafael Sanchez, Professor Gordon Schott, Dr. Cynthia Schubert-Irastorza, Professor Kwame Seku, Professor Lana Sherman, Professor Juliet Shirr, Dr. Jacquelyn Spacek, Professor Maxine Stewart-Carlson, Professor Thomas Syage, Professor Richard Walsh, Professor Ann Weegar, Professor Lois Wilson, and Dr. Melvin Zeddies. I am grateful to the following reviewers for their helpful comments: Barbara Holmes, University of Charleston, and Mary C. Ware, State University of New York College at Cortland.

A very special thanks to Dr. Thomas MacCalla, Vice-President of Multicultural Affairs at National University for his guidance in the service learning component. Finally, I would like to express my appreciation to Dr. Clifford Russell of the Teacher Education Department at National University for his initial encouragement and enduring wisdom.

unit :1

Corner Stones

The Competent and Caring Teacher

Q: Why is it that some teachers give off vibes that they would rather be doing something else than working in a classroom? It seems that teachers who have enthusiasm and care about their students are harder and harder to find. What's going on here?

A: Teaching today requires that an instructor become a full-service professional. A teacher needs to be not only competent in his or her field, but also a genuinely caring person. Accordingly, the modern instructor must be an academic mentor and have answers to the broader social dilemmas students now face as we enter the 21st century.

Even with these overwhelming challenges, many teachers must work with out-of-date textbooks, large classes, limited administrative support, and a constant drumbeat of politically motivated criticism. To top it off, teachers make the lowest salaries of all professionals with similar levels of education.

Who would want such a job? Who would keep such a job? It has become a real problem. In surveys over the last twenty years, half of all teachers say they are seriously considering leaving the profession.

This bleak picture answers the first part of the question. The second half of the query mentions teachers who do have enthusiasm and care about their students.

These are the kind of teachers who always seem to have fun doing their job, and that spark of delight seems to be passed on to their students. Of course, part of the reason why this select group of educators appears so content with their profession may be in how they conceptualize their true value to the community.

It is difficult to argue that you can have great scientists, statesmen, physicians, clergy, or leaders in any vocational field without great teachers. In short, competent and caring teachers see themselves at the hub of a successful society.

Their attitude can be characterized as one of going after the lost sheep. For example, teachers who are truly committed to all students accept disruptive, unsuccessful, "castoff" students in their classes because, as professional educators, they believe they can make a difference with any pupil. They simply refuse to give up on a child.

In many ways, their attitude is not unlike that of the U.S. Marines. When the Marines are in combat and waiting for a helicopter to pick up the wounded, they have a saying—"No one is left behind."

Teachers who truly understand that their job is not to separate the wheat from the chaff (successful students from unsuccessful students) simply dedicate themselves to the proposition that all students can learn. This gives them a different view of their life's work and allows them to expand their professional role to do whatever it takes to make students successful.

The outcomes for these competent and caring teachers are different from the 50 percent who are thinking seriously about leaving the profession. Studies show a teacher's positive attitude serves as a model for students. This outlook then creates an atmosphere where learning can more readily take place. A positive series of teacher–student interactions becomes a powerful self-energizing learning cycle.

Correspondingly, research indicates that in this kind of learning and compassionate environment, students simply achieve more. For those who dedicate themselves to being competent and caring teachers, it is a profession of great public service and immense satisfaction. ●

U.S. Schools Need an Educational Philosophy for a Democratic Society

Q: Who decides what and how a school teaches? Every state has its own framework and guidelines, but where did those come from?

A: Of course, in a democratic society, ultimately the people decide the "what and how" of a school carrying out its mission by electing state superintendents and local board of education members. That being said, this question is a most interesting one because it is quite unusual today, in a sound-bite society, for policymakers to pay any attention to philosophy. Philosophy to many seems too distant, too complicated, and too abstruse to be viewed as critical to the day-to-day process of formal education.

This unfortunate point of view has been around for a long time. Over two millennia ago, a certain Greek philosopher told a tale about a ship's captain who spent a considerable amount of time stargazing. The crew of his ship thought him to be a do-nothing and even worse—a freeloader. The philosopher pointed out that without the efforts of the captain (who was unbeknownst to the sailors navigating by the stars), the crew would wander aimlessly at sea. The philosopher,

Plato (c428–347 BC), argued the need to understand the big picture—that which we call the "what and the how."

Perhaps the foremost educational philosopher in the United States was John Dewey (1859–1952). Dewey was interested, as a philosopher and a psychologist, in observing empirical evidence to evaluate different educational theories. He traveled and studied the educational systems of Turkey, Mexico, China, Japan, and Russia. He also tested his principles in education at the Laboratory School sponsored by the University of Chicago.

Dewey came to the conclusion that authoritarian methods provided a poor educational model for children growing up in a democratic society. He favored education through various activities (learning by doing), and believed education should prepare a student to become a problem solver and encourage the student to define the boundaries of a democratic society.

Like Plato's ship captain, Dewey cared (as we should care) about finding a way to reach a certain destination. In Dewey's case, his goal was a self-directed, educated citizenry, the foundation of a vibrant democratic society. ●

What Early Schools Taught

Q: What did the first schools teach, and when and where did school start?

A: The first schools we know of in recorded history taught religion and the traditions of their people. For example, in Egypt, the ancient temple schools taught religion in addition to mathematics, architecture and the sciences. In India, education in ancient times was administered by the priests. The Buddhist doctrines they taught were learned in their schools by Chinese scholars. As a result of this educational experience, the teachings of Buddha were spread to many parts of Asia. The Chinese teachers also passed on many of the teachings of Confucius and Lao-tzu, along with a system of civil service examinations that lasted more than 4,000 years.

Finally, the Bible and the Talmud were the fundamental sources of information for the ancient Jewish people. Subjects urged by the Talmud included swimming and the study of foreign language, as well as religious instruction.

These schools may not have had bells, chalkboards, and cafeteria lunches, but they had many of the aims and methods that we still employ, even in the most modern of schools. ●

How Public Education Began

Q: How did public education start in the United States? Why is it that today every discussion about public schools becomes so political?

A: The idea of public education began shortly after the American Revolution. However, public schools, or "common schools" as they were called, were not widely established until about 75 years after the birth of the United States. From colonial times to the early 19th century, education was unsystematic. Depending on your social status or church membership, education could be freely attained or denied altogether.

Significantly, the first proponents of public education reasoned that the new democracy needed to educate all its children. Public schools were to be organized and financed by the states. Public education, as a democratic institution, has been a political decision from the very outset. The founders of the American democracy viewed public education as critical to the nation's success. They believed an educated citizenry would understand and act on the issues of the day, use the vote, and protect its freedoms.

This deep and fundamental belief was enunciated by leaders such as Thomas Jefferson, who wrote in 1787: "Above all things, I hope the education of the common people will be attended to, convinced that on this good sense we may rely with the most security for the preservation of a due degree of liberty." ●

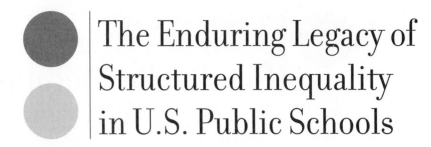

The Enduring Legacy of Structured Inequality in U.S. Public Schools

Q: What is the early history of schooling in the United States, and what traditions still remain in the contemporary classroom?

A: American public education has traditionally experienced conflicting value systems. Deeply held beliefs premised on a perception of inclusion emanate from a web of connections embracing a vibrant democracy and an educated citizenry. These lofty ideals go hand in hand with the concepts of personal and societal improvement. This notion of inclusion originating from a dynamic faith in the learning process, seen as vital to a participatory democracy, can be traced to the beginning of the American Republic.

Nevertheless, there is an opposite view in the United States, also genuine—that of exclusion, the vision of a type of intellectual meritocracy, a traditional biosocietal pecking order justified and enabled by the use of empirical data to efficiently categorize society into a layered hierarchy. The idea of exclusion grew out of the 18th- and 19th-century ideas of racial superiority that were adapted into philosophical notions such as Social Darwinism. Later exclusion, both in law and custom, was promoted and institutionally implemented by means of human intelligence test-based findings in the 20th and 21st centuries.

Accordingly, from de jure and *de facto* segregation to IQ rankings and standardized evaluations, the notion of exclusion to limit or effectively bar access to certain aspects of public education has been executed methodically over the last century.

Tracking (i.e., separating students into rigid homogenous groups based on perceived ability) comes from the tradition of exclusion. Within the historic dialectic between the philosophies of inclusion and exclusion one encounters a fundamental paradox: public education that continually postures to be ever more inclusive while perpetuating an exclusive system of structured inequality.

The history of public education in the United States may be viewed as a constant struggle between those who consistently espouse a message of hope and inclusion and those who systematically plan for the layered hierarchies of exclusion. If promoting the common good by strengthening participatory democracy via an educated citizenry through the public schools has become, over time and trials, a deeply held American conviction reflecting the nation's core values, this struggle must be resolved.

Adlai Stevenson once observed in the mid-20th century that, "The most American thing about America is the free common school system." The remark, made in a 1948 speech, was surely meant to applaud the idea of a free public school system—a common school where every citizen is accepted and the American democracy is celebrated. Yet today, just as in the Pledge of Allegiance with the often recited egalitarian promise of "liberty and justice for all," the assurance of an equal educational opportunity for every citizen remains not only an unfulfilled goal—but in danger of becoming an empty slogan. Viewed from the reality of public education at present, a more conflicted (if unintended) yet more historically accurate meaning may be gleaned from Stevenson's remark.

Today tracking is widespread in U.S. public schools. There can be little question that the differences in the course-specific tracks students take (e.g., advanced versus regular or remedial offerings), especially in math, science, and foreign language, have a profound impact on student scores in the current high stakes testing environment.

Research indicates that the more rigorous the curriculum, the greater the opportunity for student achievement and consequently the higher the standardized test score. Those qualifying test scores, the product of student work based to a great extent on exposure to enriched curricular content and concepts, can virtually open or close the door to a college education.

Who succeeds and who is left behind in today's competitive rankings-based society is subject all too often to a quantitative measure taken on an unbalanced playing field. To understand the enduring legacy of structured inequality within the U.S. educational experience demands an examination of traditional perspectives, which continue to guide the public school at the beginning of the 21st century. ●

Philosophical Roots of American Education

Q: What are the philosophical roots of American education?

A: Although the contemporary public school is a direct descendent of the mid-19th-century common school (supported by property taxes, tuition-free, open to all (white) children, state regulated with local control), the philosophical root of this institution goes back to the 18th century. Benjamin Franklin wrote in 1749, "The good Education of Youth has been esteemed by wise Men in all Ages, as the surest Foundation of the Happiness both of private Families and of Common-wealths."

It was Thomas Jefferson who in 1778 proposed to the Virginia Assembly "A Bill for the More General Diffusion of Knowledge" (subsequently voted down three times between 1779 and 1817). The bill promoted the concept of education that aimed to provide a natural aristocracy for the American experiment in democracy. Jefferson (1814) promoted a two-tiered educational system, with different tracks for "the laboring and the learned." Moreover, the Jeffersonian vision of the common school, universal free education of every (white) boy for three years, and then a university education for the elite of this group, was revolutionary for the times: "By this means twenty of the best geniuses will be raked from the rubbish annually, and be instructed at the public expense" (Jefferson, 1787).

Significantly, Jefferson's ideas are a product of a conflicted sociopolitical reality. Jefferson was a slave owner (said to own over 200 slaves) who at the same time believed in individual freedom and a type of intellectual meritocracy. During Jefferson's lifetime slavery was sustained by brutal force. Unlike George Washington, Jefferson never freed his slaves. He seemed quite willing to profit from the bondage of others. Jefferson's dual nature is striking. Here was a man who wrote passionately about liberty and independence but who nevertheless had a personal socioeconomic acceptance of slavery, a practice which excluded an entire race of people (estimated at 20 percent of the population at that time) from the benefits of liberty—and the educational opportunities needed to sustain a participatory democracy.

Revolutionary for the time, yet divisive in nature, Jefferson's twin schoolhouse ideals: a more inclusive brand of universal education and the inherently exclusive notion that "geniuses will be raked from the rubbish," is an expression of classic American pedagogical dualism. Although spreading the first glimmer of hope and inclusion for some who had been traditionally shut out of a formal education, it is notable that his utopian vision did not include the same opportunities for women (there was a three-year limit to school for girls). Correspondingly, consistent with Jefferson's practice of holding slaves, people of color were not considered for formal schooling of any kind; indeed, it was among the gravest offenses to teach African Americans to read and write. Thus the concept of individual freedom in the reality of the late 18th century excluded the majority of the population and was restricted to freedom for certain individuals.

In many ways Jefferson's plea for more schooling embodies a recurring schizophrenia in American education. There is the clear impulse for the hopeful notion of inclusion—the egalitarian side of the Jeffersonian mind promoting education for all "without regards to wealth, birth, or accidental condition." It is an argument that rhetorically soars in the laudatory quest for an informed democracy. Jefferson's writings are replete with the stated conviction that democracy can best function with an educated citizenry. In

an 1816 letter to Colonel Charles Yancy, Jefferson intones, "If a nation expects to be ignorant and free, in a state of civilization, it expects what never was and never will be." Notwithstanding Jefferson's eloquent instruction that public education is imperative in securing and maintaining liberty, one is also presented with the dehumanizing image of clearing away the "rubbish," presumably producing a strain of students to become a merit-based elite.

Although Jefferson's words and practices may seem to some inconsistent or even misunderstood within the context of our times, the unambiguous historical record of exclusion toward all but certain white males begs for understanding the fundamental rationale of those 18th-century leaders (e.g., attendees at the Constitutional Convention of 1789) who freely chose to make a distinction between races.

In Jefferson's case it could be argued that his opinions were not (solely) based on blind bigotry or the avarice of slave owners, but a far more seductive theory that stems from 18th-century study of natural history. Based on ideas of hierarchies in nature, Jefferson expresses among his many concerns about race relations a "suspicion" that his own race was naturally superior. Thus among the intelligencia of that time there was a kind of naturally designed discrimination. This type of racism based on empirical observation and naive extrapolation took root early on American soil.

From its very beginning and from its best and brightest intellectuals there is a tradition in American civic institutions in general and American public education in particular of accepting forms of structured inequality—nurtured in racist, sexist and classist law and custom that has existed for hundreds of years and continues to shape and skew society by way of public schools into the 21st century. ●

The Contemporary Debate in 21st-Century American Education

Q: What is the general condition of American education today in terms of racial diversity and an equal opportunity for a quality education?

A: Current scholars such as Gary Orfield and Jonathan Kozol have entered into a vigorous civil discussion on the reality of the resegregation of U.S. public schools. Since the landmark decision of *Brown v. the Board of Education of Topeka* in 1954, meant to integrate the public schools, a movement toward resegregation fueled by Supreme Court decisions from 1974 and into the 1990s, clearly continues to take place as schools become more and more racially isolated.

In the 1974 case of *Milliken v. Bradley* the Supreme Court emphasized the importance of local control over the operation of schools. Significantly, it posited that desegregation, "in the sense of dismantling a dual school system," did not necessitate "any particular racial balance in each school, grade or classroom." In overturning a previous district court ruling by a 5-to-4 decision, the Supreme Court held that the district court's remedy (busing students to achieve racial balance) was "wholly impermissible" and not justified by 1954 case of *Brown v. Board of Education*.

A human link between *Brown v. Board of Education* and *Milliken v. Bradley* was literally embodied in Thurgood Marshall. In 1954 Marshall, who was an attorney for the NAACP Legal Defense Fund, argued and prevailed in a case for the inclusion of African American students into a formerly segregated school district. A generation later he was in the minority as a Supreme Court judge. The 1974 decision (dealing with transporting students between the inner city of Detroit and the more affluent suburbs to achieve racial balance) effectively ended busing as a desegregation tool and as a direct result returned the public schools to a previous pattern of court-sanctioned racial exclusivity. At the time Marshall judged that in the short run it might seem easier for the court to permit a city to divide itself into white and black schools, but sensed that ultimately the American people would regret it. He concluded, "For unless our children begin to learn together, there is little hope that our people will ever learn to live together."

Census data plainly demonstrate that the schools of the early 21st century are more racially and economically isolated than they have been since the 1960s and as a consequence are becoming increasingly unequal. Kozol's writings unmistakably reveal a nation that has simply, if stealthily, reaccepted the original 18th-century status quo of separate and unequal—a tangible injustice to the 21st century's most vulnerable demographic—poor children. Those educators who desire a more inclusive school and society and genuinely wish to dispatch racism, sexism, and classism make the case that a transparent societal regression has occurred.

Orfield, Kozol, and others have constructed from the historical record convincing demographic evidence that racism continues to influence and plainly organizes society via the school to sustain and perpetuate tangible social injustice. Yet in the first decade of the 21st century there is no popular political will to integrate the schools.

Thus, in terms of the body politic at the beginning of the 21st century, the reality of separate and unequal goes virtually unquestioned. Yet the problem is even more ingrained in the public school system than typical school-to-school segregation. In fact, an easily identifiable segregation, which is a form of *intraschool* tracking (i.e., schools in the same or neighboring school districts which have strikingly different racial populations) could end tomorrow, and *interschool* tracking (i.e., grouping students within the same school into clearly superior and inferior academic tracks) with its obvious socioeconomic and racial divides would still preserve the enduring legacy of exclusion in America's public schools and virtually nullify the effects of integration.

It has been argued that the school within a school model is a recipe for segregation. For geographical proximity (students attending the same integrated school) is no guarantor of an equal educational opportunity if all students are not taking the most enriched courses. In other words students from diverse backgrounds need the intellectual challenge of working together to form respect and develop friendships based on a public school experience that is *common* in the most democratic sense of that word.

Those who propose inclusion argue that since tracking is so widespread—existing in 80 to 90 percent of all public schools—educational progress has been and will continue to be substantially impeded. Those who view inclusion as being an unfulfilled promise hold that public schools practice a form of social stratification via a layered hierarchy that in essence determines *who gets what—and why they get it.*

Certain individuals and groups are seen to traditionally promote, implement, and enforce a homogeneous-elite model (i.e., white as opposed to nonwhite, wealthy as opposed to poor, English-speaking as opposed to non–English-speaking); therefore, the children of the privileged are awarded the best curricular options (e.g., honors and/or advanced classes). The model is thus regenerated.

Significantly, inequality may or may not be accepted by most in the society; however, supported by economic reality, it is has been codified to become accepted custom. An underlying argument for exclusion appears to be that "excellence in education" is more important than racial equality or gender equity. Those who believe in inclusion as imperative see that idea as a false dichotomy. They would posit, in general, that in a participatory democracy there can be no excellence in the classroom without equality and equity. Specifically, they would articulate that until tracking is abolished the cavalcade of well-intentioned ideas and programs from Jefferson's "A Bill for the More General Diffusion of Knowledge" to Bush's "No Child Left Behind" will be continued evidence of mighty efforts that produced mighty little.

The conflicted American psyche struggles each generation with the key issue that has always been central to the fundamental rationale of the very existence of the American Republic, one of genuine social justice for all people residing in the nation. As long as tracking is the preferred pedagogical option in the public schools—the last great meeting place of the our democracy, American public education is destined to continue the traditional paradox—matching the impulse of inclusion to the reality of exclusion, yielding an enduring legacy of structured inequality. ●

How Teachers Stay Good

Q: With all the things teachers have to put up with nowadays, how can they keep up with all the changes? From computers to teaching kids who arrive at the door speaking no English, how are teachers supposed to do their job? How can teachers stay relevant and interested?

A: Academic expectations for all students are increasing on a local, state, and national level. At the same time, our country's schools are more ethnically and linguistically diverse than at any time in our nearly two-and-a-quarter centuries of existence.

Continued improvement of a teacher's professional skills and the opportunity to acquire the knowledge needed to instruct and prepare all U.S. students for the next century are critical. As schools transform themselves into learning centers for the 21st century, it is clear that the effectiveness of any school will be measured by a faculty that is both caring and competent.

Professional development programs from preservice to in-service must evolve a new model to better serve teachers from the novice to the advanced practitioner level. Teacher education must be thought of in terms of lifelong learning that extends from the first day in the profession until retirement.

The entire concept of what has been called "staff development" must be changed. The typical staff development experience, such as one-shot workshops or one-time conferences, clearly lacks the kind of long-term sequenced training needed to build new strategies for the diverse challenges schools of today and tomorrow must face.

What is needed is "action research." That is, a program under the auspices of a school of education at a college or university where classroom teachers in the role of researchers identify questions that interest them. In order for this to happen, new relationships between schools of education and school districts must be formed.

A well-trained, enthusiastic university faculty can present an extensive, ongoing training program constructed on a solid theoretical basis to help teachers plan, implement, and evaluate their research designs. The teachers themselves conduct a systematic inquiry in their schools about their students. They report their findings back to the school of education in the form of field studies.

Sound relevant? Sound interesting? That is what professional development is all about.

As teachers participate year after year in these programs, university continuing-education credit would eventually and incrementally add up to increased salary and enhanced teaching credentials for these more highly trained professionals. Because of this ongoing program, school districts could greatly reduce or even eliminate waivers—a district practice in which instructors of sometimes dubious competency are given teaching responsibilities due to the lack of qualified teachers.

In the current state of educational reform, professional development of teachers has taken on a new urgency. The main goal of teachers' enhanced caring and competency must be in promoting successful student learning. Educational reform depends on continual professional development programs that establish an environment where teachers choose to be empowered to investigate and construct solution sets to the challenges faced in the schools of the 21st century. ●

The Best Way to Teach a Class

Q: What is the best way for a teacher to teach class?

A: The best approach in the classroom has three separate components. First, there must be a rich curriculum administered to all students. The lecture and readings given to students must be of the highest quality. A good teacher always teaches to the highest level of the class and has the highest expectations for all students.

Second, a peer-review component must be established. Students should be put in a position to give positive input to fellow students. This student-to-student help is a win-win situation. The student who is in most need of help can access it, while the student giving the help reinforces what he or she already knows.

Third, time must be set aside for individualized education. For example, a teacher might decide not to accept essays or reports until she has sat down and reviewed them with each student face to face, line by line, idea by idea.

Remember, a teacher may be an English teacher, a math teacher, or a history teacher, but she is really a teacher of human beings. Individualized education gives the teacher a chance to establish a personal rapport, and gives the student the kind of help he or she needs most on a one-to-one formal basis. ●

Become a Nurturing Teacher

Q: How can you help students who seem to go from class to class in high school experiencing either boredom or frustration? People say there is no quick fix, but that is precisely what is needed. How can these students become interested in school to do better and learn more?

A: This is a tall order. However, the following two suggestions can make a significant difference.

First, become a nurturing teacher who believes that every student can be successful. You can become this type of teacher by remembering that:

- Learning is broken down into logically sequenced units of about two weeks in duration.

- Students are tested at the end of each unit.

- Alternative assessment and individual attention are given for students who do not master first-time tests.

- Students work at their own pace.

- Real rapport with students through consistent individual attention is imperative.

Second, be sure you use a metacognitive approach. Simply stated, teach the students not just what to learn, but how to learn. Instead of asking the question,

"What did you learn today?" you should ask, "How did you think about that?"

Become a nurturing teacher who practices a form of mastery learning and who teaches students how to learn, and students might well find school an interesting and compelling place to be. ●

Mentors Help Students Succeed at High School

Q: What is the answer for the many first-year high school students who just don't adapt to school at this level? At some schools, more than half of the freshmen fail at least one out of six classes in their first semester. Are there any fresh solutions, other than just telling kids to study harder?

A: One response to the problem is volunteer mentorship on a large scale. This program has three steps.

- First, the students with low academic achievement must be identified. A quick trip to the registrar's office should do the trick.

- Second, the school staff is asked to contribute their time and talents. This means that teachers, secretaries, principals, counselors, school police, custodians, and perhaps senior honor students are asked to donate their time to mentor a single student.

- Third, consistent activities before school, at lunch, or after school are scheduled between mentor and student. Field trips, brown bag lunches, or study sessions can make up the mix of valuable experiences between mentor and student.

The result is a kind of safety net which lets the student know that he or she is valued and has a friend who cares. Sometimes a struggling student has needs which range from immediate help with coping skills to consistent instruction in basic skills. Whatever the case, just knowing someone cares, is patient, and "is on your side" can make a significant positive change in the academic direction of a young student. ●

Why Are Some Teachers Better Than Others?

Q: Why are some teachers so much better than others? How can a parent tell if his child's new teacher is one of the better ones?

A: When judging a teacher, you might think the first consideration would be the teacher's competency in the subject being taught. Because almost all teachers are credentialed in a certain field of study, it would be most improbable to find a teacher who was not competent in his or her field.

That is not to say that a curricular mismatch never occurs. Mismatches are quite possible when schools scramble to find substitute teachers. For example, if a monolingual English instructor had to substitute teach for the regular Spanish instructor, we could agree that the English teacher was not competent to teach in that situation.

Yet, competency aside, there are teachers who are demonstrably better than others. The reason is that teachers do not simply teach English or history or science—they teach human beings. In order to be a good teacher, one must be able to deal success-

fully with students. The teacher's feelings about the students are crucial. A professional educator must be prepared to accept both the student's weaknesses and strengths in order to teach the whole child.

So how can a parent tell if a teacher is doing the job? See how many of the following attributes the teacher possesses in order to determine if a teacher makes the grade:

- Sends home a course syllabus (what is to be taught in the upcoming term).

- Phones your home consistently (at least once a month) to talk about your child's progress and/or problems.

- Does not assign "disposable work." Keeps all work in a portfolio so you can inspect your child's developmental progress.

- Has an objective grading policy that is clear and based on the individual student's development—not an artificial curve.

- Never uses sarcasm in class and accepts different cultural styles. The teacher, through word and action, should celebrate diversity.

- Makes himself or herself available, by appointment, before or after school for consultation.

- Keeps up to date with current research in the field. You can easily find this out by asking the teacher why he or she teaches a certain way.

- Appears cheerful in class. A parent has the right to visit the class. A teacher who loves what he or she is doing appears positive, at ease, and well-adjusted.

- Works individually with students. Many "teachable moments" arrive when the teacher can review work with the student one-on-one, line by line, face to face.

- Has the affection and respect of the students. After all, the learners' academic and social growth is affected by their attitude toward their teacher.

Score card:

10–9:	A master teacher
8–7:	A good teacher
6–5:	A mediocre teacher
4–0:	Time to ask for a transfer

We should expect our teachers to be more than just competent in their fields. They must be warm, success-oriented people who have the social skills to work with students and share the wonder and excitement of learning. ●

A Classroom Conducive to Learning

Q: Too many classrooms today appear to be mismanaged. How can a teacher make the classroom more conducive to learning?

A: Having an environment suitable for learning is a top priority for any teacher at any level. Classrooms that are constantly dealing with interruptions, from any quarter, result in a lack of academic focus and subsequent learning.

To find out if a classroom is managed to be conducive to learning observe whether the following behaviors are seen (this can be done as a student teacher):

- Does the teacher greet students as they enter the classroom? Calling a student by name seems like a simple thing to

do, but it can have a positive impact in terms of feeling welcome.

- Does the teacher appear to be organized? For example, is there an outline of the day's activities or the subjects to be learned on the board?

- Does the teacher introduce new material to the class with enthusiasm and interest? Disruptive class activity can occur when a student, perhaps reading on his or her own, "can't get it" and then vents his frustration with unacceptable behavior.

- When a student "goofs off," does the teacher chide him or her in front of the class? Berating a student in the presence of all is very poor class management.

A student should be admonished privately to change their behavior.

If you do not observe these behaviors, the classroom is probably not as conducive to learning as it should be.

An excellent way to manage your students is to explain the "culture of a classroom" to them. You can ask students what kind of classroom they want during the first days of class. The students can then propose and select rules for the classroom.

Often the rules students propose and eventually choose are even stricter than those you would select. In any case, as a teacher, you will have consensus and class "buy-in" of the notion that the classroom is a place of common courtesy, a sense of a common mission, and—most of all—a scholastic enterprise. ●

Professional Development: Who Teaches the Teachers?

Q: With all of the changes now taking place in school, who is teaching the teachers? How does all the new knowledge and new ways to teach kids find its way to teachers who are already teaching in the classroom?

A: One thing is certain: continued improvement of a classroom teacher's professional skills, needed to teach all students for this new century, is imperative.

Without a doubt, academic expectations for all students are growing at the school, district, state, and national level. Correspondingly, our nation's schools are each day more ethnically and linguistically diverse than at any time in the last two centuries of our country's history.

As classrooms evolve into learning centers for the 21st century, it is clear that a faculty that is both competent and caring will be the measure of the effectiveness of any school. Unfortunately, the old 20th-century model of professional development traditionally followed by school districts has not proven effective.

Historically, school districts have lacked the faculty of experts, the warehouse of courses, and the essential continuity in training to produce verifiable improvement in what students are taught and how they are taught (i.e., curriculum and methodology). The traditional staff development experience (e.g., one-shot workshops, one-time conferences) has an inherent flaw—a lack of continuity.

A model, based on action research (teachers using new approaches and reporting on their efficacy), is needed to build new strategies and techniques for the diverse challenges of the school of today and of tomorrow. What is called for is increased collaboration among colleges of education, state departments of education, and school districts.

Colleges of education are the logical institutions to provide the core of experts, the wealth of courses, and the continuity exhibited by graduate programs. Of course, colleges of education have always been able to supply fundamentally what is needed for teacher professional development programs.

Why haven't schools availed themselves of this resource? School districts have wanted to control staff development for a variety of reasons. Thus, school districts have not traditionally offered the option of prepaid courses to teachers to allow them to grow in the field of education the way private industry pays for its employees to increase their expertise.

Private industry views professional development courses (a growing number of them online) as an investment; school districts historically have not invested in a similar manner. If school districts continue to lag in staff development efforts, teachers' unions should ask for guaranteed prepaid online university courses as a bargaining position during contract negotiations. The new online models could make profound changes in the conceptual core of professional development.

Whatever new form of staff development evolves, it must be thought of in terms of lifelong learning that extends from the first day in the profession to the last day on the job. In an ever-changing technological and diverse society, the continuous training of faculty is essential if the needed systemic educational reforms of the 21st century are to succeed. ●

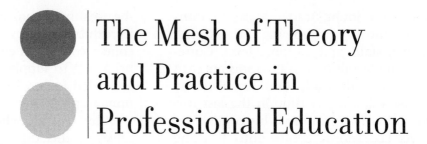

The Mesh of Theory and Practice in Professional Education

Q: What is the best way to teach adults new information they need to know in order to enter a profession?

A: Anytime we encourage adult learners to critically examine the profession to which they aspire, we are off to a good start. Every career, whether it is medicine, law, education, or any other professional endeavor, continues to go through inevitable periods of change. A professional development program that expands adult capacity using both theory and practice is an excellent way to prepare for a new career.

A learning agenda that centers on reflection and action inherently synthesizes new knowledge. Challenges—both old and new—are identified, and solutions are proposed. What is created is a community of co-researchers and co-learners. These candidates, in a given profession, learn not just from theoretical constructs, but also from practical experiences.

One approach to bringing aspirants of various vocations into contact with the everyday challenges of a particular profession is the field experience method. For example, medical students serve internships and residencies in order to observe and work with actual patients. Likewise, students in a teacher education program should work with actual (preschool through twelfth grade) students, teachers, curricula, and methodological strategies, in actual school settings.

These field experiences can be of great help to those who hope to become teachers. Those taking teacher preservice programs can participate in the classroom by tutoring individuals, working with small groups of students, preparing curricular materials, grading student projects, and recording classroom management policies that really work.

There is recent research in teacher education programs that indicates that the more field experiences the better. A study of nearly 2,000 teacher candidates in the mid 1990s indicated that less than 5 percent of them who were prepared through field-based programs had left the profession, as compared to a 12 percent attrition rate of those prepared in traditional programs.

The rationale for field-based programs is rooted in the notion that the meshing of theory and practice forms a strong learning paradigm. For the adult learner who wishes to become an adult practitioner, a collaborative effort between universities and practitioners to increase the number of authentic field experiences would appear to be the best learning model for those preparing for a lifetime of professional service. ●

Programs for At-Risk Students Do Pay Off

Q: Where is the best place to spend money on education? It seems every school is always pleading poverty, but there is only so much money to go around. Where can the public get the most bang for its education buck?

A: More than many other educational innovations, quality programs for preschool children living in poverty (e.g., Head Start programs) seem to give a greater return on an initial investment. Studies following these children, who were at special risk of failure, appear to document the lasting benefits of these early childhood programs. In judging the effects of these programs, it was found the children had significantly better intellectual performance than other children who lacked such a quality preschool experience, even two years after the program ended.

In an analysis of 50 Head Start students, immediate positive gains in intellectual and socioemotional performance and overall health lasted several years after children had finished the program. There is also concrete evidence that fewer program participants than nonparticipants, in a matched control group, were ever placed in special education classes. Furthermore, the program group had a significantly higher high school graduation rate than the no-program group.

In terms of a program like Head Start paying for itself, listen to this. Men who had been Head Start participants earn more money, have fewer arrests, and are more likely to own a home than men who had not participated in the program.

A systematic analysis of the costs and benefits yields the following long-range outcomes for program participants:

- Savings in schooling, due to lower special education costs
- Higher taxes paid by participants, based on their higher earnings
- Savings in welfare assistance
- Savings to the criminal justice system and to potential victims of crimes

Add it all up and we find that preschool programs for children living in poverty have a wonderful return on investment. How much? How about more than $7 of return for every $1 invested! Some may say that spending money on these young children is purely speculative. To me, in terms of "bang for the buck," it is one of the best investments that a community can make. ●

Quality of Charter Schools Depends on Many Factors

Q: Have charter schools been proven to be better than the regular public schools?

A: First, let's define what a charter school is; then we can examine whether or not they are providing a high quality of education. Charter schools, which do not have the regulatory constraints imposed on conventional public schools, are created and managed by different groups of people depending on the specific school site. The entity involved in running such a school could be any of the following: for-profit businesses, nonprofit organizations, parents, teachers, or community and/or business leaders.

Twenty-five states now have publicly funded independent public schools chartered by a school district or a state department of education. No single study has attempted to evaluate the hundreds of charter schools in the nation on any single measure of effectiveness. However, surveys have been taken on students attending the schools and instructors teaching the students. The results are interesting.

Charters are attracting urban students, but not always the most vulnerable minority or disadvantaged students. Although charters cannot charge tuition, they can impose fees, and some aggressively solicit contributions from families. There is concern that the pressure to raise funds may make charter schools inaccessible to low-income families.

Charters also have higher rates of parent involvement than other schools. There is obviously a great advantage in, and universal support for, encouraging parents to participate in their children's education. Innovations, such as regularly scheduled parent–child activities and habitual homework assignments that require parent participation, are part of this proactive parent involvement model.

One downside in asking for full parent participation is that some parents feel unable to contribute to their children's education. This is especially true when a charter school contractually requires parent involvement. Research indicates that parents culturally conditioned to leave their youngster's education exclusively in the hands of the school are frequently discouraged from enrolling their children in a charter school.

As for the teachers of charter schools, they have the opportunity to become school "owners" rather than just salaried employees. It is argued that with increased responsibility and commensurate authority will come increased professionalism. Some charters are exempt from the hiring requirements of other public schools and from teacher union contracts. There is a legitimate question whether some charter schools that hire unlicensed instructors at a lower wage can provide the best faculty for students.

Certainly the goal for every school should be to hire teachers who are competent, caring, and certificated. Although the ability of charter schools to provide a better educational model has not been proven, it has set off a flurry of innovations and has welcomed teachers, parents, and the public at large into a new process—all in support of education. ●

Small-Scale Schools Offer a Consistently Better Education

Q: With all the classroom disorder, rude behavior, drug use, and violence in today's schools, isn't there a better way to educate kids? Are there any kinds of schools that are free from the type of senseless acts of violence and vandalism that we read about in the newspaper every day?

A: Many researchers have concluded that small-scale schools (no more than 400 to 500 students per school) are best in terms of positive social effects on youngsters, kindergarten through high school. Before listing the social advantages of small-scale schools, it's important to note that academic student achievement in small schools is equal, if not superior to, scholastic achievement in large schools (enrollment of 2,000 or more).

The research on the social effects of school size shows that compared to students in large schools, students in small schools:

1. Experience an increase in social bonding to both school and teachers
2. Participate at a higher rate in extracurricular activities
3. Have higher attendance rates
4. Have lower dropout rates
5. Are less likely to steal, use drugs, or exhibit aggressive behavior
6. Have a lower rate of gang participation
7. Are less likely to vandalize or commit acts of theft
8. Have higher rates of parent involvement

Smaller schools seem to provide a better school environment because the people in those schools come to know each other and therefore care more about others on campus.

Learning activities in small schools tend to be more individualized, and subject matter content is more integrated. In addition, a greater emphasis on multi-age and cooperative grouping, along with team teaching, appears to bring about a more inclusive and accepting atmosphere.

Just a note about educational equity: the states with the largest schools and school districts have the lowest academic achievement and the poorest social outcomes. Minority students tend to populate these large schools. The research is clear; students who stand to benefit most from small schools are economically disadvantaged students and minority students. Large schools are contrary to the best interests of minority students in particular.

Unfortunately, the trend toward school consolidation creating ever-larger schools is alive and well. Perhaps the research on small-scale schools, which shows such positive academic and social outcomes for students, should outweigh the various political and economically charged short-range arguments that lead to large schools and the myriad of social problems they produce. ●

School Size Is Crucial to a Child's Success

Q: Can the size of a school make a difference in a child's education?

A: Each school, large or small, has its own "culture"—its philosophy and practices. Parents and their children should definitely visit schools they are considering, preferably during a regular school day, before making any decision.

Having said that, studies over the last 30 years demonstrate that there are real advantages to a small school. Research indicates that people (the entire school community—students, parents, staff) have a greater sense of belonging in a small school, one that serves between 100 to 1,000 students.

Students in schools with a student population of less than 1,000 have demonstrated better attendance, retention, behavior, attitude, and engagement. Given those advantages, it is not surprising to learn that these small-school students attain enhanced academic performance as well as increased involvement in extracurricular activities.

Teachers in a small school (especially one of their choice) frequently are more committed. They participate more in ensuring the goal of every good school: student achievement. Because there are fewer students, there is more time to give extra attention to young scholars (who is taught), curriculum (what is taught), and methodology (how something is taught). In sum, the small school has an advantage

L. Berlin

in making all within its walls feel part of a real community.

Incidentally, this is especially true for disadvantaged students. When people know you, they normally care about you. When familiar problems—academic or social—have a human face, more emphasis is given to finding solutions.

Students and teachers benefit from a small school because it simply enhances the opportunity of both students and teachers for active participation and recognition. At the end of most school days, the small-school experience usually translates into measured success and satisfaction. ●

Small Classes Yield Big Results

Q: Is there any proof that the added cost of hiring more teachers to lower class size is really worth it?

A: Common sense would argue that if a teacher had fewer students in the class, she could give more individual attention to each student. Moreover, she would have fewer discipline problems, provide more opportunities for student participation, and probably have her students produce higher test scores. In fact, research demonstrates that these commonsense conclusions are accurate.

In 1984, Tennessee State University investigated the effects of a pupil–teacher ratio of 15 to 1 on students in the first through third grades. Specifically, they focused on four kinds of student outcomes: achievement in reading and mathematics, behavior, attendance, and self-concept.

The results of this study were reported by the Colorado Department of Education's publication *Of Primary Interest*. The research indicated that the experimental smaller classes, when compared to the typical larger class sizes, had shown statistically significant gains in both reading and mathematics.

Moreover, these smaller classes were quieter and had fewer interruptions. Discipline problems could be identified and resolved more quickly, students showed a greater desire to participate, and more learning activities took place. As for the teachers—they had more time to work individually with students, to instruct, reteach concepts, and provide depth as well as breadth in classroom activities.

The study was expanded to include more than 6,000 students per year from

1985 to 1989. The evidence again was clear: students in smaller classes (13 to 17 students per class) consistently outperformed typical-size classes (22 to 25 students per class) on achievement measures at every grade level.

Smaller class sizes also proved to have lasting benefits. The long-range effects of the smaller class size in grades one through three demonstrated that these children retained a consistently strong academic advantage over their typical larger class size peers. Results of all achievement measures for the experimental smaller class students showed that they consistently did better than typical larger class size students in the fourth, fifth, sixth, and seventh grades.

In this case, common sense and research appear to agree. Smaller class size yields a measurably superior educational experience. ●

Why Do Some Schools Just Work Well?

Q: Why do some schools, even in poorer neighborhoods, seem to be so well organized? When you walk on the campus or visit a class, everyone appears to be working. Is there a secret why some schools just seem to work so well?

A: There are more than a few schools that don't function well. For those institutions, effective instruction appears to be an elusive mystery. The mission of a school is to educate. Schools that "just seem to work well" are led by educators who make effective decisions based on a systematic analysis of research data.

Accurate data yield true (and sometimes previously unseen) patterns of student behavior, and lead to a healthy review of a school's approach to the No. 1 goal: enhanced student achievement combined with continuous social growth. The simple fact is that data not only can be used to improve education, it must be used.

Schools do evaluate reading, writing, and math achievement. However, as a rule, schools don't interpret the data in ways that truly facilitate program changes. What kind of program revisions are possible? Basically, two major components leap out: curriculum (what is taught) and methodology (how a course is taught).

The idea is to get accurate data on students. Then teachers can make adjustments in teaching styles or curricula in order to gain eventual measurable student improvement. In schools that don't work, different educators use different data (or no data) and don't communicate with each other. Unfortunately, when a student experiences a lack of academic success, the student is blamed rather than the blame falling on what is being taught or how it is being taught.

The problem is not in data collection. Schools are gathering data (attendance, grades, standardized tests results, student ethnicity, family income levels, etc.) all the time. The real problem, according to researchers, is that schools must more carefully consider gender, ethnicity and/or socioeconomic background. These discrete categories can reveal important patterns of success or failure that should be routinely studied. These studies, in turn, can suggest areas that a school must improve.

In other words, it is all a question of how to break the data down into a meaningful description of who is learning and who is not, and then of attacking the problem intelligently. The classroom teacher has unique, firsthand knowledge about students that can and should be systematically investigated.

In order to make schools more effective in the future, it is the teacher "in the field" who must become an active researcher. Teachers must observe the classroom closely, create a research record for each and every student, let the student and parents know their baseline scores and skills, and devise action plans to enhance student achievement.

Viewing the classroom as a laboratory is what enlightened professional educators do in order to better understand and better serve every student. Effective decisions, based on accurate data, are the hallmark of schools that "just seem to work." ●

How Schools Can Get More "Bang for Their Buck"

Q: How cost-effective is public elementary and high school education in the United States? What innovations should taxpayers look for to be sure that their money is being spent wisely in their local schools?

A: This is a multibillion-dollar question. In fact, public education in the United States is a $300 billion endeavor. The public is right to question dramatic increases in educational funding when little or no improvement in student academic achievement is seen.

Seemingly, the measure of the relationship between educational funds and student success is a question of correlating input (expenditures) to output (academic achievement). However, the historic problem has been that public education is a complex process. This is due to the fact that many schools serve different communities with distinct mixes of socioeconomic, cultural, and language backgrounds.

Thus, when we look at measures of typical school-based outcomes—attendance patterns, dropout rates, standardized test results, or graduation rates—it is difficult to isolate a one-to-one correlation that would then lead us to a budgetary formula for school success. Having said that, it appears that smaller class size, highly educated teachers, and reduced noninstructional expenditures lead to more "bang for the buck" in terms of factors that directly impact the student.

There are, of course, other fundamental changes that could bring more value for the taxpayer's dollar into the classroom. For instance, can you envision school without a traditional principal or vice principal? Instead of the traditional nonteaching principal, a headmaster who actually teaches students could serve as a master teacher for the entire faculty. He or she would head a shared decision-making administrative process at a school site.

Under this kind of mutual collegial format, the entire faculty would have access to school-level spending data and consequently could develop ways to reallocate the surprisingly high noninstructional expenditures into the classroom. What percentage of a typical educational budget is in the non-instructional category? According to research, regardless of available funding, school districts spend about 40 percent of their money on noninstructional support services. The regular dissemination of reliable budget information among professional on-site practitioners could lead to more efficient planning and a more equitable distribution of taxpayer money. What is called for appears to be a straightforward way to put educational decisions back into the hands of practitioners (those who teach)—making the educational management of the school more decentralized and participatory.

A practical solution may be to redesign the public school system into a model where those most knowledgeable about the needs of students (i.e., a headmaster and his or her faculty) provide budgetary and planning input. Such a strategy could well lead to a systematic positive relationship between "input and output," which taxpayers have a right to demand.

In that event, the regular expenditure of public money will lead to consistently successful student outcomes. ●

Solving the Dropout Problem

Q: What is the real story behind the dropout problem? Is it worse today than ever before? Who is dropping out of school and why? What can be done to encourage kids to stay in school?

A: Dropouts remain a major concern of educators, politicians, and the public at large. Taking a historical view, dropout rates have actually been falling. In 1940, fewer than 40 percent of people between the ages of 25 to 29 in the United States had completed twelfth grade. By the year 1985, more than 85 percent had completed high school.

Dropout rates today continue to decline, but remain disproportionately high in major cities and among certain non-English-speaking populations. One reason for concern is that many of the jobs for unskilled workers that existed a half-century ago have long since disappeared. An undereducated person will almost certainly find the job market restricted to minimum-wage opportunities with little or no chance for advancement.

There are certain identifiable factors that reveal which students are more at risk of dropping out. A powerful predictor is school attendance. Sadly, a student who does not regularly attend school is actually dropping out by degrees.

Clearly, the dropout problem needs to be solved. Our nation's economy simply can't afford to have large numbers of people leading unproductive lives on public assistance. Likewise, our country's democratic system cannot fulfill its promise with a permanent uninformed underclass.

Any meaningful solution to the dropout problem must have at least these major components:

- Expand the parents' role in school from kindergarten to twelfth grade. Regular teacher phone calls to parents are a good way to open the lines of communication. Parents then know and and are able to monitor what their children are studying, when projects are due, and how their kids are doing in class.

- Provide all students the richest curriculum. Many schools still track students into higher and lower levels. This simply hinders student achievement. The end of tracking would be the beginning of equal and quality education for all students.

- Commit to individualized education. Teachers must plan to sit down with each individual learner and work together on projects and reports, day by day, line by line, face to face. This kind of learning model builds a special rapport based on trust and understanding. It keeps kids from falling through the cracks.

- Expand gifted education. The most recent groundbreaking brain and behavioral research indicates that we must broaden our definition of intelligence. The fact is, we all have gifts. Training teachers to view all students as gifted is essential to nurture and strengthen every student.

- Develop and maintain high academic standards. Instead of students competing among themselves for high grades on a theoretical bell curve (assuring both winners and losers), let them compete against high standards.

High standards should not be lowered. Instead, the efforts of teachers and parents should help the hardworking student to come up to standard. With these components in place, the phenomenon of the high school dropout could well become a thing of the past. ●

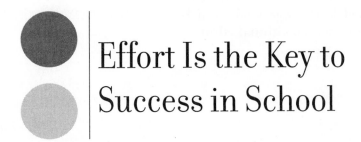

Effort Is the Key to Success in School

Q: Why is it that some students don't seem to even try to do school work? There are many, many kids who don't bring a book, a binder, or even a pencil to class. As for doing homework or studying for tests, forget it! These kids have simply given up. How can these kids be made to get on the ball?

A: For many unproductive students, fear of failure is at the heart of the problem. Anticipated failure is far more destructive to motivation, effort, and achievement than many people realize. The fear of being blamed, rejected, or even ridiculed prevents many students from even trying to do well in school.

Students who consistently give little or no effort typically try to avoid or escape any learning situation in which they believe their performance might be substandard. Their strategy is to "play dumb," believing that if they don't make an effort they can protect their self-esteem by claiming to themselves and/or to their friends that they really didn't fail because they really didn't try.

This only compounds the problem, because the student who refuses to try automatically omits the very learning task he or she needs so much to experience.

An often heard response from the student who comes unprepared to learn is the "I just can't do it" defense. This "I just can't do it" attitude is really a "I just won't do it" approach. The difference is enormous.

Once students are counseled, by an enlightened teacher or parent, to admit that an "I can't" is really an "I won't," we can begin to focus with precision on the real reason for academic failure, which is lack of student effort.

In order for a student to consistently put forth effort, he or she needs to understand four things:

1. Schools are places to learn knowledge and skills. Being uncertain or ignorant is part of the reality of learning. If you already knew what was being taught, you wouldn't need school to learn it.
2. Students must realize to err is normal. Errors are both expected and necessary to learn. Perceptive teachers respect and honor students who work hard and still make mistakes. It gives the teacher a chance to instruct using a variety of approaches, as well as reinforce the notion that continual effort is needed for ultimate success.

3. The student must feel he or she will eventually be successful. In other words, there must be an unshakable belief that hard work will pay off in the end.

4. All must understand that learning is a cumulative process. In an enlightened classroom, both reachable short-range goals, and clearly defined long-range goals, can be achieved with continual effort.

Finally, two insights will become apparent to the student who continually works hard:

1. Learning is a journey that happens step by step.
2. The road to success is always under construction. ●

Nutrition Affects Intellectual Performance

Q: A typical meal for most kids in the school consists of a cheeseburger and potato chips, washed down with chocolate milk. If fruit cups and vegetable portions have even been served, they usually land unceremoniously in the trash!

How important is good nutrition, and what can parents do to be sure their kids are eating healthy meals at school?

A: Good nutrition for children is quite important—and not only at lunchtime. Research clearly indicates that not having breakfast can adversely affect a child's intellectual performance. Moreover, even moderate undernutrition may have lasting effects on student achievement. This is not surprising; after all, the brain is part of the body. Starve the body—starve the brain.

As to what parents can do, here is a five-point plan of action:

1. **Eat lunch at school with your child.** If more parents did this, perhaps they would join in making appropriate changes in the school's menu or even the cafeteria's atmosphere.

2. **Get a weekly school menu.** Make sure you circle the most nutritious choices, so that your child knows what to order.

3. **Work with the PTA.** Raise the issue and support the notion of spreading the word about good nutrition—not only in the lunchroom but also in the classroom.

4. **Go to the top.** Discuss your attitudes about good nutrition and ask for the principal's or local school board's input and cooperation.

5. **Have a tasting party at school.** Introduce new and nutritious foods (e.g., fruits and vegetables) to children who may never have seen or tasted such a flavorful variety. ●

Teachers as Leaders

Q: When the question of school leadership comes up, it seems that most people think of school principals or district superintendents. What role can teachers play to direct the delivery of educational services?

A: To be effective, an authentic leader must have a practitioner's background, along with the talent to direct others. In other words, anyone who wishes to "show the way" must be experienced in the field they want to lead.

Leadership is especially critical in a time of change. Schools in the early part of the 21st century are facing ever-increasing academic and social demands. The potential impact of teacher leadership in which a teacher's authority is commensurate to his or her traditional responsibility can lead to a renaissance in U.S. classrooms.

The model of teacher as leader stands in sharp contrast to the traditional top-down, hierarchical paradigm that has existed since the common schools of the 18th century. Instead, the teacher-as-leader model promotes ideas of community-building in a diverse setting and decision-making on curricular and methodological issues by those who best know what takes place in the classroom—the teachers themselves.

What is called for is genuine teacher empowerment, through real decision-making authority, continuous faculty collaboration, and ongoing reflective professional development organized by and for teachers.

To sum up, a teacher as a leader

- Has as a top priority to do what is best for children
- Implements approaches via phone and the Internet (from laptops to PDAs), generating effective communication with faculty, staff, parents, and community
- Understands the value of continuous action research projects to measure the efficacy of current classroom practice, by taking on the role of teacher-researcher
- Questions, acts, makes professional judgments
- Attends conferences and publishes what works in the 21st century classroom
- Mentors other teachers
- Makes expert decisions on
  - what is taught (the curriculum)
  - how curriculum is taught (the methodologies)
  - what is assessed and evaluated
  - how it will be assessed and evaluated
- Cultivates approaches that keep a positive focus in the school and the community it serves
- Identifies with the role of a change agent
- Uses teacher leadership to model leadership for their students ●

A Teacher's Legal, Ethical, and Moral Responsibilities

Q: What legal, ethical, and moral responsibilities do teachers have inside and outside of today's classroom?

A: Teachers hold a very special place in society by providing a real-life model of lawful, ethical, and moral behavior to the children they see and teach each day. Let's look at these three different facets of every teacher's responsibilities.

A key to comprehending a teacher's legal obligations is the Latin phrase *in loco parentis,* which means "in the place of a parent." As a teacher you have to act responsibly to your students—as if you were a reasonable parent.

The parents and the community have a legal right to assume that you will take precautions regarding the student's well-being and safety. As part of your legal responsibility you must stay informed of and carry out school rules, district regulations, and state laws as they apply to your students.

An important part of your duties as a teacher is to report the *suspected* abuse of a child, even if it occurs outside the school. In most states you have the legal responsibility to report a child's allegation of abuse or your judgment of suspected abuse within one to two days of finding it out. Of course, if you feel the child is in immediate danger, you must take immediate action (e.g., by contacting your school administration, Family and Protective Services, the Police Department, calling 911, etc.).

Let's now turn to the ethical responsibilities of teachers. It is useful to think of a teacher's ethical responsibilities as a kind of professional judgment based on principles emanating from core values—a code of ethics for teacher behavior.

The following principles might well be included in such a code dedicated to the well-being of your students:

- Be a student advocate by teaching the whole student. As a teacher you are bestowed a great deal of trust to nurture both the academic development and social growth of every student.

- Foster a student's potential. High expectations are crucial. Every student deserves the most enriched curriculum taught by the widest variety of methodological approaches.

- Value cultural diversity. Respect every student's inherent dignity by learning about his or her culture and language. Value and use a student's prior knowledge as an integral part of the learning experience.

- Set a genuine learning environment. Provide an atmosphere in which students choose to become inspired, motivated, and ultimately empowered.

- Use the latest research. Be informed and implement practices proven to lead to active student engagement and greater student achievement.

- Be a role model. Set a standard for behavior in terms of language, work habits, critical thinking, and intellectual curiosity.

- Collaborate with others. Participate as a decision maker in curriculum, instruction, and assessment along with school governance. Consult the community for ideas to enhance the teaching and learning experience.

Now let's consider a teacher's moral responsibilities. Morality is about doing the right thing. Schools have traditionally reflected the moral values of their communities. Teachers are crucial carriers of those values by word and deed.

The moral question is more complex that it may first appear. For example, as late as the mid 20th century legal school segregation was an accepted social arrangement that valued some people (white children) at the expense of others (children of color).

The practice of apartheid was not only seen as legal and ethical but had the moral buttressing of biblical certainty. We can all agree that during that sad chapter of U.S. history, moral responsibility was turned on its head.

Today at the beginning of the 21st century teachers are still confronted with societal inequities and still must make moral judgments that directly impact the lives of real human beings. A teacher's moral role is multidimensional and deals with both day-to-day practices and long-range commitments.

Teachers demonstrate their moral duty to students and the community when they set a learning environment in which students choose to become actively engaged to improve themselves and the world in which they live. Teachers can demonstrate their commitment by:

- Being a competent and caring teacher
- Putting the needs of the group ahead of the wants of an individual
- Being on campus and accessible to students throughout the day (before and after class—that includes lunchtime!)
- Going to school governance meetings to defend the interests of students
- Being on the cutting edge of designing and implementing the most challenging curriculum and effective teaching methods
- Taking on the responsibility to grow as a teacher by professional growth activities
- Being aware of how a teacher's actions affect others
- Working on an continual basis for a better school that fosters high student achievement
- Being available to consult and work with parents and the community at large

Legal, ethical, and moral considerations are part of the warp and woof of the day-to-day life of a teacher. From issues involving free speech, gender equity, racial equality, and child abuse, teachers must be aware of the law, have a professional code of ethics, and be committed to the success of every child when making moral judgments. ●

The Future of Education Needn't Be Bleak

Q: Sometimes it seems that too many kids are falling through the cracks in our public schools. What does the future hold? Are things bound to get better or worse? Is there any advice that schools should follow to be sure they are doing their best so kids won't fail?

A: A good guess as to the future of public education can be gleaned from demographic research. Looking ahead 20 years, the future looks quite bleak. Researchers estimate that the trend toward higher percentages of homeless and poorly housed, malnourished, and neglected children will take a predictable toll in student achievement. These projections indicate that 20 years hence, more than half of the public school students in the United States would be considered at risk of educational failure.

Of course, the future doesn't have to be that calamitous. What is needed is a clear school-operating core philosophy—one that both reflects and promotes a certain mindset. Such a philosophy simply rejects the notion of failure on the part of students. It has been suggested that schools today that successfully serve at-risk students are more than just caring, cohesive institutions. These schools operate under a philosophic commitment similar to high-reliability organizations.

So what are high-reliability organizations? Consider air traffic control towers. They must operate under a standard of a 100 percent failure-free operation. This means that whatever is necessary to get the job done is provided, one way or another. There can be no excuses, no exceptions, and no room for error. What is set in mo-tion is a standard of freedom from failure. That standard promotes a mindset which is shared by the air traffic controllers, the pilots, and eventually the public. Such a mindset doesn't just occur. The resources and the enthusiasm must be continually supplied for the belief in air safety to be commonly held by the public.

There are a number of factors to take into consideration in order to make the schools a failure-free operation. First, like air safety, it must be something we just don't simply value, but demand. This demand for failure-free schools must be a vision shared by all concerned. There must be a shared sense of purpose, trust, teamwork, and recognition of genuine success. The "mission" (to educate all using the richest curriculum) must be clear to and valued by all. Failure in the core curriculum is unacceptable. Therefore, vigilance against failure is imperative. Resources are available and well maintained. The school environment is attractive, comfortable, and functional. Budgets are focused, like a laser, on the true purpose of the school: academic success for all students.

The attitude of faculty and parents toward students must be, "We are here for your success." Anything less than this societal commitment simply has proven inadequate to the task. Until schools become failure-proof, they will continue to cycle down into a state of perpetual mediocrity, physical dilapidation, and general disarray. Of course, this is not a question of lowering academic standards to make the school failure-proof, but of providing the resources and enthusiasm to bring all children up to standard.

High-reliability operations provide high expectations, high performance, and high public confidence. The future can be determined by an enlightened public consensus that expects and, indeed, demands that all children succeed. ●

SUGGESTED READINGS

Aronson, J. (Ed.). (2002). *Improving academic achievement: Impact of psychological factors on education.* Boston: Academic Press.

Benninga, J. S., Berkowitz, M. W., Kuehn, P., & Smith, K. (2003). The relationships of character education and academic achievement in elementary schools. *Journal of Research in Character Education, 1*(1), 17–30.

Berends, M., Kirby, S., Naftel, S., & McKelvey, C. (2001). *Implementation and performance in New American Schools.* Santa Monica and Arlington: RAND.

Burke, M. A. (2003). *Leveraging resources for student success: How school leaders build equity.* Thousand Oaks, CA: Corwin Press.

Chall, J. S. (2000). *The academic achievement challenge: What really works in the classroom?* New York: Guilford Press.

Corbett, D., Wilson, B., & Williams, B. (2002). *Effort and excellence in urban classrooms: Expecting, and getting, success with all students.* New York: Teachers College Press.

Covington, M. (2000). Goal theory, motivation, and school achievement: An integrative review. *Annual Review of Psychology, 51,* 171–200.

Character Education Partnership. (2002). *Practices of teacher educators committed to characters. Examples from teacher education programs emphasizing character development.* Washington: Character Education Partnership.

Cibulka, J. G., & Boyd, W. L. (2003). *A race against time: The crisis in urban schooling.* Westport, CT: Praeger.

Esteve, J. M. (2000). The transformation of the teachers' role at the end of the twentieth century: New challenges for the future. *Educational Review, 52*(2), 197–207.

Francis, B. (2000). *Boys, girls, and achievement: Addressing the classroom issues.* New York: Falmer Press.

Giroux, H. A. (2002). *Schools for sale: Public education, corporate culture, and the citizen-consumer.* In A. Kohn & P. Shannon (Eds.), *Education, Inc.: Turning education into a business* (pp. 105–118). Portsmouth, NH: Heinemann.

Hill, P., Campbell, C., & Harvey, C. (2000). *It takes a city: Getting serious about urban school reform.* Washington, DC: Brookings Institution Press.

Howell, W. G., & Peterson, P. E. (2002). *The education gap: Vouchers and urban schools.* Washington, DC: The Brookings Institution Press.

Jacobson, L. (2001). Moving targets. *Education Week, 20,* 32–34.

Kyriacou, C. (2001). Teacher stress: Directions for future research. *Educational Review, 53*(1), 28–35. (EJ 622 519)

Penuel, W. R., & Davey, T. (2000). Meeting the educational needs of homeless youth. In J. Stronge & E. Reed-Victor (Eds.), *Promising practices for educating homeless students* (pp. 63–78). Larchmont, NY: Eye on Education.

Popp, P. A., Hindman, J. L., & Stronge, J. H. (2003). *Students on the move: Reaching and teaching highly mobile children and youth.* New York: ERIC Clearinghouse on Urban Education.

Roderick, M., Nagaoka, J., Bacon, J., & Easton, J. (2000). *Update: Ending social promotion.* Chicago: Consortium on Chicago School Research.

Stronge J. H. (2000). Education, homeless children and youth: An introduction. In J. Stronge & E. Reed-Victor (Eds.), *Promising practices for educating homeless students* (pp. 1–19). Larchmont, NY: Eye on Education.

Troman, G., & Woods, P. (2001). *Primary teachers' stress.* New York: Routledge/Falmer.

Wong, K. (2000). Chicago school reform: From decentralization to integrated governance. *Journal of Educational Change, 1,* 97–105.

unit :2

Culture to Culture

21st-Century Roll Call

Q: The United States is a nation of immigrants with diverse racial and ethnic minorities. What will children coming to school in the next few years look like? What will the teachers who greet these youngsters at the classroom door look like? What has been the recent track record of success or failure of students from racial and ethnic minorities?

A: Today the population is 14 percent Latino, 13 percent African American, and 4 percent Asian, as well as many others. Let's look at who is coming to our classroom door in the next few years. The under-5-years-old population reflects significant demographic changes. Today, one in three United States residents is a racial or ethnic minority; however, 45 percent of children under the age of 5 years are from that group.

Taking a closer look at racial or ethnic minority children, the under-5-years-old group are 22 percent Latino, 4 percent African American, and 15 percent Asian. According to the U.S. Census Bureau, Latinos are the nation's largest and fastest-growing minority group. They accounted for 49 percent of the country's growth from 2004 to 2005. In fact, the increase in young children is largely a Latino phenomenon, driving 70 percent of the growth in children younger than 5 years of age. It may surprise some to learn that Latino births in the United States added more to the population growth than Latino immigrants have in this decade.

How well have these students done in the recent past? Let's look at the dropout rate in terms of high school graduation. The nation's overall graduation rate is only 70%. That means 30% don't graduate on time with their class. Even more disturbing is a study released in 2006 by researcher Christopher Swanson who reported that students in a handful of big-city school districts have a less than 50-50 chance of graduating from high school.

Fourteen urban school districts (which typically have a heavy ethnic minority student body) have on-time graduation rates lower than 50 percent. Among the cities were Detroit, Baltimore, New York, Milwaukee, Cleveland, Los Angeles, Miami, Dallas, Denver and Houston. Here are the dismal high school graduation rates from three of those cities: New York City (38.9%), Baltimore (38.5%) and Detroit (21.7%).

The study, which uses 2002 and 2003 data, stated that about 70 percent of four million eligible students graduate each spring, meaning about 1.2 million students likely don't graduate. That yields a dropout rate of 7,000 students each school day.

And who will be meeting these students at the classroom door trying to stem the tide of dropouts? Nearly nine of ten teachers, according to the National Educational Association are white, only 6 percent of teachers are African American, and 5 percent are Latino, Asian, or come from other ethnic minority groups. There is a significant gender imbalance as men represent barely a quarter of teachers—the lowest level in forty years.

Clearly new steps must be taken by a new generation of teachers with a goal (and with action plans) clearly geared to student success. A new message of hope and inclusion from elementary through secondary school must be articulated—and acted on. ●

Schools Should Celebrate Ethnic Diversity

Q: What can be done with students who come to school with racial or ethnic prejudice? How can this problem be confronted so all students can feel more accepted?

A: This question of prejudice clearly transcends a particular school or community. Bigotry toward another human being because of race or ethnicity is an ugly worldwide phenomenon. Witness recent wars and unrest in Iraq, Darfur, and the Middle East. These are but a few contemporary examples of the brutal and deadly lengths to which this kind of hatred can lead.

One might feel resigned and say that when the world changes and rids itself of prejudice, then the school will reflect this change. Of course, with that philosophy, everyone waits for everyone else to cure the obvious malady of racial or ethnic bias.

Schools themselves are first and foremost learning institutions. Students are always learning something—either intended or unintended. The problem is, in racially and ethnically divided schools, students essentially see prejudice as unchallenged. Moreover, in the absence of proactive solutions to racial or ethnic bias, bigotry may be viewed as acceptable.

Schools must be in the forefront of not only accepting diversity, but understanding the positive aspects inherent in a diverse student body as students prepare to live and work in a multicultural world. Schools must create opportunities for students to experience diversity through cooperative education, heterogeneous

L. Berlin

(untracked) grouping, and working with neighborhood groups and churches to foster respect and appreciation of other cultures.

Schools have a long way to go in achieving real diversity. If you doubt that, just look at the national dropout rates by race or ethnicity, or visit a large high school at noon and notice the lunchtime phenomenon of racially segregated seating patterns around campus.

To counter this all-too-frequent pattern of exclusion, examples and illustrations must be given so that students can see the power and strength of inclusion through diversity. Here is a short lesson any parent or teacher can use to illustrate the positive side of accepting diversity.

Picture in your mind three artists standing next to their easels on the rim of the Grand Canyon. One artist is Japanese, one

African, and the third French. Each artist is asked to draw the Grand Canyon from virtually the same viewpoint at the same time of day. Do you think all three paintings would be the same? Of course they would be different. Do you think because all three paintings are different, only one work of art is necessary? Without a doubt, the three works of art are of value because each would bring a unique perspective and add to our knowledge.

Three different portrayals of the Grand Canyon's natural beauty from three representatives of vastly different cultures celebrates the strength of diversity. Within a diverse society, there are different people with different approaches. To every challenge, from art to science, diversity provides more ways to find solutions to every problem under the sun. ●

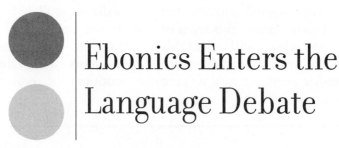

Ebonics Enters the Language Debate

Q: What is the controversy about Ebonics? Should schools be teaching students how to misuse the English language?

A: The primary goal of every English language program should be to teach students standard English. Having said that, it is important for the teacher to know as much as possible about the students he is teaching. That knowledge includes Ebonics.

Ebonics literally means "black sounds," and has its roots in the languages of West Africa. For teachers to be aware of and understand different languages, dialects, slang, or jargon that their students use is valuable knowledge.

I know of no program that actually teaches Ebonics to kindergarten through 12th-grade students. However, there is a movement to have teachers understand Ebonics so they can better comprehend what students are trying to express.

It is important not to think of any language or dialect as beneath another. Languages don't exist on a totem pole. It is better to think of places (what linguists call domains) where a certain type of language is appropriate.

Most of us don't speak the same language at a game or a party that we would in a formal classroom situation or when addressing a group of parents. At a game or a party, informal expressions are quite

We are pleased to present our group report on···

appropriate. In school or in a business setting, standard English is best.

In terms of what goes on in the classroom, three elements are part of any effective language program:

- Students must understand what kind of language is appropriate for a given place or situation.

- Teachers must speak standard English in classroom situations. Modeling standard English is a crucial part of instruction.

- Students must have daily opportunities to practice standard English orally and in written form as the rich, dynamic, and primary language of our nation. ●

 # Two-Way System Solves Bilingual Problem

 Q: We seem to have more and more non-English-speaking kids entering the schools. What is the practical value of bilingual education? Shouldn't kids be learning English from the first grade, since the language of this country is English?

A: There is no question that all children in this country should master the English language. It would be beneficial if native English-speaking children could learn a foreign language.

There is a program that has proven successful in accomplishing these twin goals. It is called two-way bilingual education. In this program, students develop dual language proficiency by receiving classroom instruction in English and another language. The student population of such a class is comprised of half native speakers of English and half native speakers of another language. Although Spanish is the most common other language, French, Portuguese, Russian, Navajo, Japanese, Korean, and Cantonese make up other two-way bilingual models.

The goals of two-way bilingual programs are high academic achievement in both languages, along with improved cross-cultural understanding. Strong academic accomplishments in both languages require strategies that include experiential or hands-on activities, as well as peer instruction. An appreciation of each individual student's learning style is essential to getting meaning across in both languages.

The results of such a two-way format are beginning to emerge. The two-way approach is effective in teaching both languages while developing academic excellence. A recent study indicates that on standardized math achievement tests, two-way bilingual students demonstrated academic progress as well as fluency in both languages. In another study, two-way bilingual students from a language background other than English made more long-term educational gains than students in other bilingual or English as a Second Language (ESL) programs.

The United States has the most culturally diverse population in the world. Given our rich cultural and linguistic makeup and the rise of a global economy, our nation has a unique opportunity to use our cultural diversity as a resource.

Selling to the rest of the world is the goal of every great exporting nation. Although you can purchase goods in English, you must sell goods in the language of the buyer. A country that possesses highly trained professionals speaking many different languages is at a clear competitive advantage. Two-way bilingual education has demonstrated high test scores, better cross-cultural understanding, and a practicality that makes solid economic sense. ●

Two-Way Bilingual Education Benefits All

Q: Proponents of bilingual education say that a two-way bilingual program teaches two languages to children. However, many so-called bilingual students don't appear to know either language very well. Isn't is true that the more time kids spend in English instruction, the more English they will learn?

A: This issue is often confusing because the term "bilingual education" has been used to describe the teaching method of almost any class with children who speak different languages. There is a plethora of different so-called bilingual programs: two-way bilingual instruction,

concurrent bilingual instruction, English as a Second Language, sheltered classes, an array of English-only curricula, and everything in between. You can see why the question of whether bilingual education is effective or not is simplistic.

An example of effective bilingual education occurred in the early 1960s in Florida. James Crawford wrote about this program in his book, "Bilingual Education: History, Theory, and Practice" (Bilingual Education Services, Inc.).

During this period, many well-educated Cubans fled the Cuban Revolution of 1959. Those first Cubans were not economic refugees, but people looking for political asylum. Many of the initial wave of immigrants were from the upper professional classes (doctors, lawyers, and professors). They came with what is called "cultural capital." They had an appreciation of the importance of a first-class education, and they were experienced in working within a formal educational system to achieve those ends.

The federal government extended generous financial aid to these particular immigrants through the Cuban Refugee Program. With the cooperation of the state of Florida, Cuban teachers became recertified and were able to teach in Florida's public schools.

In just two years, the Dade County Public Schools had established a true two-way bilingual approach to education at Coral Way Elementary School. This was not a remedial program for refugees. Neither was this a compensatory curriculum for the "culturally deprived." Instead, this was an educational approach that was clearly aimed at fluent bilingualism for both Spanish speakers and English speakers.

The Cuban children began each morning with lessons in Spanish. Lunch, art classes and recess were spent with the English-speaking children. Afternoon lessons for the Cuban youngsters were in English. Conversely, the native English-speaking Floridians began each morning being taught in English. Lunch, art and recess were spent with the Spanish-speaking Cuban children. Each afternoon, lessons were taught in Spanish.

Sounds pretty evenhanded, but was it effective in terms of the Cubans learning English? Both the English-speaking Floridians and the Spanish-speaking Cubans did as well or better in English reading than their counterparts at all-English schools.

Why did the two-way bilingual program work so well in terms of the Cuban students acquiring English? Researchers from cognitive psychology and linguistics have theorized some basic elements of an effective bilingual program. Bilingual students experience positive academic achievement when they develop both their native language and their second language. The question is not whether bilingual education should focus on either a transition to the target language (English) or maintenance of the native language (Spanish). To be a success, a bilingual program must focus on both.

A student who comes from a non-English-speaking environment needs to be provided, in a language which the learner clearly understands, an equal opportunity to experience and learn the same enriched content and higher-level skills as any other student. Remedial programs tend to produce remedial students. Low expectations are a self-fulfilling prophecy.

Bilingualism enriches every student and should be the goal of all students. Clearly, the ability to communicate in more than one language enriches the cognitive and social growth in the classroom, and assists in understanding diverse peoples and cultures outside the school.

As to the second part of the question, whether more time in English instruction yields more English learned, the answer may surprise you. Actually, the more time spent on a student's first language, the easier it is for that student to transfer those skills to a second language. If a student has not built up sufficient skills in the mother tongue, there is a problem. You can't transfer skills you don't have.

The United States has been, is, and for the foreseeable future will be, a home to millions of people who come to our schools speaking a language other than English. We have options. The first option is to view these non-English-speaking children as a problem and order them not to speak their native language in school. The state could simply offer all-English instruction for all courses in a "sink or swim" edict. The results would be a continuation of higher dropout rates and lower achievement scores.

On the other hand, we can view these children's ability to speak another language as a valuable resource—a rich linguistic and cultural gift that can be shared with other English-speaking students. Similarly, those English-speaking youngsters can share a wonderful English-language heritage with the newcomers.

One option leads to isolation and a well-documented record of schools failing new immigrants. The second option, in this case the two-way bilingual format, points the way to academic success and enhanced acculturation by all students. Such a bilingual format would be a boon to our English-speaking population.

Presently, only 5 percent of all college graduates in the United States reach a meaningful proficiency in a second language. As for foreigners, learning English doesn't seem to be a problem. Two-thirds of the one billion people who speak English learned it as a second language.

Did you know that for every American who learns Chinese, 10,000 Chinese learn English? It seems so ironic that in the United States, a nation of immigrants, we continue to view children who come to school with a language other than English as a problem rather than a resource. Given an ever-shrinking world and our clear need to be successful in a global economy, using the resources and talents of all of our people should be an absolute imperative for our schools and our country.

Schools that understand the elements of a quality bilingual program, where the goal for all students is bilingualism, are on the right track—a track constructed nearly four decades ago by Cuban refugees. ●

Roots of Intolerance

Q: How does intolerance start in a child? What can we do to reduce intolerance, bias, and racism in the schools?

A: No one is born intolerant, biased, or racist. Many children, however, notice that people around them have differences. Children also notice when some people are treated with less love and respect than others. Children are always learning. They surmise, early on, that human differences are in some way related to power and privilege. The seed of intolerance is planted when a child believes certain groups of people are to be loved or respected less because of their gender, race, religion, sexual orientation, or ethnicity. The child can quite easily develop misconceptions and/or anxiety about different members of our diverse human family. These initial negative feelings, from the seed of ignorance and fear, can grow into a hateful violent prejudice.

What is the answer? The answer to ignorance and fear is knowledge and hope. The more a child learns about and comes into contact with people of diverse backgrounds through firsthand experience, the greater the chance that an appreciation of everyone's basic humanity can take hold.

The key is for children to have working relationships with a diverse group of people. When children work together toward a goal, such as a group project for science class, as members of an athletic team, or as participants on a student council, their commonality as members of the human family comes to the surface.

It is not too long before children realize that all of us want to love and be loved and wish to feel safe and respected. When children realize that others have the same desires and needs, their differences become secondary to their similarities. Friendships are made, intolerance gives way to tolerance, ignorance to reason, and fear to hope. ●

Teachers and Parents Can Help All Students Succeed

Q: There seems to be a lot in the news about a return to racial segregation in schools, especially at the college level. What is going on here? What is the problem and how can we fix it?

A: The problem is that colleges have seen affirmative action admissions policies face legislative and judicial challenges in the last few years. If these colleges are forbidden to assist historically underrepresented minorities in the admissions process by using race as a consideration (as in California or Texas), there will be a greater reliance on standardized tests. These tests will act as a filter. Who is admitted to college and who is rejected will depend more than ever on a certain score, on a certain day, on a certain test.

Here's the problem in a nutshell: Latino and African American students, as a group, score below others who take the standardized tests. Although there is much research to show that SAT scores and other professional school standardized tests are poor predictors of scholastic and career success, colleges are forced to lean heavily on these results due to the sheer number of applicants and the cost of evaluation.

Is there an answer to this seemingly intractable problem? Here's a threefold long-range solution: First, recognize that not all students receive the same educational opportunities in elementary and high school. Studies show that nearly 90 percent of all public secondary schools offer different courses to students based on their perceived ability. In other words, they track students.

As long as we have high and low tracks in schools, we will have two different sets of curricula with two different outcomes, one superior and one inferior. It is no secret that high tracks and so-called gifted programs have a disproportionately low number of African American and Latino students. Therefore, it should be of no surprise that on standardized tests, a disproportionately high number of African American and Latino students score lower than other ethnic groups and, in effect, forfeit their entrance to college.

An answer to the dilemma is to abolish tracking and require schools to offer the most enriched curriculum to all students. The research is clear: Students do best when an enriched curriculum is offered by an enthusiastic teacher.

Second, parents must be involved. Parents must be kept better informed of their children's progress. One way of accomplishing this is by a teacher's weekly phone call giving an update on the child's achievement. Too often, parents are left in the dark until their child is floundering in a course and it is too late to do anything about it in a particular semester.

Perceptions some parents have must change. School should not be thought of as a dog-eat-dog jungle where students hoard information so as not to lose a theoretical competitive advantage. Instead, parents and students should understand that learning improves when students work with other students from diverse backgrounds, sharing knowledge and teaching each other. You cannot argue in the name of pedagogy that less knowledge is better. The more diverse the group, the more learning and social skills can be developed.

Third, the actual de-tracking of schools depends on teachers who are trained through meaningful professional development classes that promote an enriched curriculum (what is taught) for all students. Correspondingly, various methodologies (how one is taught) that allow for different ways of learning for a diverse student body are imperative.

To de-track a school means that the teacher must assume that all students can learn. Planning how the new enriched curriculum will be administered to all students is critical. When students from any of the diverse groups in school find the curriculum difficult, it is the teacher's and the parents' responsibility to reteach the material until it is mastered.

What is being argued here is not lowering standards but, through will and skill, bringing all students up to standard. What is even more crucial is that teachers understand that the strongest indicator of success in school is not racial, ethnic, or economic status, but the curricular expectation of the school itself.

Research indicates that students matched (by race, ethnicity, gender or family income) in a high-track curriculum do better than their counterparts in a low-track curriculum. Accordingly, it is what is taught, not who is taught, that seems to be the key. It should be obvious that historically underrepresented groups in colleges and universities can do just as well as others if they are given the same curricular educational opportunities at the elementary and secondary levels. ●

Multicultural Education Is the Right Way to Go

Q: What are the benefits of multicultural education? I was always taught that we are the world's melting pot. It seems to be only good common sense that our schools' curricula should be based on our common culture. Isn't it time to admit that politically correct multiculturalism is really something which divides us? We're not the Divided States of America; we're the United States of America!

A: From an educator's point of view, multicultural education has five things going for it. First, it is a proven strategy for improving academic performance and bolstering self-esteem among students who do not come from the predominant Anglo-European culture.

Second, when a curriculum is inclusive, harmony between groups of students increases, and conflict based on stereotypical ideas decreases. Third, all students benefit from knowledge about other ethnic or language heritages. The National Education Goals (No. 3) speak of increasing the level of knowledge all students have about the country's diverse heritage.

Fourth, multicultural education views students' diverse cultural backgrounds as a resource rather than a problem. In short, it proposes to capitalize on them, rather than ignore or even belittle them.

Fifth, the goal of multicultural education is the same as all education—to present the truth. Truth should not ignore our commonalities or our differences.

It is important that in a search for an enriched view of the world within a school's curriculum, we evaluate instructional materials for cultural relevance. Researchers have indicated that forms of subtle or blatant bias find their way into instructional materials.

These kinds of biases include invisibility and the "sidebar" approach. For many years African Americans, Native Americans, Asian Americans, and Latinos were simply ignored in instructional materials in terms of their obvious historical accomplishments. In many of today's textbooks, these ethnic groups are relegated to a sidebar or box, clearly out of the mainstream of the text. There is a none-too-subtle message given to all students when some ethnic groups are mentioned in only a few historical events, isolated from the main historical narrative.

We are one nation, the United States of America. We are also a nation of immigrants. As for the melting pot, at times it appears to be a bubbling cauldron of discontent. Blind assimilation has historically been a game of winners and losers. Perhaps a better strategy to bring peace and harmony to the schools and the country is acculturation.

Acculturation is based on the knowledge and appreciation of all people's contributions. People learn each other's languages and can function in each other's cultures.

In understanding our different backgrounds and respecting the diverse history and common dignity of all under the Stars and Stripes, we truly can become a united people in the United States of America. ●

Inclusive Schools See Diversity as a Strength

Q: What should schools be doing to teach students who come from foreign countries? Of special concern are newly-arrived kindergarten-through-high-school students. How do schools approach this problem?

A: The answer to this question encompasses a number of steps that can lead to successful outcomes for all students, native-born and newcomer:

1. Express respect. It is critical that the newcomer and his or her parents feel that they are understood and appreciated by the school.
2. Express empathy. This is as simple as school personnel understanding someone else's point of view—to walk a mile in another's moccasins.
3. Withhold immediate judgment. The trick is for the school to remain objective. Decisions should not be made until enough information and understanding about the cultural and family background of the newcomer have been gathered.
4. Have patience. Sometimes, due to cultural differences, academic and social tasks cannot be accomplished immediately.
5. Ensure the richest curriculum for all students. Schools should avoid tracking (perceived ability grouping), which traditionally presents an advanced curriculum for the selected native students and a watered-down or "dumbed-down" curriculum for the newcomer.
6. View the newcomer's linguistic and cultural heritage as a school resource, not a problem. Schools that set up rigorous two-way bilingual programs (where every student learns a second language) end up with students who have attained superior cross-cultural skills, a real plus in our multicultural society.

Accordingly, a school's awareness of diversity means that the old "melting pot" idea of cultural unity is a bit passé. The melting pot theory suggested that people from all over the world could be blended into one particular kind of American steel.

It is quite obvious that many groups have never fully been part of this melting pot process. African Americans, Latinos, and Native Americans, among others, found that their languages and cultural practices were, at times, not welcomed into the school—if not expressly forbidden.

On the other hand, an inclusive school accepts a wide range of culturally different groups without ranking them as better or worse than any other group. An inclusive educational institution holds the promise of a new kind of school—a place of expanding knowledge that views diversity of language, thought, and culture as a learning opportunity. In short, diversity is seen as a strength. Such a new way of viewing schools recognizes the richness inherent in each culture. These new schools are in the image of a rainbow—made up many colors in a single unified arc, committed to academic growth and social harmony. ●

Some Children Develop Skills Faster Than Others

Q: Everyone says the early years of education are the most important. At what age do children really take off as learners? Why do some children seem to start from way behind and remain behind?

A: Today, 98 percent of all children attend kindergarten before beginning the first grade. These children increasingly come from different language, racial, family, ethnic, cultural, and socioeconomic backgrounds. It is the mission of the school to provide all children with enriched activities and instruction to make sure that each and every child gets off to a good start.

As to when children really "take off" as learners, let's look at emerging literacy skills. Findings from a U.S. Department of Education study of 3-to-5-year-old children are quite enlightening. The percentage of preschoolers who can recognize most letters of the alphabet more than doubles between the ages of 3 and 4. The number of preschoolers who are able to write their own name more than triples between their third and fourth year.

It is true that some children develop these emerging literacy skills faster than others. Here is a list, from the same study, of five risk factors that are associated with learning problems after children start school:

- The mother has less than a 12th-grade education.
- The family is below the official poverty line.
- The mother speaks a language other than English at home.
- The mother was not married at the time of the child's birth.
- Only a single parent is in the home.

The research indicates that one or more of these risk factors affects 50 percent of all preschoolers. Of even greater concern, three or more of these risk factors affect 15 percent of these children.

Interestingly, race does not appear to be a risk factor. In fact, apparent differences between races are wholly explained by the preceding five risk factors. Programs like Head Start and other center-based preschool programs have a positive impact in raising the literacy scores of 4-year-olds, regardless of whether the family backgrounds were high-risk or low-risk.

A solution to meeting the needs of children who are demographically and developmentally diverse can be found in a commitment to provide all children with the most enriched curriculum at the earliest opportunity. ●

School Vision Begins
with Educational Platform

Q: How can schools change? Everyone from the president of the United States to my next-door neighbor has an opinion, but what exactly can or should change? What is the key ingredient for real change in our schools?

A: Schools change when the people who actually do the teaching in a school share an explicit agreement on an educational platform with the community they serve. Much like the platform of a political party, this educational platform incorporates the values, methods, and goals of a school. Each educator shares in this same vision and action plan. A school is thereby transformed.

Research indicates that school principals play a pivotal role, for better or worse, in shaping the vision of a school. Although principals can be key players in creating a coherent vision, many administrators are not risktakers. Neither are principals active practitioners; they seem to lack the time or the inclination to teach in the schools they administer. In fact, many administrators seem detached from current educational research.

For example, eight of ten American schools are tracked. These schools offer different curricular tracks for students of presumed higher and lower ability. Yet tracked schools are routinely decried in educational research as unfair to many students—minority students in particular. Historically, principals have been unable or unwilling to end tracking and all the downstream problems it creates (minority underrepresentation from colleges to boardrooms).

The roadblock to real change has to do in large measure with delegating author-ity. Unfortunately, many principals are not willing to release personal ownership and embrace shared decision making with the community and the faculty when new programs must be implemented. However, new leadership models (charter schools) can evolve from an alliance between the local community and empowered teachers. Such a powerful combination would join the community's enthusiasm for change with the faculty's expertise in academics to produce a shared vision for a restructured school.

For example, here is a progressive vision of a school operating without regard to race, ethnicity, home language, or gender:

- All children receive the most enriched curriculum; tracking is not allowed.

- Teachers do not give grades; students earn them.

- Children who speak a language other than English are viewed as a resource, not a problem. Two-way bilingual programs are set up so every student is proficient in more than one language.

- The school articulates specific academic standards. Standards are not lowered; instead all students are "brought up to standard" by using a variety of teaching strategies, including reteaching.

- Teachers are in a continual professional development program administered by a local university. Without unrelenting assessment and analysis by a college of education, a common progressive vision for the school may not be sustainable.

For such a vision and corresponding action plan to be successful, teachers must be involved and empowered. After all, teachers are the true school administrators of curriculum (what is taught) and methodology (how something is taught). Without the teachers, mighty efforts to change a school for the better will add up to mighty little. ●

Teaching the Bilingual Student

Q: How are teachers supposed to teach children who don't even understand English? With all the problems education has, how can a teacher who speaks only English cope with this situation?

A: This is a question that becomes more important with each passing day. Classrooms in the United States are increasingly more multilingual, multiracial, multicultural, and multiethnic.

Clearly there are two basic curricular items that must be delivered by a professional educator to the student: language instruction and content instruction. Research indicates that a second language is most successfully acquired in conditions similar to those in which a first language is learned.

When a person learns his or her native tongue, the focus of instruction is on meaning rather than form. In other words, fluency precedes accuracy. Therefore, in the second-language classroom, the focus should be on meaningful information, such as academic content.

The target language (the new language you are trying to learn) should be modified so language acquisition is facilitated while academic content becomes accessible to second-language learners. To put it another way, two things must happen at once. Students must continue their academic development while they acquire second-language proficiency.

Another point should be made to understand how long it takes to become proficient in a new language in order to function well at school. There are two types of language ability: basic interpersonal communications skills and cognitive language academic proficiency.

Social language (basic interpersonal communications skills) can take about a year or two to acquire. However, the level of proficiency needed to read a history book or solve a word problem in mathematics (cognitive language academic proficiency) can take five to seven years to develop.

Teachers need to present integrated language and content instruction so second-language students can continue their academic development as they acquire a new language. To accommodate an increasingly language-diverse population, content-area teachers need to know how to integrate certain methods (demonstrations, visuals, and/or cooperative education) into everyday instructional activities. Likewise, language teachers need to learn how to integrate academic language and content in the classroom.

Educating the educators with the techniques to better serve language minority children must be a top priority for every teacher in every school in every district. The ultimate goal of teacher in-service training is enhanced student achievement for every learner from every language background. ●

Multicultural Heritage

Q: What is all the controversy about what language kids should speak in school? If we want to prevent language separation and a breakdown in national unity, only English should be spoken in the schools. People who come and live in this country should want to learn English or they should not be allowed to enter.

As far as the United States is concerned, English was the language of yesterday, is the language of today, and will be the language of tomorrow.

A: In fact, when the United States of America was formed, speakers of many different languages populated this country. Besides English, there were Spanish, German, French, and hundreds of Native American languages, among many others.

The founders decided not to declare an official language, understanding that tolerance for linguistic diversity within the population had economic and social value. In addition, at that time, there was no desire to restrict the cultural or linguistic freedom of those living in the world's newest democracy.

Today, there are groups that promote the idea of English as the official and exclusive language of the United States. Others, who view cultural diversity as a national strength, oppose those who would, through legislation, make English the official language of the United States.

Those opposed to English as an official language, however, are not opposed to immigrants learning English quickly. In fact, they support access to bilingual services and education to provide a way for non-speakers of English to acquire English as soon as possible. They point to research that demonstrates that native language development has a positive influence on second-language proficiency.

Significantly, studies also indicate that the lack of native language development can inhibit the level of second-language (English) proficiency. Since language acquisition occurs only when incoming messages are understood, successful bilingual programs result in faster acquisition of English.

Today there appears to be no organized resistance to learning English. Research indicates that immigrant groups have a great desire to learn English. In a survey of nearly 3,000 Americans, including those of Mexican and Cuban descent, more than 90 percent of the respondents believed citizens of this country should learn English.

As for tomorrow, although knowledge of English is necessary, it may not be sufficient as our nation moves into a global economy. Acquiring languages in addition to English is highly recommended. Some states, such as New Mexico, Oregon, and Washington, have adopted resolutions declaring that proficiency in more than one language is beneficial to the nation, that English needs no special law to support it, and that acquisition of other languages should be encouraged.

With this philosophy, tomorrow's classrooms should have more and more people who can support and defend America in more than one language. ●

The United States: An English-Speaking Nation or a Multilingual Nation?

Q: We have always been an English-speaking nation. But more and more people come to the United States each day speaking less and less English. Isn't this a prescription for cultural disaster?

If we are not to become a "Tower of Babel," these new immigrants have to understand that learning English is their responsibility. It is the schools' job to make us a literate nation.

A: In fact, the United States is and has been, since its inception, a multilingual nation with English serving as the dominant language. Historical research is quite clear on this point. At the time of our country's first census in 1790, many different language groups existed in America.

About 50 percent of the population was of English origin, just less than 20 percent came from Africa, a little more than 10 percent were Scottish or Scottish-Irish, less than 5 percent were Irish, and slightly less than 15 percent were Dutch, French, and Spanish. Unfortunately, but predictably, the indigenous Native Americans were basically ignored by the first census. However, their languages were no less a part of the American mosaic.

It is true that through the mid 19th century, immigrants came from predominantly English-speaking areas. However, by the end of that century, the majority of newcomers entered the United States speaking a language other than English.

At present, we have more and more immigrants entering the United States, but we are still behind the high mark for the 20th century. Although recent statistics show that close to 10 percent of the current population was foreign-born, the number of foreign-born in 1910 was closer to 15 percent.

Another point about language is important to consider. One should not confuse the lack of competence in English with illiteracy. Because literacy in the native language of millions of people who enter the United States is not often surveyed, claims of illiteracy among immigrants are highly suspect.

The perception that today's new wave of immigrants are less eager to learn English than were the immigrants of prior generations is unsubstantiated. In fact, there are vast numbers of adult immigrants on waiting lists for English as a Second Language instruction (ESL) across the nation. For example, in Dallas alone there have been 6,000 people on a one-year waiting list to take the basic introductory course in English. The numbers in Los Angeles have historically been six to seven times that number.

Language diversity is not the problem. Learning English must be a priority for all residents of the United States. However, in the 21st century's world economy, knowledge of English alone isn't always enough.

Quality schools must promote English literacy and biliteracy for all students. After all, you can't argue, in the name of education, that the knowledge and practical application of one language is better than the understanding and use of two languages! ●

What Has to Happen for Standards to Work

Q: There has been a lot of talk about state-wide and even national standards. Will these standards work, or is it just a lot of wishful thinking?

A: Almost everyone who is truly committed to making our educational system work believes in some kind of standards. Let's investigate what standards really are and then discuss whether, under the current widespread school policy of homogeneous grouping, such standards are doomed to failure.

To begin, we can all agree that mere "seat time" in a class is no real measure of a student's knowledge. On the other hand, standards focus on student performance and are a means of translating broad notions of improvement into fairly specific criteria that should encourage intellectual vitality.

We are not talking about uniform or fixed goals, but an intellectual process consisting of behaviors and skills. Moreover, standards should emphasize that attitudes toward education are as important as what is taught. Instead of traditional

testing methods, more innovative forms of assessment, such as portfolio reviews (e.g., reflecting the development of a student's writing skill), are considered a more valid reflection of what a student has learned than "fill-in-the-bubble" examinations.

This is all well and good. Standards seem like an enlightened way to hold all students to high expectations. But there is a problem. The practice of homogeneous grouping is quite prevalent in the United States. Unlike many other countries, U.S. schools commonly divide students into advanced (higher perceived ability) and regular (lower perceived ability) groups. The problem with standards is easy to identify by asking the following question: How can all students be expected to achieve the same high standards when the two curricula (literally what the students are expected to learn) are so radically different?

The practice of perceived ability grouping, or tracking, is based on the widespread notion that students' intellectual differences are so great that a common curriculum would either slow down the higher-tracked students or hopelessly confuse the lower-tracked students. These notions, as educational researcher Jeannie Oakes has pointed out, are built on four assumptions. First, students learn better when they are grouped with those of similar ability. Second, lower-track students develop more positive attitudes when they are not grouped with higher-track students. Third, there exists a fair method of deciding who goes into which track. Fourth, it is easier for teachers to individualize instruction in homogeneous groups.

The problem with these four assumptions is that they are not only unproven, there is substantial educational research indicating that all four assumptions are erroneous. For many years there has been a large body of consistent research that indicates that heterogeneous (mixed-level) groupings best serve all students. In a mixed or untracked group with a diverse student population, the emphasis is on effort rather than perceived ability.

Success in school is viewed as a function of hard work. Effort is the ethic stressed as the key component for student success. The problem with fuzzy notions such as perceived ability, talent, or giftedness is that they have a track record of excluding certain groups of our diverse population with alarming consistency.

African American, Latino, and Native American students have been historically underrepresented in gifted programs. These students may be underrepresented by as much as 30 to 70 percent, with an average of 50 percent. In January, 2003, the National Academy of Sciences reported on the seeming overrepresentation of minorities in special education and underrepresentation in gifted education. The claim is substantiated by more recent statistics nationwide that reveal about 7 percent of all white students and 10 percent of Asian students are in gifted programs. At the same time, 3 percent of African American students, 4 percent of Latino students, and 5 percent of Native American students attend gifted programs. The underlying core assumption about standards is that all students can learn more and can learn at high levels. There is a plethora of evidence to suggest that when all students are encouraged to work with enriched content and enthusiastic teachers, they make far better progress than those students who receive lower-track basic skills instruction.

If standards are to work, parents, administrators, and teachers must dismantle the structured inequality inherent in a tracked school. If we want standards to work, all students must receive a quality education. There is no quality education without equality in education.

High standards for all students in a tracked system are plainly incongruent, unworkable, and doomed to fail. Until we solve the tracking problem at the elementary, middle, and high school level, the standards movement will be just another high-minded idea that never gets off the ground. ●

Meeting Standards

Q: Everyone is in favor of meeting standards—but what are we really talking about? Is there national, state, and district agreement on which standards should be followed and how these standards should be taught?

A: The idea of attempting to meet every national, state, and district standard from so many disparate sources has the potential of creating mass bewilderment. To be sure, there are not only national standards; in addition, 50 states have standards in disciplines ranging from English, math, history, science, and physical education, to fine arts and foreign language. As for school districts, there are over 17,000 districts in the nation and all of them have their own—and frequently modified—standards. How can we pull these separate entities together into a coherent aligned framework under the banner of meeting standards? Where does one start?

To attempt to align or even reconcile these ever-changing and in some cases incongruent standards among so many different political structures would surely be a fool's errand. Yet there is little doubt that standards are critical and can form the basis of benchmarks, projected outcomes, assessments, and evaluations to see where we have been, where we are, and where we are going in terms of student achievement.

Let's first recall that "meeting standards" should not mean simply attaining fixed goals but continually developing behaviors and skills that are inherently dynamic in nature. To ensure a student develops academically and grows socially, standards are integrated into a curriculum so that structured learning experiences occur and outcomes are assessed (e.g., by teacher-to-student conversation and day-to-day observations) and evaluated (e.g., by test scores, rankings, and grades).

This being understood, we can now formulate a game plan to "meet standards." A curricular framework is made up of content standards (what is to be achieved) and harmonizing performance standards (how students might achieve). As a teacher you are in the position to choose and implement a culturally responsive standards-based curriculum with goals, task-specific objectives, research-based procedures, and you can judge its effectiveness by assessments and evaluations of outcomes as a pathway to meeting standards.

Initial and continual collaboration with authentic local input is essential in building a curriculum that serves the needs of that community. Recognition of the significance of cultural and linguistic differences, the analysis of the new technologies—from laptops to PDAs (affecting *what* we learn by means of *how* we learn) are all part of the process in selecting and carrying out meaningful standards in today's culturally diverse and technology savvy world.

As content standards become part of a school's curriculum, explicit expectations arise concerning skills and knowledge as well as procedure (how a task is accomplished). This is where higher-order critical thinking skills (analysis, synthesis, and evaluation) come into play. Learning is a problem-solving enterprise.

Of course, within any plan of action there are long-range and short-range targets that need to be specified. Accordingly, when we look at a specific stage of student performance at a given level of development we use the term *benchmarks*. To put benchmarks in context, teachers create and evaluate an evolving curriculum that is modified based on student achievement at a given point (benchmark). In the day-to-day classroom teachers observe, monitor, and record student outcomes as they assess their curricular choices and their methodological approaches.

Understanding the rationale behind benchmarks we can now see why perceived ability grouping, commonly known as tracking, is an anathema to standards-based curricula. By setting up two contrasting curricular models (clearly distinguished by greater and lesser academic rigor) unequal educational experiences based on contrasting levels of teacher, student, and parent expectations lead to a self-fulfilling prophecy. Research indicates that curricular differences are at the heart of the disparity between the achievement and standardized test scores of those who were exposed to an enriched curriculum and those who were

not. Tracking has been shown to be an exclusionary practice that creates a classroom wall of structured inequality.

Teacher preparation to productively engage in the process of creating and implementing standards is imperative. Effective practice requires a wide variety of methodological approaches that can become part of a teacher's repertoire. This can be accomplished by quality professional development programs, in which knowledge of new methods is the first step to developing and practicing innovative teaching approaches to meet an ever greater diversity of learning styles.

Living in what is called the information age, in which the amount of knowledge on teaching and learning seems to grow exponentially, it should be obvious that a standards-based curriculum is anything but static. Changes during the teaching and learning process not only can but should be implemented to improve curriculum, assessment, and instruction, as new information and groundbreaking strategies become known. After all, raising student achievement trumps both curricular and methodological orthodoxy. ●

What U.S. Schools Could Learn from Japan

Q: We hear so often that high schools in other countries are much different from our own. Newspapers report that test scores in math and science show that U.S. students trail this country or that country. How is the daily life of a high school student different in Japan, for instance, from here in the United States? Can we really learn from cultures so different from our own?

A: By following Japanese students through a normal school day, you see some significant cultural differences between the high school experience in Japan and the United States. To begin, Japanese students do not typically drive cars. If their school is close, they may ride a bike or walk. If they live a great distance from the school, they may ride an hour or two on a train. Because schools start at 8:30, they must get up around 6. Students are easily identifiable in public because they wear a uniform unique to each school.

While on the train, the students are under the rules of their school. School policy, for example, may prohibit eating snacks, chewing gum, or any other activity that reflects poorly on the school's reputation. Some schools even require students to stand on buses and trains when coming or going to school, leaving seats for others in order to demonstrate courtesy.

When the students arrive at school, they put their street shoes in a locker and slip on school slippers (blue for boys, pink for girls) and head for their homeroom. As in the United States, the school day starts with class management tasks. The difference is, in Japan, students usually take attendance and make announcements. These activities are part of a rotating duty schedule called the *toban*.

Homerooms may be overcrowded by U.S. standards: They contain from 40 to 45 students. Another difference is that except for physical education or laboratory sessions, the students stay in their classroom the entire day. It is the instructors, who have a central teachers' office, who move from room to room.

Japanese students spend 240 days a year in school, which is about 60 days more than American students. The Japanese Ministry of Education determines course selection and textbooks. Schools have only limited power to change the curriculum.

Some of the subjects in academic high schools include mathematics, social studies, English, Japanese, and science. Electives are few. At the academic day's end, all students participate in *o soji*, the cleaning of the school. We are talking not about just sweeping the classroom, but the hallways, the restrooms, and any other unkempt area of the school.

Every day after school, club activities are held. While teachers sponsor the clubs, it is up to the students to determine the clubs' activities.

Students making their way home may stop at a "cram school," many times located near a bus or train station. Here they can go for supplementary lessons. Approximately 60 percent of Japanese students attend these after-school institutions.

High premiums are placed on learning. Admissions to the most prestigious high schools and universities are on the basis of examinations. The outcome of such examinations can influence a student's destiny, affecting not only what school he or she can attend but also the prospects of finding a good job.

Clearly the Japanese have a distinct approach to education. Seemingly much more responsibility is delegated to the student than in the United States. This call for the Japanese student to be increasingly self-directed in his or her studies stems from a belief that all young people possess the same innate intellectual capacity. Therefore, it is only the effort of the person that determines his or her ultimate success.

Some Japanese customs may not find acceptance in our culture, but the high premium on learning and hard work is instructive. The importance of education to a people and the emphasis placed on individual effort are values from which all can learn. Such values transcend time, place, and culture. ●

How Can All Students Experience Success?

Q: Given the number of poor kids, non-English-speaking kids, and slow learners, how are we going to get all of these young people to be successful without simply inflating grades to make it look like something good is happening?

A: The challenge to serve the learning needs of an ever more diverse student population has a "how to" that can work in any school. One thing that must happen, so that all students receive the most enriched education, is to coordinate efforts by every faculty member as to what is taught in the classroom.

The five-dollar term for this is "curricular congruence." How does this work to allow all students to receive the most enriched curriculum and experience academic success?

Instructional activities are planned among faculty so that schoolwork can overlap from one class to another. Let's say a student—we'll call her Joan—takes American history first period. This week's essay topic is how Thomas Paine's book *Common Sense* influenced Thomas Jefferson.

Joan has been taught the importance of the words, "We . . . do . . . declare, that these united colonies are . . . free and independent states. . . ." She also knows that in June of 1776, when these words were written, they were dangerous to speak or write, for they represented rebellion against the British government.

Nevertheless, Joan isn't sure of the connection between Thomas Paine and Thomas Jefferson. She is stuck and at risk of not attempting this week's essay.

During third period Joan has a study hall, or what some schools term a learning center period. Unfortunately, many schools still furnish a separate instructional unit (all too often made up of generic and mind-numbing workbooks!) for a study hall, a learning center experience, or any other form of pullout. Joan, however, is lucky. At her school, the learning center staff knows what she has been studying in her social studies class. What she really gets is a double period of American history. By having staff available to reteach and provide supplementary materials, Joan is able to grasp facts and concepts she had not realized before.

Now she finds out that Thomas Jefferson read Thomas Paine's book, and that, to some degree, *Common Sense* influenced Jefferson in writing the Declaration of Independence. Sounds like a fun essay to write. Here Joan can use her critical thinking skills of analysis, synthesis, and evaluation. She can also ask for help in more than one class when she gets stuck.

In order to make the curricular congruence plan work, teachers must have a set time each week to meet, plan, and discuss the learning progress of individual students. If the English teacher joined this group, then Joan would have three teachers during the day who knew the curricular demands as well as Joan's strengths and needs.

Therefore, to set up an enriched curriculum in which all students can succeed, some form of curricular congruence is necessary. Put it this way: Sufficient opportunities for every student to engage in real learning can occur by creating curricular links among classes. ●

Fostering the Bilingual Child

Q: Is it fair to ask a child to learn two languages when so many people have a hard time mastering one?

A: As our nation becomes more and more culturally and linguistically diverse, many children now live in a community where more than one language is commonly heard each day. These children face linguistic demands, not out of choice, but due to migration patterns over which they have no control. Because children are growing up in a multilingual world (e.g., teachers and students speaking English, mother and father speaking Spanish), they confront two languages on a daily basis and are not afforded the option of living in a monolingual world.

In this brave new multilingual world, one can observe a plethora of opinions as to the beneficial or detrimental effects of a child's multilingual experience. Politicians and voters are continually expressing strong notions concerning children growing up in a multilingual society. The concerns may be summed up in the question, "Is it fair to ask children to cope with more than one language?"

Many teachers, counselors, speech therapists, and even medical doctors have recommended that children growing up in a bilingual environment stop using one of the languages. They argue that the children will experience less confusion and one language (the main or higher status) will be acquired more easily without competition from a second language.

The problem with this "time on task" solution is that it flies in the face of known linguistic theory of how languages are acquired in a multilingual society. Besides the fact that no causal relationship has been shown to exist between a bilingual environment and language learning problems, there is simply no evidence that giving up one language redounds to the benefit of improving the retained language.

On the contrary, language and personal identity are so closely linked that any abrupt change in the use of a language can lead to social disorientation and troubling behavioral patterns. Further, as counterintuitive as it may first sound, building and maintaining a child's first language are of real benefit in the acquisition of a second language. Learning is an associative process, and the rules of language are transferable.

Having said that, acquiring a language is not an effortless task. Languages are complex. Engaging in a simple conversation on the playground does not provide the kind of cognitive academic learning proficiency needed in the classroom. To learn the complexities of any language, children need a nurturing environment in their first language. One cannot transfer language skills to a second language that have not been acquired in the first language. ●

Nurturing the Bilingual Child

Q: How important are parents and teachers in getting a child to feel good about speaking more than one language? What can they do to help a child learn two languages?

A: The emotional bonding between a child and parent in the initial phases of language learning should not be overlooked. An enriched language atmosphere and a strongly supportive environment in the home provide a strong foundation for building language skills.

Listening generates speaking; reading promotes writing. Without children having someone to speak to them in many different circumstances, and read (to and with them) many different kinds of stories, the early stages of language development will be stunted.

The quantity and quality of language learning experiences provided by a caring teacher (the parent is a child's first and most important teacher) play a critical role in developing a child's linguistic abilities, including the fostering of second-language development for the bilingual child.

Bilingualism is a process that occurs in phases. As more and more teachers confront the challenge of teaching the bilingual student, they must be made aware that helping a child to maintain his or her home language will increase that student's ability to acquire a second language.

Research indicates that the cultural, cognitive, and future economic advantages of a child growing up bilingual are real. Furthermore, if children do not maintain their home language, vital communication with their parents is put at risk.

Teachers can foster a climate of well-being in a culturally and linguistically diverse classroom by using methodological approaches that promote the development of all students into caring and literate human beings. Understanding different cultural patterns in how language is used is a good way to avoid a cultural clash based on misunderstanding. For example, we have known for decades that due to home environment, some students do not join in class discussions. At home they may have been taught that speaking up in public is a form of calling attention to yourself. This is considered by some cultures to be aggressive and even arrogant behavior.

Culturally sensitive instruction includes curricula and methodological approaches that pay respect to those who are being taught. Accordingly, writing about people, places, and activities important to the bilingual child encourages that student to take linguistic risks that would probably not occur in an artificial assignment not geared to the learner's previous experience. Subject matter that deals with a child's previous linguistic and cultural knowledge in a positive way validates the learner. Thus the simple phrase "Your mother and father will be pleased," may be much more meaningful than "You should be pleased with yourself."

Another notion that both parents and teachers should realize is that in language, fluency comes before accuracy. Therefore, the bilingual child needs to feel free to experiment and produce utterances that are original (if initially inaccurate). The patterns and rules of grammar come into play as the teacher rephrases the child's linguistic expression into a standard pattern.

Teaching is modeling. Appropriate feedback from the instructor helps the bilingual child reformulate standard patterns and embed appropriate expressions.

Bilingual children will internalize a second language better if they are engaged in meaningful activities that require using the target language. Activities such as demonstrations, modeling, and role-playing, along with presenting new information within the context of known information, are highly recommended. ●

Attracting Minority Students to Science and Math

Q: Are we attracting enough minority students to math and science courses to keep up with the nation's need for scientists and engineers in the 21st century?

A: The short answer is no. In fact, minorities are underrepresented in quality math and science classes at every level from the elementary classroom to the graduate seminar. Historically underrepresented minority students (i.e., African American, Latino, and Native Americans) are a large part of the total equation of the overall shortfall of scientists and engineers America will face in the 21st century.

Over the next 20 years, minority students will outnumber the total white population of elementary school children. In the last decade, historically underrepresented racial and ethnic minorities comprised 19 percent of the civilian labor force, yet only 8 percent of the nation's science and engineering labor force. As we enter the 21st century, 85 percent of the new workers in the United States will be members of minority groups and/or females.

There is a lack of enriched elementary and secondary schools programs in science and math, which after all are the gateway to college courses and ultimately career choices in the new technologies. Some of the obstacles to success for minority students, which lead to the unequal participation of these groups in science and mathematics education, are:

- Perceived ability grouping (tracking)
- Understaffed and underequipped schools
- Relatively low number of quality science and math courses offered
- Lack of qualified science and math teachers
- Poor access to resources

Furthermore, there is an unfair expectations game being played in which minority students have traditionally come out as losers. Unfortunately, teachers of classes with high minority enrollment are most likely to expect less from their students. These teachers, therefore, emphasize getting students ready for standardized tests (a watered-down competency-based education) rather than preparing them for challenging college-level studies in science or mathematics.

The ultimate answer to this problem is to ensure that all students receive the same enriched curriculum and that teachers use a wide variety of methodological approaches to best serve each student. Improving the opportunities for minority students means moving toward more individualized learning, as well as cooperative learning. Simply put, teachers have to be ready to accommodate many different kinds of learning styles.

America's future depends to a large degree on the amount of enthusiasm, interest, and enriched science and math curricula that teachers present to those too often left behind. The results for the underserved minority student seem clear—enhanced school achievement, based on the acquisition of skills and knowledge, lead in turn to successful professional careers in an increasingly technological society. ●

Mathematics for the English as a Second Language Student

Q: What are some of the ways teachers can build mathematics skills for students who are still learning English?

A: Teaching mathematics or any other content course to an English as a Second Language (ESL) student is a unique challenge. Teachers must understand that when a student comes into a new cultural and linguistic environment, he or she may well have trouble making sense of course content without the same background that a native student possesses. This, of course, can lead to a frustrating experience on the part of the ESL learner.

While the coursework must be modified for the ESL student, every student, ESL or otherwise, must have access from the very beginning to the most enriched mathematics curriculum. Teaching the enriched core curriculum to all students, regardless of their cultural or linguistic background, demands that educators use a wide variety of methodological approaches. Thus, by using the enriched core subject matter along with a variety of approaches to set the environment for learning, math teachers can better teach all students to:

- Learn the value of mathematics
- Become mathematical problem solvers

- Attain and maintain a level of mathematical self-efficacy
- Understand how to reason and communicate mathematically

Here are three approaches any mathematics teacher can employ to better serve the ESL student:

1. Use a mixed grouping procedure. ESL students benefit from a variety of group settings. Whole-class work is essential in providing all students with the most enriched core curriculum while building listening and responding skills. Small-group work allows students to use a "buddy system" with native speakers to enhance conversational skills and social rapport. Individualized education gives the student the necessary one-on-one contact with the teacher or peer tutor to permit the ESL student to work at his or her own pace.

2. Choose math assignments that spur a student's intellectual curiosity. Frequently, ability to perform mathematical operations is based on practice. The more practice a student has with a mathematical

task, the more proficient he or she will become. Students tend to work with problems that interest them. Therefore, calculating percentages can be a dull or interesting task depending on the subject matter (e.g., baseball statistics, comparative sales of a pop star's latest CD, world birth rates, etc.). Knowing the cultural backgrounds of students can help the teacher develop connections to previous and developing knowledge, which in turn produces a more interesting set of mathematical developmental tasks.

3. Incorporate technological tools to increase math awareness. The use of the computer, calculator, ruler or protractor breaks away from the single dimension of the spoken or written word and allows the ESL student to learn yet another language—the universal language of mathematics.

The overriding assumption is that both mathematics and language acquisition are skill-based operations based on understanding concepts and putting that knowledge to practice. Any skill gets better with practice. Thus, when a teacher becomes more and more acquainted with the cultural and linguistic heritage that an ESL student brings to the classroom, intellectually stimulating connections can be made to both the target language (English) and the content of an enriched mathematics curriculum. The result is an ESL student who gets a first-rate mathematics education, while concurrently learning the English language. ●

Changing Public Schools to Serve All Students

Q: It appears that all is not right in today's public schools. Mediocrity appears to be acceptable. What are the facts, and what can be done to make things better?

A: American schools continue to present a dual result. Some students are truly prepared for the world of work and/or college, and others are left behind. The Fordham Foundation reports that since the early 1980s, about ten million seniors in high school did not learn to read at a basic level.

Of course, without basic skills students become frustrated and give up. Witness the nearly six million students who, since the early 1980s, have dropped out of high school altogether. Did you know that in 1996, 13 percent of all African Americans from ages 16 to 24 neither attended school nor possessed a diploma?

Seventeen percent of first-generation Latinos were high school dropouts, including 44 percent of Latino immigrants from the same age group. Clearly, even though dropout rates nationally continue to decline and college attendance is increasing, a dual educational system—an anathema to equal educational opportunity—is too often a reality for poor and minority children.

What is the answer? Let's start off by giving practitioners (classroom teachers) more of a say in setting up a system where learning can take place for every student.

Teachers know that there are four basic components that must be fulfilled for a student to be successful. A student must understand what is being taught (curriculum), how the material is being taught (methodology), that the subject is of value (cultural relevance), and that if a student demonstrates genuine attempts, a successful outcome can be achieved (effort creates ability).

Frankly, the traditional "top-down" approach from superintendents and principals, many of whom have been out of the classroom for decades, has not proven to be an efficient model. What might a new administrative paradigm look like?

With teachers in charge, a headmaster could be appointed at each school. This headmaster would be an administrator who is also a classroom teacher, thus providing a pedagogic role model for the faculty. The headmaster would have the responsibility of being not a traditional principal (preoccupied primarily with management functions), but a true instructional leader.

By the way, so many of the daily nonacademic functions performed by a principal (work for which they have never truly been trained), such as ordering supplies, allocating room space, directing the gardeners, and filling out insurance forms for school activities, could be handled by a business manager at a fraction of the salary of a principal.

With practitioners in charge of their profession, as in medicine, law, or even at the university level of education, K–12 schools might more readily be transformed. The initial mission of the school would be for the teachers to adopt the most enriched curriculum for all students (regardless of social or economic status or race), devise various methodological approaches to best reach different learning styles, and commit resources to a meaningful ongoing staff development plan.

A systematic professional development plan is a key part of educational reform. Such a professional development model that links with a partner institution in higher education is a logical way to keep the faculty updated on the latest pedagogical practices that enhance student achievement and social growth. What is called for is systemic change. Incorporating the expertise of those who actually teach the classes may provide the best route to give equal access to a quality education for all. ●

Girls Still Getting the Short End of the Education Stick

Q: Girls still don't seem to be getting the same chances as boys to get a good education. Why is this so? What can be done?

A: Subtle and sometimes unintended messages create powerful—although incorrect—notions among parents, teachers, and the students themselves that girls, because of their gender, cannot be successful in certain subjects. For example, the tra-

ditional cultural belief that women's roles are secondary to men ("... behind every good man stands a good woman") has been woven deep into our subconscious.

The idea that males excel in math, technology, and engineering, whereas women excel in more artistic endeavors, is part of this often observed, but seldom challenged, modern mythology. Gender equity is a critical issue because it recognizes that inequality in educational opportunity promotes subsequent unequal educational treatment and ultimately results in unequal educational outcomes.

As long as women are primarily seen in secondary roles—nurses rather than doctors, secretaries rather than managers—college applications and careers will reflect this self-fulfilling prophecy. Of course, there is nothing wrong with a woman choosing to be a nurse or a secretary, as long as she did not make that choice simply because she felt incapable of choosing other professions.

If you think the problem today is being overstated, just look at the schools themselves. The lower-paying and/or less prestigious positions (in elementary schools) are staffed with a preponderance of females, and the higher-paying and/or more prestigious positions (principals, superintendents, faculty at colleges and universities) are numerically dominated by males. This reality presents a constant, if unchallenged, model.

Make no mistake; gender-biased attitudes are alive and well! For instance, research indicates that many girls attribute their success to luck. Unfortunately,

we don't control luck, and it frequently changes. On the other hand, many boys attribute their success to ability. Ability appears more meritorious, more valid, and more stable. Is it any wonder that many girls, although they may be academically outperforming their male counterparts, have lower self-confidence than boys do?

When one attributes her success to luck, such a fickle friend, we can understand why she might lack a high level of confidence. The work of parents and teachers (parents for this generation of children, teachers for the next two generations of children) is to provide the most enriched curriculum to all students. This can, in part, be accomplished by disposing of curriculum materials that are biased in content (be it language or illustrations), reinforcing the misguided notion that certain fields of endeavor are gender specific.

A fair and equitable education must be based on the idea that all students have an equal opportunity, without gender-biased limitations, to relate to all aspects of the world in which they live. ●

Gender in Children's Literature: Cinderella or Cinderfella?

Q: Anyone who has been in an elementary school realizes that boys act very differently than girls. Who sets these gender roles? What can be done so that kids, male or female, are not stereotyped, and instead grow up to be all that they can be?

A: There are a lot of sociocultural factors that shape gender roles inside and outside of school. One significant factor which

contributes to how boys and girls think of themselves is the image of males and females portrayed in children's literature. When it comes to many traditional children's books, there can be no doubt; gender bias in content and illustrations clearly exists.

Research indicates that male characters dominate the majority of books in children's literature. According to one recent study, male names outnumbered female names by nearly two to one.

Perhaps the archetypal example of male–female stereotyping is the classic story of Cinderella. Cinderella, for all her noble qualities, is fundamentally portrayed as being acted on rather than active. She is seen as conforming, dependent, and obedient. Only with the help of her fairy godmother, a favorite (bibbity bobbity boo) empowered character, can Cinderella have a chance at a better life. Even at the royal ball, she is not in control—except to escape the palace and seemingly accept her fate as a henpecked housekeeper.

In contrast, the strong, independent, and capable role is embodied in the prince. Romance, affection, marriage, and a happy ending appear solely dependent on his choice, not hers.

When children read these stories they immediately pick up on a variety of none-too-subtle messages. Boys are to be the rescuers; girls are in need of rescuing. Boys are to be active and assertive; girls are to be passive, waiting for that knight in shining armor or the prince who sweeps them off their feet at the royal ball.

So what's the answer? Should Cinderella be banned? That would be a nutty idea. Instead, after children experience a story like Cinderella, parents and teachers should be sure to introduce a narrative where females are presented in active and dynamic roles. In this way children will begin to see individuals in stories as distinct personalities who act irrespective of their gender.

After all, virtues like courage, wisdom, understanding, and honesty are not gender specific. In order for children to understand this, we should focus more on the stories in children's literature in which characters act in a rational or emotional way depending on the situation in the story—not on some stereotypical notion of gender. ●

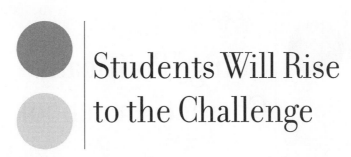

Students Will Rise to the Challenge

Q: Is there a survey to show the kind of classes students really want? Do they really want failure-proof underwater basketweaving kinds of courses, or do they want to be challenged? Has anyone bothered to ask the students themselves?

A: To begin, students are influenced by those at home and school to set their sights high or low. Parents' and teachers' expectations and assumptions about a student's potential have a real effect on student achievement and on the student's own feeling about his or her ability. Students internalize the beliefs about their ability and adopt their parents' and teachers' perceptions of them.

Unfortunately, many students from particular ethnic or low socioeconomic groups discover that their teachers consider them capable of doing only a less-demanding course of study. The result of this kind of educational predestination is that the student either rises up to or (more often) lowers himself or herself to the teacher's expectation.

In this atmosphere of predestined assumption, innate ability is viewed as the main determining factor in scholastic success. For the underachiever, poor performance means low ability, and low ability is viewed as immune to change. Factors such as quality instruction, parental involvement, a nurturing teacher, or a student's efforts are summarily discounted or even dismissed.

In such an environment, we might reason that students with low expectations of themselves would look forward to lax teachers with low standards. If we believed that, we would be wrong. In recent surveys of high school students, four major concerns are worth noting:

- Students want to be engaged. The most memorable work in school was their most challenging. They equated hard work with success and satisfaction.

- Students want order. Students feel personally insulted by "dumbed-down" curricula. In short, they would work harder if more demands were put on them.

- Students want more individualized instruction. Closer and better monitoring from teachers, and expanded after-school classes, were requested.

- Students want fairness in the classroom. Teaching the values of hard work, honesty, and effort were seen as a way to combat cheating.

It seems obvious that students want to be challenged by the most enriched curriculum. Teachers and parents who view intelligence as a changing element, rather than a static one, are on the right track.

They can avoid the rigid preconceived notions or unconscious biases of what students can or cannot achieve in school. Students are asking for high standards and interesting courses. Are we listening? ●

Being "Politically Correct" in School

 Why is it that education today all has to be politically correct? Anytime a student or teacher steps out of line and "offends" women or minorities, you can forget about free speech.

Is it fair that either you practice political correctness in school or you have a problem with certain students and teachers?

 Everybody has an opinion about the term "politically correct" (or PC). This term has been around since the mid 1980s, becoming a pejorative expression that casts a negative pall on any number of progressive initiatives. Such ideas as affirmative

action, multicultural education, incorporating women's issues into the curriculum, and renaming different groups of people (e.g., Native Americans instead of American Indians) all fall under the umbrella of political corectness.

If we eliminate the confrontational tone of what can easily turn into a partisan knock-down, drag-out fight, we can shed some light on political correctness. For example, today it is right and proper to address a woman as Ms. instead of Miss or Mrs. Likewise, the groups of people once known as blacks are now called African Americans.

The key issue is not what is PC, but something our mothers told us many years ago. It was, quite simply, to address people by the name they wished to be called. Sounds fair, and it's pretty hard to disagree with Mom.

There are those who see political correctness as an organized movement that threatens free speech and the very fabric of our nation. Of course, one is free to believe in such a conspiracy theory. However, there is no evidence of such a tacit, subversive agreement among teachers or professors at any level of education. In fact, faculty meetings at the elementary, secondary, or collegiate level demonstrate that far from consensus on any subject, the opinions on any subject usually vary in the exact quantity as the numbers of teachers or professors present!

One problem with the anti-PC crowd is that they have no suggestions for what would substitute in place of political correctness. Do they wish to march with flags unfurled back to the 1950s? The world is changing, and new words are needed to try to describe current variations.

How we address human beings, especially in school, should be accurate and should take into consideration the wishes of those being labeled. ●

SUGGESTED READINGS

Bergstrom, A., Cleary, L. M., & Peacock, T. (2003). *The seventh generation: Native students speak about finding the good path.* Charleston, WV: ERIC Clearinghouse on Rural Education and Small Schools.

Boyle-Baise, M. (2002). *Multicultural service learning: Educating teachers in diverse communities.* New York: Teachers College Press.

Campos, C. (2006, May 2). National Teacher Day Spotlights Key Issues Facing Profession. *National Education Association.* Retrieved September 27, 2006, from www.nea.org/newsreleases/2006/nr060502.html.

Cohn, D., & Bahrampour, T. (2006, May 10). Of U.S. Children Under 5, Nearly Half Are Minorities. *Washington Post,* p. A01.

Deloria, V., Jr., & Wildcat, D. R. (2001). *Power and place: Indian education in America.* Golden, CO: Fulcrum.

Fry, R. (2003). *Hispanic youth dropping out of U.S. schools: Measuring the challenge.* Washington, DC: Pew Hispanic Center.

Gale, T., & Densmore, K. (2000). *Just schooling: Explorations in the cultural politics of teaching.* Philadelphia: Open University Press.

Gibson, M. A., & Bejinez, L. F. (2002). Dropout prevention: How migrant education supports Mexican youth. *Journal of Latinos and Education, 1*(3), 155–175.

Harris, H. L. (2002). School counselors' perceptions of biracial children: A pilot study. *Professional School Counseling, 6,* 120–129.

Henze, R. (2002). *Leading for diversity: How school leaders promote positive interethnic relations.* Thousand Oaks, CA: Corwin Press.

Martin, J. R. (2002). *Cultural miseducation: In search of a democratic solution.* New York: Teachers College Press.

Osterman, K. F. (2000). Students' need for belonging in the school community. *Review of Educational Research, 70*(3), 323–367.

Pewewardy, C. D. (2002). Learning styles of American Indian/Alaska Native students: A review of the literature and implications for practice. *Journal of American Indian Education, 41*(3), 22–56.

Russell Chaddock, G. (2006, June 21). US high school dropout rate: High, but how high? *The Christian Science Monitor.* Retrieved September 27, 2006, from www.csmonitor.com/2006/0621/p03s02-ussc.html.

Sadler, N. (2002). *Multicultural connections: Creative writing, literature, and assessment in the elementary school.* Lanham, MD: Scarecrow Press.

Siraj-Blatchford, I., & Clarke, P. (2000). *Supporting identity, diversity, and language in the early years.* Philadelphia, PA: Open University Press.

Sorensen, B. (2002). The community-based education model: Bringing validity to education and careers. *Winds of Change, 17*(4), 60–62.

Stansfield, J. (2002). *Writers of the American West: Multicultural learning encounters.* Greenwood Village, CO: Teacher Ideas Press.

Vavrus, M. (2002). *Transforming the multicultural education of teachers: Theory, research, and practice.* New York: Teachers College Press.

Yamauchi, L. A., Ceppi, A. K., & Lau-Smith, J. (2000). Teaching in a Hawaiian context: Educator perspectives on the Hawaiian language immersion program. *Bilingual Research Journal, 24*(4), 333–351.

unit :3

The Why and How of Classroom Psychology

There's More Than One Way to Be Smart

Q: What are the standards for intelligence? How do we know someone is smart? How is it possible to be smart in math but not in English, or be a great musician but a poor speaker?

A: We know someone is intelligent when they demonstrate an ability to learn. Someone may be intelligent without demonstrating learning, but then we would have no way of gauging their intelligence.

If we take the demonstration of learning as a standard, we can attempt to answer your questions. It is not useful to think of intelligence as a once-set, never-changing thing. Howard Gardner has proposed eight intelligences, with each demonstrating a certain kind of learning:

- Linguistic: use language effectively in both oral and written modes
- Logical/mathematical: use numbers and patterns effectively and reason well
- Visual/spatial: recognize form, space, color, line, and shape; draw, create, and build
- Musical: recognize rhythm, pitch, and melody; make music
- Bodily/kinesthetic: use the body to dance, move, touch, gesture, and solve problems
- Naturalist: recognize and classify plants, minerals, and animals
- Interpersonal: understand another person's feelings, motivations, and intentions; work in groups
- Intrapersonal: be self-directed, based on self-knowledge

This would explain how one can be so "smart" in one activity and not so successful in others. Gardner further contends that each intelligence "learns" in a different way. This notion has real implications for everyone, especially teachers. New materials and strategies should be developed to reach a wide variety of learning styles. The more ways an idea is explained, the better it will be understood by different learners approaching it from different learning styles. ●

Bell Curve Isn't the Best Learning Indicator

Q: What is the fairest and most accurate method of grading students' exams?

A: Teachers who use a so-called "balanced" curve base the use of that grading method on the notion that a bell-shaped curve in some way "proves" the reliability of the scores and the validity of their test. They believe that a test that results in a few A's and F's, a larger number of B's and D's, and a great majority of C's has somehow proven their test valid and their evaluation fair because such a scale resembles the "perfect" bell curve.

These beliefs are unwarranted and may do great harm to students. In order to understand why, we must first understand something about curves. When a researcher makes continual observations, she may perceive that many physical and psychological factors follow a pattern called normal distribution. The right side of this curve is the mirror image of the left. In these situations, most observations cluster around the center of the curve.

Imagine pinching a half-filled toothpaste tube at both ends (keep the cap on!). The paste is forced to the middle of the tube while the ends flatten out. Unfortunately for teachers using the bell curve, students do not in any way resemble toothpaste in a tube. In fact, a perfect normal distribution does not exist in nature; it is only a theoretical concept.

Furthermore, some curves based on research observation look nothing like a bell at all. These curves, just as valid as any other, are skewed to one side of the graph or another. In other words, depending

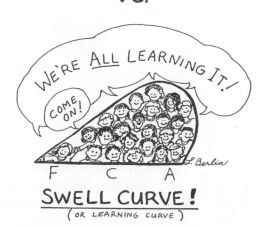

on what you are observing, curves can be bell-shaped or very lopsided.

If a teacher is anchored to the bell curve in scoring tests, that same teacher would logically assume that failure of a given number of students on a test is normal—and even desirable. Now you can understand the potential harm of grading tests on a predetermined normal distribution. This approach fails to realize that the reason to give tests is not to produce a normal distribution curve but to measure what the students have learned.

When a teacher is truly doing the job, high expectations and a can-do attitude are called for, not the expectation of predicted failure. A teacher whose students do poorly cannot consider herself to be doing a superior job.

For an example of how the bell curve mentality operates against setting and then achieving lofty goals, look at the real world. If you were a football coach who, season after season, won as many games as you lost, would you consider your record "perfect" and expect a new coaching contract each year? If you were a car manufacturer who turned out as many good cars as lemons—with a great many average cars in between—how long do you think this "perfect" distribution would keep you in business?

When a teacher finds that a certain segment of the class is not "getting it," the instructor can either accept the failure as part of a "bell curve" or intervene to make sure no one is left behind. A good teacher gives a "fair" chance to all by reteaching the material, using different approaches to appeal to different learning styles, and contacting parents (elementary school through high school) to enlist their support when students appear to be falling behind.

This is not about lowering standards but actively working to bring all students up to standard. A good teacher is a committed student advocate. That teacher judges her success not on a theoretical perfect balance of failure and success but on the number of students who have learned. ●

Teachers Don't "Give" Grades

Q: What should a parent do when her child complains that the teacher gave her a low grade that she didn't deserve? Everybody knows different teachers grade differently. Are there some basic rules in giving fair grades?

A: The issue of grading is central to the integrity of a school. Unfortunately, it is a topic that is frequently misunderstood. First, let us clear up a major misconception. Teachers should not be "giving" grades. Grades should be earned by the students.

An analogy to sports may be helpful. Students are the players who score the points, and teachers, in assigning grades, are merely the scorekeepers. Grades should be the product of student achievement, not something "supplied" by the teacher.

Having said that, the teacher must take the responsibility of calculating the grades most seriously. You may have some sincere and quite legitimate questions for the teacher.

If you think your child's teacher graded her unfairly, or you do not know how your child was evaluated, it is time for you to talk to your child's teacher. Here is a short list of practices to which a good teacher adheres. You can think of them as the basic rules of assigning fair grades.

- Grading policy must be clear, objective, and understood by the students and their parents. A concise handout outlining the grading policy should be distributed by the teacher at the beginning of each term.

- Students should have immediate and up-to-date access to their current grade at any given point during the term.

- Teachers should give periodic updates to the parents. This can be accomplished most easily by phoning parents with progress reports.

A teacher's grading procedures should never be a mystery to students or parents.

The idea must always be that it is the student who controls his or her academic future by earning good grades.

After the final exam is over and the last essay is turned in, points are summed up by the teacher to reveal the grade each student has earned. It is the student, both in theory and practice, who should be the one truly responsible for his or her grade. ●

Halting Grade Inflation

Q: There is a lot of talk these days about grade inflation. Does it occur and what can be done about it?

A: The problem in the minds of many seems to exist at all levels of education from elementary school through college. Here are the facts. Prestigious schools such as Harvard, Dartmouth, Columbia, and Stanford have experienced grade inflation for decades. The *New York Times* reported that

83 percent of all grades at Stanford were A's or B's from 1992 to 1997, whereas only 69 percent of all grades were in that range from 1973 to 1977.

Many have voiced their notions concerning the phenomenon of grade inflation. Opinions as to why grade inflation occurs include the following:

- Societal pressures for students to excel

- Faculty reluctance to risk unpopularity

- The (spurious) charge that more and more students are simply grade-grubbers

Whatever the reason, the important thing is that there is a way to lower traditionally inflated grades and increase student satisfaction at the same time. Sound counterintuitive? Lowering grades while increasing the student's contentment with a class may seem, to many teachers, not only a distasteful task but also an impossible goal.

School administrators who simply request an end to grade inflation without presenting a coherent plan to accomplish this task use what I call the "magic wand" approach. They recognize the need and have a sincere desire to end grade inflation but simply fail to present a coherent strategy to get the job done.

Fortunately, a program that can be used at any level of schooling was developed at a major university to lower a school's grade point average, while increasing the students' approval of the program. In a nutshell, here's how this was accomplished:

- The premise of a standardized course "design and rigor" gave students a familiar approach to a changing sequenced curriculum. In other words, the *what* changed, but the *how* remained the same.

- Three functional graded curricular components were thoroughly described to both teachers and students. Specifically, those three items were essays, class participation, and the final exam. Bloom's taxonomy of thinking skills was used to assure grades were based on a continuous demonstration of the students' higher-order critical-thinking skills (analysis, synthesis, evaluation)

- An explicit grading policy (each component was weighed by a point total) and objective scoring scale were presented in the course syllabus. The scale was as follows:

100–93 = A
92–85 = B
84–75 = C
74–60 = D
59–0 = F

- A two-pronged policy for grading the final exam was constructed. Students were advised that they had the opportunity to earn a B only if their final essay exam reached a certain requisite length (e.g., 1,500 words) and was of high quality. Correspondingly, a final exam essay that reached a requisite length of 4,000 words and was of high quality allowed the student, due to the demonstration of greater fluency, the opportunity to earn an A.

- Obviously, word totals, which can be adjusted downward for elementary and secondary students, were only part of the criteria. Grading elements other than length were included. For example, the complexity of ideas (within a coherent response to specific questions), the quality and quantity of detail (e.g., explicit connections to research), the organization (e.g., APA or MLA format), and correct usage of grammar and syntax were all taken into consideration by the teacher.

- The general philosophy—teachers do not give grades but students earn them—was articulated in the course syllabus. Because students had detailed and specific goals, objectives, procedures, and evaluations they had clear and concise information about the *what* and *how* of the course that provided unambiguous direction. As students finished each task successfully they gained a growing sense of self-efficacy. In short, this straightforward approach reinforced the concept that to a great extent, effort creates ability.

- Teachers were asked after each term to submit their class grades to a program coordinator via email. The coordinator did the math, came up with a collective GPA, and immediately reported that information back through email to all the teachers in the system.

- A third party polled students, by means of an anonymous questionnaire, as to their satisfaction with the courses they were taking. These results were released to all the teachers as well as to the administration.

The final results were surprising to some and gratifying to all. Grade point averages fell from a decade-long, seemingly intractable 3.8 to a more respectable 3.2. The 3.2 GPA is even more impressive due to the fact that student satisfaction rose during the study from a low of 75 percent to a high of 96 percent.

Thus, even though grades were lowered, students were more contented. The reasons seem to be that both students and teachers understood the grading criteria and felt the evaluation was fair and accurate and gave the student the choice to excel.

Let's review the three basic steps to implementing this program:

- First, a rigorous and fair format must be designed.
- Second, the newly designed model must be communicated to the teachers and the students.
- Third, the GPA and student satisfaction outcomes must be reported to, and monitored by, the entire faculty.

In the end, avoiding grade inflation is a function of professorial leadership. ●

Does the Size of Your Brain Matter?

Q: What are the newest discoveries about human intelligence? Is someone with a larger brain more intelligent than someone with a smaller brain? What should teachers and parents know about the brain?

A: Exciting research about the human brain seems to be in the news on a frequent basis. Much of the new research on that three-pound mass of gray matter centers on better understanding the connections inside the brain.

An infant's brain is made up of trillions of unconnected neurons that have the potential of connecting with other neurons. It is these connections (roughly 100 billion) that cause the brain to function.

Scientists examined photos of Einstein's brain just recently. In terms of size, his brain was considered quite normal. Einstein's brain was the same weight and had the same front-to-back measurements as the other brains in the study. Size, therefore, does not appear to affect intelligence.

The distinguishing physical factor about Einstein's brain (which used to sit in a jar in a cardboard box behind a beer cooler in Kansas!) was that the inferior parietal region was 15 percent wider on both sides than normal. Correspondingly, a groove (the sulcus) that normally extends from the front of the brain to the back was smaller than normal. This might

have allowed more neurons in this area to establish connections among each other. It is this evidence of very rich connections between the brain cells that may be the key to understanding intelligence.

The leader of the study of Einstein's brain, neuroscientist Sandra Witelson, remarked, "... it shouldn't be seen as 'anatomy is destiny.'" The point is that environment is crucial to the development of intelligence. The brain is not a static organ.

Brain capacity is actually something that we physically build up. Recent research appears to prove that growth of new brain cells can take place in mature mice. This is consistent with the idea that a rich learning environment stimulates brain growth. What we know now can be summed up under the "use it or lose it" principle:

- Neuron patterns in the brain form from the amount of input.

- Neurons connect when we learn by doing.

- Review and feedback refresh and fine-tune the brain.

With this new knowledge, parents and teachers should understand two basic notions. First, the earliest years of a child's life are the most critical for developing intelligence, because this is when neural connections are made. Second, hands-on learning is of great importance in making these neural connections that will last a lifetime.

There are three ways to make the latest breakthroughs in brain research work for you. Plan firsthand experiences. A field trip provides the kind of multisensory experiences that can stimulate a variety of intelligences.

Include the arts. Enrich your life while those neurons connect by incorporating music, drawing, and other forms of artistic endeavor into the learning experience.

Finally, offer a wide range of activities. The more diverse the activities, the more ideas and concepts to understand and the more ways to learn them—all of which continue to stimulate those neurons into making those crucial connections.

When it comes to developing intelligence, a strong case is now being made that nurture, even more than nature, may be the critical factor. ●

Brain Growth: A Second Bite of the Apple

Q: How might teaching in the classroom change in light of current developments in what we now know about the brain?

A: First, let's review the latest research about the human brain. We know now that intelligence (brainpower) is not static, but dynamic—it changes as we learn.

The brain goes through very dramatic changes at least twice in our lifetime. The first, of course, is after birth when the brain produces an "oversupply" of brain cells and neural connections.

The second time the brain grows (at about age 11 for girls and age 12 for boys) is in adolescence. In this second growth phase, the gray matter of the brain actually thickens behind the frontal lobes—areas that control judgment and decision making. This "bulking up" at the adolescent stage of life includes both new brain cells and new neural connections.

Significantly, it appears that if an adolescent "uses" these new cells and connections (e.g., in a stimulating classroom environment), they can be retained. Therefore, important choices have to be made at this time, because a youngster's brain seems to become "hard-wired" for whatever endeavor—profound or frivolous—he or she is pursuing at that stage

of life. The hard-wiring occurs because as teenagers grow, a substance called myelin wraps around the brain cells and neural connections. Myelin gives the brain cells better insulation and faster connections—but at the same time, limits new growth.

Using this information as background, educational reformers have been suggesting a curriculum that cuts across subject matter lines. Accordingly, integrating a school's curriculum has been promoted as the best method of stimulating learning.

It is believed that integrative education provides a better learning model than the traditional breaking down of ideas into different disciplines (English, math, history, etc.). The reasoning is that the brain can more securely encode and retrieve information when it perceives a web of connected meanings. It has been argued that an integrative education allows the child to be educated through a more holistic context, without the artificial divisions that traditional single-subject curricula present.

Knowledge is both additive and interdependent. An integrative curricular model, which cuts across traditional subject matter lines, may well prove to be the kind of enriched environment best suited to a learner's dynamic growing brain. ●

Disposition Drives Cognition

Q: How important is it that students enjoy what they are about to study? Do they learn more? Do they learn better?

A: To understand the importance of disposition let's consider the three learning domains that teachers deal with every day in the classroom: the affective, the cognitive, and the psychomotor. One simple way to explain each domain is to assign them to the "heart, head, and hands." The affective deals with emotions and values (heart), the cognitive with thought (head) and the psychomotor with physical activity (hands). You can now realize why learning is such a multidimensional pursuit.

Central to all teaching should be the merging of "heart, head, and hands." Although all three of the traditional realms constantly interact with one another, it is the affective domain that is seen to initiate learning. In other words, the affective (one's disposition to learn) leads the way to the cognitive and the psychomotor. The affective domain functions first (has primacy), for it is in the affective domain wherein you as the teacher initially set a positive learning environment so that the cognitive and psychomotor domains can flourish.

Today we know more than ever about the apotheosis of learning—the brain. In scanning the brain with new high-powered technological tools, we now have the ability to examine billions of neurons and trillions of connections between cells. The brain represents an incredible universe of complex circuitry that grows and contracts with the learning experience. No chaotic universe this, amazingly every cell has a "preprogrammed" position and cor-respondingly every link between neurons is part of a meticulous order.

Although parts of the brain have specialized functions these actions are shaped by learning. Hence, both nature and nurture sculpt the brain. Our new understanding of genetics and environment has both obvious and profound ramifications for teaching and learning. We now understand how different learning environments continually grow and prune neural connections in a brain of amazing plasticity. By continuing to comprehend how the human brain learns best, teachers have a wonderful opportunity to adapt their teaching to better meet the needs of the learner.

Let's be clear; the very foundation of learning, which has its origins in personal discovery and idiosyncratic invention (as we "sculpt" our brain), is to a large degree premised on how we feel about what we are about to do. Furthermore, it is the synergistic interaction among the three domains that produces learning. The human brain presents multidirectional pathways where meaning is valued over mere information and where nurture (given the brain's plasticity) can overcome nature (the brain's past capacity).

As we have noted, the affective domain deals with attitudes and values that shape both academic development and social growth. Common notions such as the love of learning, the spirit of discovery, the dedication to science, or the honoring of civic duties are all examples of the emotions and values that make up the affective domain. They are clear examples of value-laden education in which a student feels self-motivated. How one feels about what is to be taught (or who is doing the teaching!) can virtually open or close the door to cognition. Inspiration, motivation, and empowerment, all affective in nature, express our deepest feelings of self-worth and commitment. In short, disposition drives cognition.

Research has discovered that

- Emotion drives the thought process and sparks decisions
- Learning is a process of deciding which neural connections to strengthen and which to prune
- Thinking involves complex reactions from different parts of the brain
- Neural pathways are multidimensional
- Nurture can overcome nature
- Meaning trumps information (we don't seek information; we seek meaning)

It is critical to understand the trigger nature of the affective domain. Although traditional approaches to learning emphasize cognitive aspects (e.g., generic lesson plans are usually based on cognitive strategies that stress a student's ability to think, learn, and apply) little, if any, sustained learning will occur without the student's intrinsic motivation (i.e., student choice), which is premised on interest being aroused, a response being generated, and a judgment being passed on the worth of the knowledge and/or skills being expressed or demonstrated.

If the initial emotion about what is to be learned is positive, there is a good chance for success in a given developmental task—in short, we learn more and learn better. Success sets the groundwork for self-efficacy. As this attitude of self-efficacy grows, a learner becomes more and more apt to find success even in new and unique environments. With what we know about the affective domain as a trigger mechanism for learning it is fair to describe humans not as thinking beings, but more precisely as feeling beings that think. Figure 3.1 illustrates that the affective domain is at the core of learning. The affective activates the cognitive and then the psychomotor domains. Think of it as a chain reaction from heart to head to hands as our values and emotions influence our thoughts and then our actions. ●

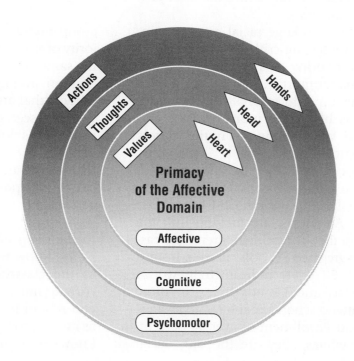

Don't Abandon the Academic Ship

Q: Are students today as good as they used to be? There seems to be a lot written about how poorly students today do compared with the kids who went to school in the past. Is the ship sinking? Can any of this be measured?

A: If we look at SAT scores over the last 30 years, we can take the measure of how well students seem to be doing. There is good news and bad news. These are uncertain waters, so let's look at the good news first.

In fact, SAT scores have risen from a combined verbal and math score of 1006 for the class of 1976 to a score of 1021 for the class of 2006. That would seem to indicate that students are doing better than those of past generations. Although a number of boats are rising with the tide, not all students are riding the crest of a wave of success.

HANG ON! SMOOTH SAILING IN SIGHT!

To be sure, large racial gaps remain, and some testing critics worry they will widen. Enduring gaps in scoring between non-Asian minorities and other students indicate an educational environment which is becoming more separate and unequal. What is going on in the schools of America?

Researchers at the Harvard School of Graduate Education point out that even though large numbers of Latinos and African Americans are moving into the suburbs, they continue to attend increasingly segregated schools. Results from a 1996–1997 study indicate that African Americans and Latinos living in these areas attend schools that have an average nonwhite enrollment of over 60 percent. As for whites, they are the only racial group attending schools in which the majority of students are white. Research from the same year, 1996–1997, demonstrates that on average, white students attend schools that are over 80 percent white.

Does segregation exact an academic price? Let's look at the class of 2004. Latinos scored about 150 points lower than whites and African Americans scored about 200 points lower than whites. A gender gap also appears to be growing; boys scored 44 points higher than girls, the largest gender gap since 1993.

We know what works for all students in the classroom: continued focus on parent/family involvement and policies to end school-to-school segregation as well as interschool segregation (tracking—also known as ability grouping) so that every learner from whatever background can receive the most enriched curriculum.

More accountability brought about by clear, challenging, and achievable standards with credentialed nurturing teachers and fully funded programs can lead to a turnaround for traditionally underachieving students. These improvements are necessary so that the rising tide of academic achievement, chronicled in the most recent tests, can raise all boats. ●

Mixed-Age Grouping Works

Q: Many schools now have children of different ages in the same classroom. Aren't such classes more difficult to teach than a class where everybody is about the same age?

A: Same-age grouping is practiced by schools all over the globe. However, age is not always an indicator of learning readiness, cognitive growth, or social development. Actually there is a big upside to having a mixed-age grouping in the classroom. When you think of it, what could be more natural than learning from your older sister or helping out your younger brother? Remember when he needed help tying his shoes? It is easy for schools to forget that by increasing the heterogeneity (mixing) of a group, we increase the chances of sharing different and valuable experiences, knowledge, and abilities. Students need the chance to observe—and yes, to imitate—a wide variety of competencies.

Youngsters also need friends who will share ideas and information based on different experiences. When you think of it, putting a same-age group into a class is based on an assumption that may not be true: that these young people can be expected to learn the same ideas, the same way, and at the same time. There is simply no evidence to support this assumption.

On the other hand, there are observable positive factors that come from mixed-age grouping. Younger children see older children as helpers; older children see younger children as in need of help. A wise teacher builds an atmosphere of mutual cooperation based on these perceptions. Information is shared; learning is enhanced.

Conversely, research experiments observing student behavior at same-age-level groups has indicated less student-to-student cooperation. Children in same-age groups have been observed playing one-upmanship, and some tend to be domineering. Mixed-age grouping can be a very advantageous model for learning.

So, on behalf of every younger child who has had a shoe tied by an older child, thank you. Little did either of you know that you helped each other's cognitive and social development while you kept someone from tripping! ●

What Is Self-Esteem?

Q: How would you define self-esteem, and how can parents and teachers help children develop high self-esteem?

A: Self-esteem is all about how you feel about yourself. If you feel good about yourself, you have a healthy sense of self-esteem. It is important that both parents and teachers show they are interested in seeing a student develop good feelings about himself or herself, as it demonstrates that they accept the student and value him or her as a person. Many students need regular parent and teacher approval to have positive feelings about themselves. In school, think of self-esteem as the personal confidence that you can do good work and overcome your mistakes. Students with healthy self-esteem try to do their best. Students with low self-esteem will not try to do certain work. They claim they "can't get it," but many times the true reason is they are afraid of what others might think of them if they fail.

On the other hand, students with a healthy self-esteem feel good about their attempt, even when the result is not perfect. They know that the people who are important to them will appreciate their effort.

Praise and effort go hand in hand. When we tell others how much we appreciate their work, a "can do" attitude is reinforced and self-esteem grows stronger. ●

Help Your Student Beat Fear of School

Q: What should you do when a child expresses a real fear about going to school? How concerned should you be?

A: When a child expresses a fear, he is revealing a feeling that deserves your attention. This fear may be based on something outside the youngster's control—the presence of a bully, a stern teacher, or a walk through an unfriendly neighborhood on the way to school.

On the other hand, the fear may be based on factors that the youngster can control but has been unwilling to do something about—fear of being singled out in class due to unfinished assignments, a poor test result, or low grades in general.

It is important that you find out exactly what the fear is so it can be dealt with immediately. We are creatures of habit. Habitual fear of going to school is certainly most debilitating.

Here are some steps to take in talking with a youngster to get to the bottom of this problem.

Find a quiet, comfortable place. You will need a calm, pleasant environment and enough time to talk in a place where you won't be disturbed.

Ask open-ended questions, such as, "When did this fear start?" These kinds of questions can yield extended answers that are more helpful in nailing down the problem. In contrast, a yes or no question such as "Are you afraid to go to school?" can lead to unenlightening single-word replies.

Devise a mutually agreed-to plan. Once the fear has been identified, the two of you must come up with a plan to confront it. Fears met head-on lose their paralyzing effect. Be sure to have a specific objective plan to conquer fear. For example, there can be no other acceptable planned behavior than being on time and in school every day.

Translate the plan into action. At the same time, be sure to endorse effort. Even if a child's initial attempts to set a new habit seem uncomfortable to her, tell her to accept the discomfort and compliment her effort.

Life is often a try–fail, try–fail, try–succeed proposition. Daily anxiety about going to school must be replaced with a positive plan to confront fears, both real and imagined. In combating apprehension, we make a decision that fear will not control our lives.

Start your discussions about the fear of going to school now. Your immediate and thoughtful intervention can replace a child's fearful anticipation with a happy expectancy. ●

Self-Esteem Is Everything

Q: How can you help children who get very low grades and easily get down on themselves? Otherwise healthy kids continually say that they get uncomfortable and tired when they have to do schoolwork. Is there a way to get them to feel better about themselves and school so that they can begin to get better grades?

A: It's important to make two initial observations. First, it should be no surprise that children who feel bad about themselves are easily distracted by their feelings to the detriment of their academic and social growth. In other words, they don't do as well as they can.

Second, it may surprise you to learn that children are not responsible for their feelings. By the way, neither are adults. Feelings are highly subjective and may be difficult to express. Furthermore, they come and go, seemingly on their own.

It is quite common for a child to be anxious or uncomfortable and not know why. Feelings, therefore, can come unbidden. Feelings, however strong, are not objective truth. They are not even the problem. What the child must understand is that one can accept either a negative or a positive view of life by controlling one's thoughts, regardless of how that person feels. Moreover, a positive thought practiced continually, over time, will defeat a negative feeling.

It has been said that a human being cannot have a positive and a negative thought at the same time. A person must choose one or the other.

When a child having a negative feeling learns to accept a positive thought ("Yes, I am uncomfortable doing this work, but I will stay focused on my work"), he or she is on the road to conquering what is, in essence, a bad habit. In contrast, when children constantly blame themselves for their negative feelings, a vicious cycle begins.

However, that vicious cycle of believing negative feelings as fact can be broken by thinking positive thoughts. Over time, those negative subjective feelings will dwindle and die on their own if not fed by negative thoughts.

The remedy is so simple, some will scoff and not take it seriously. Deliberately having a positive thought is simple, but it is not easy. It is not easy because one is faced with breaking a long-established habit of defining oneself only by one's negative feelings.

The power of the positive thought should not be underestimated. Discouraged, apathetic students with low self-esteem can completely reverse themselves into becoming, over time and with practice, confident and creative youngsters.

Children need to be taught that unhealthy personal feelings can be dealt with effectively. A positive objective thought can override a negative subjective emotion. ●

Students Will Behave with Proper Guidance

Q: How can parents and teachers get kids to behave?

A: Behavior is an interesting topic. There is a true story about a chicken that explains how behavior works and how it applies to humans. This story begins on the beautiful lush island of Puerto Rico. A teacher from the States had been invited to teach high school English classes in the town of Corozal, right smack in the middle of this tropical island. One weekend, the teacher was invited to a farm owned by a grand old man named Don Manolo. Early one Saturday morning, over a cup of Puerto Rican coffee, Don Manolo, who was approaching his 80s, asked the teacher if she wanted to see "la gallina ballerina" (literally the dancing chicken). The teacher agreed, not knowing exactly what the old man was talking about. Don Manolo went to the chicken pen and pulled out a chick. Then he continually dropped little corn kernels just to the left of the chick. As each kernel hit the ground, the chick would hop to its left, grab the kernel in its beak and swallow.

The chick, watching Manolo's hand, began to learn to move to the left as Manolo's hand went there, with the expectation that a kernel of corn would soon drop. The chick's anticipation became so strong, it even continued to hop to the left without a kernel dropping each time. In very little time, Manolo was circling his hand, dropping a kernel only now and then, and the chick would continue hopping in a circle. Manolo smiled, then proudly said, "Damas y caballeros, la gallina ballerina" ("Ladies and gentlemen, the dancing chicken").

The teacher, however, was taught more than how to make a chick dance. Behav-ior, she reasoned, is based on performing for something. If we wish for humans to behave (kids at home or school), there has to be some form of payoff. Depending on the child and the desired behavior, the payoff could be a certain privilege: money, hugs, a toy or, on a higher level, the child's own self-satisfaction. It also could be something even nobler—something chickens can't experience—that special feeling one gets when he or she helps out someone in need.

Parents and teachers should remember what wise old Don Manolo knew. Behavior patterns can be set if one provides an appropriate enticement to stimulate the desired behavior. ●

Student Motivation

Q: What can parents and teachers do to have motivated students?

A: A major goal of education is to develop lifelong learners who continue to seek knowledge through self-directed learning. Motivation, which can be characterized as the reason one carries out an activity, is central to becoming a self-directed learner.

The major outcome of motivation is effort. For effort to occur, a person must understand the task, value the task, and have the clear expectation of successful completion of the task. A student who doesn't know what the assignment is, who doesn't see any payoff in doing it, or who believes that failure is the probable outcome will simply not try.

What is called for, then, is an understanding of motivation and strategic components for setting an environment where students choose to become motivated. It is important to realize that genuine motivation comes from within a person. Therefore, it is not possible, under this definition, for another person to truly motivate anyone to do anything.

You could argue that if you gave a student one million dollars to eat an apple, you would stimulate that student to devour the fruit in an instant. However, you must understand that a million dollars is an incentive (just as grades or honors certificates are). That is to say, they come from outside the person. Recall, motivation comes from within the person.

Incentives (such as money) are rewards from the outside. Motivation (the wish to be a doctor to cure illnesses or the desire to practice law to see social justice done) is stronger than incentive (the wish for monetary gain in medicine or law).

The teacher's role in the classroom is to set up an environment that nurtures a student's choice to become actively engaged. In other words, the classroom should be a place where the student is not afraid to try, struggle, and make mistakes before eventual and inevitable success occurs. Such a classroom should have standards-based instruction that is interesting and relevant enough to encourage (self) motivation on the part of the student.

In order to accomplish this, the student must know what is expected, see the value of it, and believe that with effort, success can be attained. Teachers and parents must continually communicate by phone, email, and personal visits in order to give a unified message to the student that his or her effort (the classic outcome of motivation) is the first and most important step to academic success. ●

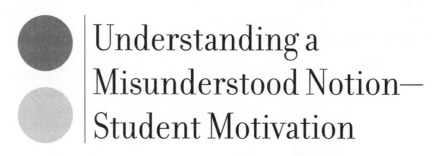

Understanding a Misunderstood Notion— Student Motivation

Q: Everyone, from the school superintendent to the principal to the parents, expects teachers to motivate students. What can a good teacher do to motivate students who seem so apathetic?

A: No word is probably more misunderstood by superintendents, teachers, and parents than that often-heard term—motivation. As students move from the elementary level to the secondary level, why is it that learning seems to be such a burden rather than an exciting exploration of new facts and ideas?

At some schools, new programs seem to appear every year to end student apathy by various inducements from raising grades, to giving awards, to even paying students money in order to "motivate" them to do better. Other schools aim to motivate students by lowering their grades, making them ineligible for sports, and even banning them from dances, in order to motivate them do better. For the majority of students, such common practices are doomed to fail because those who make and attempt to carry out such school policies don't understand the notion of motivation.

To begin, genuine motivation comes from within. Offering rewards or penalties to motivate a student doesn't work well because what is really being offered is an incentive—that is, something outside of the student, to be attained or avoided. Think of it this way, motivation (from within a person) is strong, whereas incentive (outside of a person) is weak.

The truth is parents and teachers don't motivate. However, they can set an environment in which students decide to become inspired. Thus, a person (e.g., a teacher or a parent) who models passionate commitment, communicates high expectations, or builds personal rapport with a student can set an atmosphere in which students can opt to become motivated.

Motivation in learning has to do with attitudes about what is expected and what is important. When a teacher nurtures a student's natural curiosity about the world around him, and applauds effort, that educator implicitly teaches the student about the courage to make mistakes and cope with inevitable, if usually temporary, confusion or even failure.

When a student grows in self-worth, personal autonomy, and becomes a self-directed learner, he or she does not fear and is not bored by a new learning task. The student has come to understand that hard work will be praised and, in the end, will lead to the attainment of new knowledge and skills.

As a teacher, don't fall into the trap that you can motivate a student. Instead, create a stimulating learning environment, provide a "can do" attitude, praise effort, and provide the opportunity for the student to change an attitude of apathy for one of engagement. ●

How to Set Up an Environment in Which Students Choose to Become Motivated

Q: Is there really such a big difference between motivation and incentive? If motivation is so strong and so important, can you tell me how it can be nurtured in the classroom?

A: True motivation is a force within an individual, and therefore stronger than a mere incentive (an outside reward). There is a growing body of evidence that students work harder to achieve when they are motivated—when they have an intrinsic interest in what they are studying.

Motivated students employ strategies that demand more effort, and use more logical knowledge-gathering and decision-making approaches, than students who simply are spurred on by an incentive (e.g., an extrinsic reward such as a grade or a "happy face" sticker). Furthermore, a truly motivated student tends to prefer an assignment that is fairly rigorous compared to students stimulated by an outside incentive. The incentive-driven students may tend to "skate by," preferring tasks with a lower level of difficulty.

Here is how to set up a classroom environment conducive to fostering students to develop genuine motivation—that is, self-motivation:

1. Set a caring, supportive classroom atmosphere.
2. Create an ambience where there is a sense of belonging and every class member feels valued.
3. Keep all tasks challenging but achievable.
4. Put a value on curiosity, a genuine motivator.
5. Define specific, short-term goals stressing effort, learning, and task mastery.

Remember that the ultimate outcome of setting such an environment is of enormous educational consequence. The final result is no less than developing the ultimate scholar—a self-directed lifelong learner. ●

An Answer for Unsuccessful Learners— Cognitive Retraining

Q: There are some students who get one low grade after another, even though they show a lot of ability in the things that interest them. Why do some kids, who are otherwise pretty smart, seem not to learn much in school, and what can be done to improve their performance?

A: There are a lot of children who fall into a failure syndrome. These youngsters tend to throw in the towel at the first sign of difficulty and consequently, when it comes to school, learn to have very low expectations of success.

Some youngsters who lack confidence in their own abilities, or feel they are in competition with others to get "good" grades, give up trying as a defense mechanism. They reason that if they don't try to do a task in school, public mockery and personal ridicule will be less than if they really made a true effort and failed.

For example, if a teacher asks a student to read in class and the student replies, "I don't feel like it," there may be a reason for this kind of defiance. Perhaps the student (who assumes inferior ability) does not want to have her performance evaluated in a classroom where inadequacy carries the stigma of public embarrassment.

Unfortunately both parents and teachers, directly or indirectly, communicate low expectations to students. This is especially true for those students who have been grouped into lower-ability classes.

Predictably, unsuccessful students develop a deep-seated belief that they lack the ability to succeed, and therefore abandon genuine academic effort and instead concentrate on not being singled out in class. In other words, the unsuccessful student walks into the classroom each day, not full of curiosity and enthusiasm for the learning experience, but feeling like a turkey the day before Thanksgiving. A "good" day in class is an invisible day.

One of the things that can be done to help these students is cognitive retraining. Basically, it is a three-step process.

1. Ask the learner to concentrate on what needs to be done instead of being preoccupied with failure.
2. Teach the learner to cope with initial failure by finding the errors and revising the work. Never lower standards. Help the learner to reach the original (attainable) standard.
3. Praise effort. Call attention to the learner's progress. Display her accomplishments in public for all to see.

A child who has learned to view herself with low expectations must be cognitively retrained. Children must be taught to be concerned about their effort, not someone else's (usually premature) view of their ability. Children may learn that the funny thing about effort is that it appears to create ability! ●

Learning Requires a Dual Investment: Time and Effort

Q: It is amazing how two children from the same family can have such different grades from the same teachers, in the same school, taking the same classes. You would think that their experiences would be so similar at home that they would get about the same grades in school. Why do some kids from the same background perform so differently?

A: This is a question nearly every family with two or more children has asked for as long as there has been organized schooling. The answer is really quite simple. Each person has two basic elements: genetic endowment and personal history. The reason two children from the same parents—who share much the same upbringing—can have such different outcomes has to do with their idiosyncratic responses to the world around them.

These unique responses are based on what has happened in an environment when one interacts with it. The famous behaviorist B. F. Skinner pointed out that a person who has ridden over a route as a passenger cannot find his way as well as a driver who drives the route an equal number of times. Although both have been exposed to the same visual stimuli (the road, the signposts, and other landmarks), the contingencies—the circumstances—were quite different.

Recent research has emphasized the importance of student effort as the decisive element in promoting successful academic outcomes. As such, the entire academic community can and should create a climate to nurture an ethic that values student commitment.

However, in the final analysis, it is the student who must empower himself or herself to take control of his or her own education. Students should realize that school is one of the last places where they are truly the captains of their own ships. Specifically, this metaphor means that each individual is free to adopt a work ethic based on the tenet that academic success stems from a personal pledge of time and effort. The more active a student becomes in taking the responsibility to develop into a self-directed learner, the better she will recognize the road, the signposts, and the landmarks to a quality education. ●

Best Efforts Are More Important Than Being Exceptional

Q: Many children don't seem at all happy about attending high school and are very anxious about school. These students' grades may not be that bad—but they put themselves under a lot of pressure to be the best.

These students want to be considered outstanding and get quite upset when they "fail" and receive only a good grade.

What can parents and teachers do to help these students perform well and still enjoy school?

A: These children have fallen into a trap. Unfortunately, this trap has been set by people who have the best of intentions. Their zealous aim is to produce excellence, but they end up producing what is now called "burnout."

Instead, educators and parents must be consistent in asking youngsters for their best effort and not for exceptionality. Many people, both young and old, do not truly make the distinction between giving their best effort and being exceptional in their daily lives.

The two notions are not the same. An individual's best effort means one's finest attempt on a task compared to that same person's other efforts. Exceptionality, on the other hand, commonly means an individual's best effort compared to everyone else.

When a person compares himself with the best attempts of others, he will usually come up short. Exceptional people, exceptional efforts, and exceptional deeds are a rarity—which is why they are exceptional.

Because of this confusion between best effort and exceptionality, there is a great anxiety, common to many students, about even approaching an assignment. The student fears his best just won't be good enough. This fear arises with every trivial error that all of us are subject to making every day of our lives.

The mistaken belief that we should be an error-free people simply goes against all we know about human nature. Even more important, this call to be faultless can lead people to become anxiety-driven and eventually quite negative about school and themselves.

In order to break this cycle of negative feelings, students should be told that all that is required of them is their best efforts on a daily basis. In other words, parents and teachers should emphasize effort over outcome. Students must come to understand that in trying their best on a day-by-day basis, and keeping a positive attitude, they actually will become better students in the long haul. Finally, advise students to take school seriously, but not be too hard on themselves. When we can laugh at our trivial mistakes, we give them the minimal attention they deserve. ●

Teacher Expectations Are a Self-Fulfilling Prophecy

Q: Is it appropriate for teachers to label students? If not, what can be done about it?

A: Some teachers label students in order to sort them out, as you would different pairs of socks or different sets of dishes. Does that sound inhuman and insensitive? It should, because it is. However, labeling students is a sad reality in too many of our schools.

Eighty percent of all schools in the country actively label, and then group, students into high- and low-ability levels based on what these educators assume is each child's learning potential. What is most troubling is the kind of screening devices schools and teachers use to sort children.

So-called aptitude tests, which are many times indistinguishable from achievement tests, are used to predict a student's academic potential. What they really do, according to many studies, is assess previous knowledge. The unfairness in such an assessment seems obvious. In a society with unequal access to certain kinds of knowledge (classically, a student's home or school located on the "wrong" side of the tracks), the selec-

tion process becomes a game of winners and losers—with the winners consistently coming from the same socioeconomic and ethnic backgrounds.

In addition, research tells us that a student's dialect, physical appearance, gender, ethnicity, home language—even the student's name—can create an expectation in a teacher's mind that leads to a first impression followed by lasting assumptions about that particular learner. How powerful are those suppositions? Very powerful indeed, because they lead a teacher to treat a given student in a distinctly different manner. Consistent differential treatment on the part of the instructor may well lead to students acting out a self-fulfilling prophecy.

Believe it or not, even the most recalcitrant children believe their teacher's assessment of them. Therefore, educators should guard against any negative expectations because they will inevitably communicate those suppositions to the child, which in turn may predictably lead to negative student outcomes. In short, teachers must realize that when it comes to low expectations, too often they get what they "expect"—or more precisely what they have unwittingly helped to create. ●

Prosocial Behavior: A Product of Positive Expectations

Q: How do you get kids to behave in school? It seems like the same kids are always the ones getting in trouble. Do they need a course in manners?

A: The best way to learn manners stems from a teacher's positive expectations of student behavior. When a teacher models appropriate classroom behavior based on mutual respect and genuine caring, most students grasp that this kind of behavior should be emulated. In other words, children who are treated with kindness and understanding are more likely to reciprocate those qualities than if they were treated otherwise.

It is true that some children learn faster than others and that some students come to the class with chronic or serious behavioral problems. In such cases, the teacher must do six basic things in order to help those students with persistent unacceptable classroom behavior:

- Isolate the student when discussing behavioral problems. To do otherwise almost always involves public rebuke, which is counterproductive.

- Question the student to find out if the student is aware that her behavior is unacceptable.

- Articulate with precision what acceptable behavior is and looks like. Emphasize what to do, rather than what not to do, in class.

- Ask the student to accept responsibility for her actions.

- Plan with the student ways in which acceptable behavior can be demonstrated and recognized.

- Work toward a goal of self-regulation by providing the student opportunities (e.g., working in groups) to develop better social skills.

In following these six recommendations, special care must be given to certain students in a U.S. culture ever more culturally and linguistically diverse. Teachers need to be culturally sensitive so as not to misinterpret a child's behavior. Accordingly, educators must become proactive in learning more each day about the languages and cultures in their classroom in order to build bridges of understanding to their students.

Research is conclusive on the following point: How a student feels about his or her teacher is inextricably linked to how well the youngster will learn. When a teacher spends time building a positive rapport with students in the classroom, that educator is constructing a pathway for student success in the classroom. Improved social skills lead to enhanced academic achievement. ●

Sidelined Athletes Grumble about Grades

Q: In the past, high school athletes could play for the team as long as they had a C semester average. Why are some schools changing the rules so any player who has a failing midterm grade is immediately ineligible?

A: Many schools have decided that when a student is failing a class, he or she should focus on getting a passing grade. The message is clear. The primary mission of the school is to educate. High school sports can be a wonderful experience, but academics come first.

There is a reason the word "student" appears first in the term student–athlete. For a high school student to believe that athletics come first is like having the tail wag the dog. Any student who is failing a class should leave the practice field and head for the library.

In the long run, schools that have high expectations for their student–athletes have better students and more competitive teams. These schools are saying that playing sports is a privilege. To earn the privilege of representing their school on the field of play, students must be successful in their studies. ●

Grouping by IQ

Q: Shouldn't we put more stock in scientific tests of intelligence in order to separate students so they can be with others of similar intelligence? Wouldn't good students do even better if they were placed into advanced classes where they wouldn't be held back by the slower students?

A: There are many problems with IQ testing. For example, IQ tests are constructed to produce a bell-shaped curve. Therefore, 50 percent of the takers of an IQ test necessarily fall below average.

The problem is the lack of any evidence that in the real world, human intelligence is distributed according to a bell-shaped curve. Thus, it would appear that the IQ test has a tendency to distort rather than clarify.

Another problem is the lack of evidence that IQ testing and subsequent measurement has led to improved schools. IQ tests are subject to examiner training or bias, examinee age, and misinterpretation

of these scores. Given our know-ledge of multiple intelligences, the stakes seem too high for schools to rely too heavily on any given test.

Perhaps a better way to help students in school is to give a variety of tests to better understand a learner's cognitive styles (the particular way we learn something). In this way, we could make a better match between educational methods and materials, and enhance the ability of the learner to take advantage of those resources.

As to the second part of your question, tracking students by perceived ability into so-called advanced classes has been shown to harm lower-tracked student's motivation and can subsequently curtail their learning. Moreover, tracking has historically evidenced social class and racial inequalities.

What are called for are approaches to expose lower-achieving students to successful peer models, demanding content, and high expectations through mixed ability grouping. ●

The Fear of Making Mistakes

Q: What can you do for a boy who is 13 and doesn't seem to have a lot of confidence? It is not that he is always failing; in fact, his grades are quite good. It is just that he gets easily frustrated when he makes even the smallest mistake. It seems if conditions aren't just perfect to attempt something,

then he just won't try. How can he feel better about himself?

A: Some people seem to lack spontaneity because they are afraid of making mistakes. They just seem to fold up their tent. Trying to be perfect will eventually lead to disappointment and can paralyze the creative spark in all of us.

Somewhere along the line, some people pick up the notion that every little endeavor, every trivial task, every ho-hum enterprise, is a challenge to the impossible "error-free" standards they set for themselves. Life then becomes a series of hoops to jump through. Each one, no matter how seemingly inconsequential, is a serious challenge to our own notion of our personal worth. It is like being forever in front of a hanging judge and jury, waiting for them to pass an innocent or guilty verdict on how well we have accomplished every task we have undertaken.

What is needed is a way out of this self-imposed exile to the land of the perfect. In order to be a person who takes on chal-lenges, one must be relaxed, spontaneous, and poised. Fear of making mistakes in everyday trivial affairs must be banished. What is called for is the fortitude to make all kinds of trivial mistakes, which are simply learning experiences with no lasting downside.

Educators and parents must teach that these kinds of mistakes are healthy. To be afraid of them leads to a paralysis of action and inevitable disappointment. A mistake, correctly handled, becomes a learning encounter.

The way to make mistakes work for you is to pursue not perfection, but knowledge. It is the courageous search for knowledge, accepting one's mistakes along the way, that is the pathway to self-acceptance. ●

Educational Research and Common Knowledge

Q: There is a lot of tax money spent on educational research programs. Why don't politicians, educators, and parents know what works? You would think there can't be all that much debate—either a classroom practice works or it doesn't.

A: There are a number of reasons why people in each one of the categories mentioned may not know "what works" in education. Educational research, although absolutely essential to moving forward in identifying best practices, presents a lexical barrier for politicians, educators, and parents.

First, almost all educational research appears solely in professional and academic journals. These publications, printed in limited quantities, do not have a wide circulation among the general public. If you don't believe me, just pop down to your local bookstore or even your neighborhood library and try to find one of these academic journals on the shelf.

Second, for the general reader, the lexical density, statistical data, and organization of educational research articles makes them very hard to penetrate. The major findings of a research article, almost without exception, seem to be hidden among very technical terminology. Although such vocabulary may actually simplify communication within a specific discipline, it can cut off comprehension to an interested member of the general public.

Is there a remedy to this cloaking of important findings about what works in the classroom? Here are four ways to open educational research findings to the general public so they can make more informed decisions concerning the kind of best practices they want implemented in their schools:

1. Simplify the language: Present the findings at the beginning of a report in short, clear, declarative sentences.

2. Create attractive charts or graphics: Dense statistical data can usually be best understood by presenting it in the form of various charts (e.g., column, pie, or linear chart).

3. Communicate findings to journalists: Mass consumption depends on the mass media.

4. Publish on the Internet: Using the first three recommendations, immediate dissemination of educational research can now have a worldwide audience.

Dissemination precedes implementation. The value of important educational research can only be realized if the ultimate policymakers (the public) know about best practices in the classroom and decide to implement them. Educational researchers would be best served by building a communications bridge to the public they wish to serve. ●

A Poor Educational Choice: Grade Retention

Q: How do you place a kid who simply does not seem to fit in with the rest of the class? Why should we promote kids who really aren't at the same level as the average kid?

A: In many schools around the nation, grade retention is the answer to this question. Roughly two to three million children a year are held back and told to repeat the year they have just experienced.

Is this sound educational policy? It's revealing to consider who is being held back. The profile goes like this: poor scholarship, frequently absent, limited English-language skills, low socioeconomic status, probably male and minority.

Another problem is that most schools have vague, if not functionally nonexistent, policies regarding grade retention. In other words, this decision is usually not tied to any known guidelines, and is basically left to one teacher's opinion on who is promoted and who is not.

The research record indicates that when a teacher holds a child back a year, the overall effect is negative. In fact, the majority of these youngsters never catch up to their peers. Their self-esteem is clearly affected, and the tendency to drop out of school is increased. Moreover, statistics indicate that a child held back twice will almost certainly drop out of school altogether.

How do youngsters feel about being held back? They rate failing a grade as nearly as stressful as the fear of blindness or the death of a parent.

Retention, like social promotion, therefore appears to be a poor educational policy decision based on good intentions (school accountability), but with a decided ignorance or simply a dismissive attitude toward solid educational research.

So what's the answer to the problem? The core of the answer begins with designing an inclusive academic program with the most enriched curricula and the most adaptive methodologies to fit the needs of a particular child. Parents are a big part of this focused intervention to help low-achieving students make the grade.

Following are strategies schools and parents can employ to help youngsters who fall behind in their studies:

SCHOOL SOLUTIONS:

1. **Individualized instruction:** It is important to know a child's learning style in order to make the best use of these one-on-one encounters.

2. **Mixed-age grouping:** In this arrangement, students can learn at their own rate based on the mastery of specific skills, without grade labeling.

3. **Smaller classes:** This is a pretty obvious solution. It simply gives the teacher more time to spend with fewer students—to the benefit of those youngsters who need the most attention.

4. **Mentoring:** This kind of approach depends on a student's rapport with a teacher, counselor, or even a community resource person who provides encouragement, guidance, and support to the student.

PARENTAL SOLUTIONS:

1. Challenge any proposed retention of your child as a poor educational choice. You might suggest some or all of the just mentioned school solutions in your efforts to oppose retention.

2. Keep the teacher informed of your unique and special knowledge of the child's behavioral patterns at home, so consistent and positive messages are being delivered in both environments.

3. Let the teacher know if major changes are taking place in a child's life—death or illness of a family member, a new baby, or a new home in a new neighborhood can all affect a child's behavior and school performance.

4. Provide the child with a clean, quiet, well-lighted place to study. Homework is a way to extend the school day—a good idea when a student needs to make up for lost time.

Retention is a poor answer to a real problem. When a student does fall behind, more attention should be paid to assuring that child is getting an enriched curriculum, is being taught through a variety of methodological approaches, and feels valued by parents and teachers alike. ●

Social Promotion or Being Held Back—Are These the Only Choices?

Q: Isn't social promotion one of the reasons why kids graduate from school not knowing much of anything? Wouldn't it be better to hold underperforming students back a year?

A: Many schools across the country deal with children who appear to be underachieving by having them repeat a grade. This practice is not rare at all; in fact, between two and three million students are retained at the same grade each year.

Who are these kids that the schools fail each year? It may surprise you to find out that many of these children are the physically smallest or youngest in their grade. They have been frequently absent from class, and many have limited English-language skills. Moreover, they are most likely male, from a minority group, and of low economic status. Finally, they are likely to have parents who—for one reason or another—don't seem to get involved with their child's education.

After looking at this profile, it might appear that some kids are destined to fail even before they spend their first full day in school. In fact, a child may be considered for retention if he or she does poorly on a prescreening assessment.

Although social promotion is clearly undesirable, major problems usually arise from having a child spend an extra year in the same grade. In most cases, according to research, the negative effects of being held back usually outnumber the positive effects.

Unfortunately, most children retained at the same grade level are never able to catch up. Even more problematic, students who are held back may get into more trouble, dislike school, and dislike themselves more often than children who are promoted to the next grade level. Research reveals that a child's anxiety involved in flunking is nearly as traumatic as the death of a parent.

Although holding a student back a grade is defended as "tough love," too often retention simply overlooks the root cause of a child's failure. Any youngster is teachable and will learn if a program is adapted to fit the needs of that particular child.

There are other options besides holding a child back a year. Here are four alternatives:

1. **Individualize instruction.** Tailor the curriculum (what is taught) and the methodology (how something is taught) to the needs of the child.
2. **Teach with a teacher–parent team.** Parents get structured and specific information about what is being taught and how to help their child form solid study habits.
3. **Reduce class size.** Smaller class size logically leads to more teacher time with each student—critical to slower learners.
4. **Utilize tutors.** Another teacher, parent, or even a student can provide the kind of one-on-one attention crucial to consistent academic achievement.

To sum up, a dose of "preventive medicine" may avoid an either/or decision regarding social promotion or retention. Early intervention with students who are suffering through a lack of initial success can prevent the two extremes of holding children back a grade or simply practicing what has been called social promotion.

Both retention and social promotion become unnecessary when a child's strengths and weaknesses have been properly diagnosed, and an action plan is set forth and implemented. Student success rates can soar when teacher, learner, and parents focus on daily academic improvement and social development. ●

Four Steps to Enhance Academic Achievement

Q: Many people are tired of hearing about low test scores on standardized tests. They never seem to shoot up, especially in the case of minority youngsters. The federal and state governments spend millions in research to get all of our youngsters to read and write better than they do, yet it doesn't seem to make a dent in low grades and low test scores.

Why don't things ever seem to change, and what needs to be done so students can achieve at higher levels?

A: First the good news: there are four steps to enhance academic achievement that could be started tomorrow under enlightened leadership within our schools, with no additional costs.

Now the bad news: erroneous assumptions continue to be made about intelligence. Some believe intelligence is innate—you are either born with a great deal of it or not. Many even contend that intelligence cannot be changed. These scientifically unwarranted opinions form the basis of the traditionally tracked educational system (high tracks and low tracks) found in 90 percent of our schools.

Following are the faulty assumptions which grow from these all too typical misguided convictions:

- Students simply learn better when they are classed with those of similar ability.

- Lower-tracked students develop more positive attitudes about themselves when they are not grouped with higher-tracked students.

- There exists a fair method of deciding who goes into which track.

- It is easier for teachers to individualize instruction when students are classed by similar ability.

Each one of these widely held assumptions is profoundly incorrect. Research over many years has conclusively shown that mixed or untracked grouping best serves all students. It is no secret that the historically underrepresented students in college (Latino and African American learners) are those who are overrepresented in the lower-tracked groups in elementary, middle school, and high school. In schools with ever more diverse populations, the emphasis should be on effort rather than on deciding which students go to the higher or lower tracks.

Although there is much more to be said about the unfair and harmful effects of tracking, perhaps it is more important to discuss a solution that increases the success of all students. There is a model being used in the public schools that really can change students' grades and standardized test scores in only 60 days. It is a four-point program that every teacher can implement, and every student and parent can understand. Following is a description of this program, using reading comprehension as an example of the subject to be learned:

1. **Diagnostic Pretest:** On the first day of school, administer a nationally normed diagnostic test in reading comprehension. Here we are interested in evaluating the literal, inferential, and critical comprehension skills. Advise both students and parents of these scores. The low

scores may shock and disappoint some people, but the truth will set you free. These scores simply mean it is time for the students with the lower scores to roll up their sleeves along with the teacher and start making up for lost learning opportunities.

2. **Curriculum:** On the second day of school, teach all students with the most enriched curriculum (consider the classics from the works of Homer, Shakespeare, and Dickens, along with authors like Villasenor and Angelou). As for discipline, all you need is two rules: arrive on time and work hard for the entire class session. Dump all the phony rules about hats or food in class. A student can ingest food (as long as they clean up) and wear a beanie if they want as long as they work hard for the entire session. Funny thing about treating youngsters like adults; they start acting more responsibly each day.

3. **Methodology:** Teachers should set an environment in which students choose to be motivated and should follow three basic steps in every class: explain, apply, and synthesize. Use computer technology to produce papers that can be read by all and that meet clearly defined standards. Praise effort. A student who continually revises his work because of errors should, when his paper finally meets standards, receive a high evaluation. The question shouldn't be how fast you did it, but if you did it. School shouldn't be a quiz show. Teachers should give parents an update every two weeks by phone on work turned in and assignments to be accomplished.

4. **Assessment:** In terms of test scores, a nationally normed posttest should be given to the students 60 days after the class has been in session. Students are not to be graded on the outcome of the posttest. The posttest is to be used by the teacher to determine how successful the curricular and methodological approaches have been in lifting student scores—in this case, reading comprehension.

And now for a reality check. Does this program really work? In other words, does effort create ability? The answer is a resounding yes. In a recent application of this program, the historically lower-tracked minority students scored near the bottom fourth of all students nationally on the pretest in reading comprehension. Just 60 calendar days later, the same students scored above the national average on the posttest!

Isn't it funny how reading and writing every day improves reading and writing? But then again, what are reading and writing? They are skills. Everyone knows that any skill will improve with practice. If we could only practice what we know.

Schools simply must stop tracking students into perceived ability groups. Teachers should instruct their heterogeneous class with enthusiasm and with the most enriched curriculum. Students should routinely write out their responses in all classes in order to continually improve their higher-order critical-thinking skills of analysis, synthesis, and evaluation. If these basic steps were followed, the direction of both in-school grades and national standardized test scores would head north in a hurry. ●

SUGGESTED READINGS

Anderson, J., Greeno, J., Reder, L., & Simon, H. A. (2000). Perspectives on learning, thinking, and activity. *Educational Researcher, 229*(4), 11–13.

Bilhartz, T. D., Bruhn, R. A., & Olson, J. E. (2000). The effect of early music training on child cognitive development. *Journal of Applied Developmental Psychology, 20*(4), 615–636.

Blakemore, S. J., & Frith, U. (2000). *Implications of recent developments in neuroscience research on teaching and learning.* London: Institute of Cognitive Neuroscience.

Butzlaff, R. (2000). Can music be used to teach reading? *Journal of Aesthetic Education, 34*(3–4), 167–178.

Davis, A. (2004). The credentials of brain-based learning. *Journal of Philosophy of Education, 38*(1), 2004.

Ellison, L. (2001). *The personal intelligences: Promoting social and emotional learning.* Thousand Oaks, CA: Corwin Press.

Gildner, C. (2001). *Enjoy teaching: Helpful hints for the classroom.* Lanham, MD: Scarecrow Education.

Ginger, Serge. (2003). Female brains vs. male brains. *International Journal of Psychotherapy, 8*(2), 139–145.

Gordon, E. (2000). *Integrative neuroscience.* Sydney, Australia: Hardwood Academic.

Goswami, U. (2004). Neuroscience and education. *British Journal of Educational Psychology, 74*, 1–14.

Hall, J. (2005). Neuroscience and education. *Education Journal, 84*, 27–29.

Ho, Y., Cheung, M., & Chan, A. S. (2003). Music training improves verbal but not visual memory: Cross-sectional and longitudinal explorations in children. *Neuropsychology, 17*(3), 439–450.

Jackson, L., & Veeneman, M. (2002). *Positive behavioral support in the classroom:* *Principles and practices.* Baltimore, MD: P. H. Brookes.

McKelvie, P., & Low, J. (2002). Listening to Mozart does not improve children's spatial ability: Final curtains for the Mozart effect. *British Journal of Developmental Psychology, 20*(2), 241–258.

National Research Council. (2001). *Knowing what students know: The science and design of educational assessment.* Washington, DC: National Academy Press.

Pierangelo, R., & Giuliani, G. A. (2000). *Why your students do what they do and what to do when they do it: A practical guide for understanding classroom behavior, grades k–5.* Champaign, IL: Research Press.

Pintrich, P. R., & Schunk, D. H. (2002). *Motivation in education: Theory, research, and applications* (2nd ed.). Upper Saddle River, NJ: Merrill/Prentice Hall.

Roberts, J. W. (2002). Beyond learning by doing: The brain compatible approach. *The Journal of Experiential Education, 25*(2), 281–285.

Stover, E. (2001). Brain research in the classroom is not a no brainer. *Education Digest, 66*(8), 26–30.

Visser, J., Daniels, H., & Cole, T. (Eds.). (2001). *Emotional and behavioural difficulties in mainstream schools.* New York: JAI.

Webb, W. H. (1999). *The educator's guide to solutioning: The great things that happen when you focus students on solutions, not problems.* Thousand Oaks, CA: Corwin Press.

Wiseman, D. G., & Hunt, G. H. (2001). *Best practice in motivation and management in the classroom.* Springfield, IL: Charles C Thomas.

unit :4

Discipline: The Rules of the Road

Classroom Discipline That Really Works

Q: Many classrooms have plenty of rules—no hats, no food, no talking, no passes to the restroom—posted on the bulletin board. Even with all these rules, the class is often noisy and disorganized, with little work getting done in class, and only a few students handing in homework regularly. How can a teacher make discipline work so the students can get their assignments done without feeling they are in jail?

A: A list of negatives (no hats, food, etc.) is not the right way to develop and maintain discipline. It sets up a negative environment that basically says the teacher doesn't trust the students. Instead, a teacher should use a positive approach by simply telling students what she wants. Two simple rules should be sufficient:

1. Be on time.
2. Stay focused the entire session.

If students do these two things, they can be permitted more and more privileges that actually help them mature. After all, social development occurs when students are given the opportunity to evolve, privilege by privilege, from a child to a responsible young adult.

For example, as long as a student is on time and totally focused on his work, he can be allowed to wear a hat, since wearing a hat typically does not pose a pedagogical impediment to one's learning. On the other hand, wearing a hat with earmuffs would be a problem if the teacher could not clearly be heard explaining material to be mastered. Rather than making an absolute rule about the prohibition of all headgear, the teacher should explain that as long as the student is working in an unimpeded fashion, wearing a beanie is acceptable.

As for food—again, as long as a student remains focused on the job at hand (and cleans up after she has eaten), no problem. In fact, if a student wants to eat a seven-course Italian meal, but continues to focus on the academic work at hand and is not disrupting the class—so be it.

Now that we have emphasized focus (sitting up straight, eyes on the teacher, the text, the computer screen, etc.), let's address "follow through"—having work turned in by all students on a consistent basis. The way to accomplish "follow through" is to start the homework in class so that every student understands not only what is to be done, but also how it is to be done.

Keeping the parents informed of a student's progress (or lack of it) is what every good teacher does, by phone or email. If the teacher is calling or emailing a student's home at least twice a month, parents will be "in the loop." A virtual blizzard of homework assignments usually lands on the teacher's desk as a result of teacher-to-parent contact.

In sum, class discipline means a few positive rules, an emphasis on student focus, and keeping parents informed. Sounds simple, but it works! ●

The Disadvantages of Punishment in the Classroom

Q: It seems we live in a more and more permissive society. Public schools often seem not to punish kids who deserve it. Student misbehavior has few, if any, consequences. It may sound old fashioned, but when did punishment fall out of favor with educators? Don't we need more of a "three strikes and you're out" philosophy in our public schools?

A: Before we consider punishment per se, let's remember that the atmosphere of the classroom plays a large role in student behavior. Teachers who make too many arbitrary rules can produce students who become confused, frustrated, or openly antagonistic.

This is not to say that a teacher should not set firm guidelines of behavior. Recall, a teacher probably needs no more than two rules:

1. Be on time.
2. Stay focused the entire session.

Notice that both of these rules are stated in a positive way—things a student should do.

Punishment can be defined as a technique that is geared toward decelerating misbehavior in the classroom. For example, a punishment can be a reprimand ("Johnny, stop talking!"), a frown or glaring stare, or simply writing the offending student's name on the board.

There are problems with this kind of public rebuke in a classroom setting. First, you embarrass a student in front of his peers—something that research indicates students fear as much as the death of a parent! Second, the teacher creates an adversarial relationship not only with the offending student, but probably with the whole class.

When a teacher publicly castigates a student, other students might well believe the teacher has been unfair, or that they are next to be ridiculed. In other words, public rebuke—in terms of classroom atmosphere—can really produce an environment where learning becomes difficult.

Of course, public scolding of a student is only one kind of punishment. There are others—for example, corporal punishment (e.g., paddling), which is still permitted by law in nearly half of the states.

One of the most troubling things about corporal punishment is the types of students who are most likely to be hit. Boys, minority children, and poor white children top the list.

The practical problems with administering punishments are many. When a teacher is enraged enough to paddle a child, the instructor might not think of what she is doing or how she is doing it. Sometimes a punishment can actually reinforce a particular misbehavior because the offender may get exactly what he or she wants—a reaction from the teacher.

Although punishment may indicate what a student shouldn't do, it may not at all indicate what the desired behavior is. Instead, many students learn through punishment that the trick is not to terminate a particular misbehavior, but simply not to get caught! Moreover, a young person might react to punishment in a very negative manner by increasing the undesirable behavior, striking back, or running away.

Due to these observable drawbacks, punishment is usually a poor first choice to modify a student's behavior. Instead, an instructor should consider isolating the student and, if a reprimand is in order, giving it to the youngster privately.

During this one-on-one "time out," the reprimand should be accompanied by information identifying what kind of behavior is expected in the class.

One phrase the teacher might use during these brief one-on-one sessions, usually outside the room, is "You are better than that." This phrase affirms the teacher's belief, in the eyes of the student, that the particular misbehavior was an aberration. It does not reinforce the false notion so many students adopt—I did a bad thing, therefore I'm a bad person.

During this time it is also important for a teacher to articulate and, if need be, demonstrate the desired classroom behavior. Finally, the instructor should monitor the offending student as soon as the pupil returns to the classroom. Such an approach can change a student's behavior, and even produce understanding and friendship between student and teacher.

Research and practical experience in the classroom make one thing quite clear. A one-on-one private meeting with a student is certainly a more effective approach in dealing with misbehavior, compared to the unpredictable—and at times counterproductive—response of many students to punishment. ●

Punishments and Rewards: One and the Same?

Q: There are a lot of teachers and parents who know that punishments can do more harm than good when it comes to prodding a student to get better grades. What is effective in getting young people to study hard and be committed to doing good work?

A: It would be nice if the answer were as simple as throwing away the stick and breaking out a bag of carrots. However, the traditional classroom practice of awarding everything from brightly colored stickers to a free meal at the local fast-food restaurant for academic excellence doesn't produce self-directed learners. In fact, promising a treat for desired academic behavior can actually be counterproductive. Simply put, the more we want students to do something, the more detrimental it is to reward them for doing it.

Research consistently indicates that incentives do not positively affect the emotional resolution or cognitive commitment that are at the foundation of long-lasting self-directed learning. In fact, the more higher-order critical thinking skills (analysis, synthesis, and evaluation) that are required for a task, the worse students do when they are promised a reward upon completion of the assignment.

To be sure, an interest in a task for its own sake (genuine motivation) is very different than doing a task in order to win a prize (incentive). Clearly, rewards impel students to win rewards. The problem is, rewards also give a person a reason to stop doing the activity when there is no longer a prize to be gained. Once the prize has been obtained, the specific activity (e.g., reading 25 books, doing a science project, learning a list of verbs in a foreign language) is actually less attractive than ever before.

In one exemplary study, students were given a new beverage. Group one was simply asked to drink it. Group two received generous praise for consuming it. Group three was promised prizes if they drank it.

As you might guess, groups two and three consumed more of the beverage initially than group one. However, after only a week, groups two and three found the drink much less appealing than before. Group one, the students offered no rewards, liked the drink just as much, if not more, than at the beginning of the week.

We may have a hard time swallowing the results of this test. Nevertheless, the conclusion is clear: rewards do not result in students retaining interest in what they were rewarded for doing, and may even cause them to lose interest.

If parents and teachers shouldn't use punishments or rewards to spur academic achievement, then what is left? Parents and teachers should provide students with an enriched curriculum, a caring atmosphere, competent instruction, and unconditional support. Such an environment, free of attempts to manipulate behavior through punishments or rewards, can produce a creative atmosphere where lifelong, self-directed learners can emerge. ●

Classroom Discipline

Q: What is the best way to discipline a child who is misbehaving in school?

A: Kids need to be told when they are acting in a way that disrupts the school day, but talking to some kids seems like talking to a wall. Here is a five-step process designed to change unacceptable school behavior.

1. **Isolate.** First, meet one-on-one with the student. Confronting students in front of a classroom full of friends only complicates the process. Kids will side with kids. As a teacher or parent, you will find yourself in a minority of one and your advice will not only be unpopular but outvoted.

2. **Ask and listen.** After you have established a face-to-face meeting place with the child, ask the child why (or if) he has misbehaved. Your primary role is to listen and understand the child's side. Model the same courtesy you will be ask-ing the child to display when your turn to talk arrives.

3. **Speak and specify.** Your role, after listening politely to the child, is not necessarily to dialogue with the young person. This may well be the time for a strong, calm, well-reasoned, focused message coming from a single voice—yours.

When you point to the student's faults, be specific and remember that although a child can do bad things, one should never refer to the child as bad. Understand that some children have initial difficulty seeing their individual wants as secondary to the educational needs of the group. Most importantly, it is never enough to tell a child what not to do; one must articulate and model correct behavior—what to do.

4. **Offer.** Human beings respond favorably to rewards. Positive reinforcement can stimulate desired behavior. Tell the student how his life will specifically improve as his behavior improves. Threats,

anger, or shaming a child are ways to stimulate fear, resentment, or even vengeance. Obviously none of these results is productive.

　　5.　**Decide and act.** Now it is time for the young person to think, plan, decide, and act on an appropriate way to behave. Support the child as he struggles to understand why the decision to behave in an acceptable manner is necessary and how to respect the rights of others. When a child comes up with an acceptable plan, he has taken part in a learning process where both the teacher and the student should feel a sense of mutual agreement.

Monitor and endorse the child's efforts to set new habits of proper behavior in a classroom setting. Remember, the student's decision to change unacceptable behavior should not be a grudging concession, but rather the child's beginning realization that he must learn to put the needs of the group first. Sacrificing individual wants for a higher group need is the first rung on the ladder to maturity. ●

What Constitutes Appropriate Discipline?

Q: How can a teacher select the most effective type of discipline for each situation?

A: Few teachers (or parents) dispute whether discipline is necessary, but many ask how it is best carried out. Let's consider how to handle two different disciplinary decisions. It would generally not be appropriate to prevent a student from going on a school field trip because she received a low grade on a test. A low test score—in and of itself—is no reason to discipline a child. Moreover, if the field trip is considered to be a learning experience, prohibiting a student from going on such a trip clearly does not educate the student. If, however, the low test score was due to the student's refusing to study or being actively disruptive, discipline of some sort may well be appropriate.

Another common disciplinary method is to require a student to write a sentence over and over again because she wasn't on task or was disruptive. Perhaps the student is told by the teacher to repeatedly write the sentence "I will not talk in class when the teacher is speaking." Since the mission of the school is to educate, is this form of discipline helpful in accomplishing that mission?

　　Before answering that question, assume that a student is required to write the same sentence 50 times as a punishment for talking in class. What will the student remember about that form of discipline? Not the sentence she had to write and rewrite or even what she did wrong to merit the arduous task. Instead, she will probably remember writing the word "I" 50 times down the left-hand column of the page, then writing the word "will"

50 times, followed by the word "not" 50 times, and so on until the sentences were finished. In other words, she was not concentrating on the message, but on the most efficient way to complete the task.

The only thing this student learned was a way to put her brain on autopilot, which was probably not the intended disciplinary lesson.

The best discipline starts with the teacher meeting one-on-one with the student and asking her what she thinks she did wrong. Unless the student realizes the problem, discipline will not have the intended positive results.

Once the problem has been identified by both the teacher and the student, any discipline involved should be focused on changing behavior. A tedious writing assignment is simply not inherently focused

on changing behavior. It can, however, foster harmful resentment of the teacher and the school.

For example, if excessive talking is the problem, jointly identify it as such with the student. Ask the student to change this habit, and observe her behavior closely, complimenting and, when appropriate, rewarding the student for the sometimes difficult effort to change a well-established habit.

This kind of enlightened discipline aims at the problem, closely monitors behavior, and guides a student to acceptable comportment. Students need to know the boundaries of acceptable conduct and be directed to change their habits when necessary. Parents and teachers should speak with a single voice when discipline is necessary. ●

Effective Classroom Discipline

Q: It seems we need a new emphasis on law and order in the schools, as kids today are getting away with more than ever before. How can teachers maintain discipline in the classroom?

A: A school has options and alternatives when it comes to setting a discipline policy. For example, the school could initiate a "one-size-fits-all" policy of cut-and-dried solutions, ranging from in-school suspension to corporal punishment to outright expulsion. Unfortunately, many students see suspension as a holiday; corporal punishment is nothing less than outright student abuse (which can become counterproductive); and expulsion merely passes a problem on to someone else.

Therefore, we must be careful not to draw a false analogy between a school's discipline policy and the criminal justice system. This particular mindset has caused schools to blame children, overreact to trivial offenses, and implement inappropriate punishments. On the other hand, discipline policies which are based on community values that emphasize prevention rather than punishment are on the right track.

Let's look at an effective school discipline program in terms of five basic components.

• **Accurate data:** Policies on student behavior should be based on factual information, not rumors.

• **Shared decision making:** Every group involved in the policy (students, teachers, and administrators) should have a hand in making the policy.

• **Flexible solutions:** Nothing can be more unfair to certain students than a one-size-fits-all policy. Different methods of discipline should be available for different problems.

• **Published discipline handbook:** Everyone (students, school staff, and parents) should have an easy-to-understand handbook outlining appropriate student conduct.

• **Fairness:** Consistent enforcement of a code of conduct is the only way the entire school community will feel the system is fair.

These five components are necessary but not sufficient for implementing an effective discipline policy. What must be added to the mix is the guiding principle of genuine personal rapport among all of the school community members (students, staff, and parents). Building rapport can be as simple as sharing a smile, commenting in a positive way about a person's clothes or hairstyle, giving an occasional pat on the back or hug, or telling a student how much one appreciates his or her effort.

So many of the daily disruptions in the school start as trivialities (e.g., wearing a hat in class, a playful shove, tardiness, daydreaming, etc.), and yet they can quickly escalate into a major discipline problem. Accordingly, we have to understand that the above-listed disruptions are really symptoms of deeper problems (i.e., wanting attention or just boredom).

Poor school discipline policies attack only symptoms and produce disciplinarians who seem unaware of or uninterested in dealing with real student problems. When a teacher, staff member, or parent has built rapport with a student, meaningful communication can get to the root of the problem. Correspondingly, trivial disruptions are dissolved (a "problem" has been nipped in the bud), allowing productive academic development and social growth to resume. ●

Homework Helper

Q: What can a parent do to help a boy who is having only some success in school? He is in the third grade and has received below-average report cards.

A: There are a number of things parents can do to help children succeed in school. First, try serving supper after the homework is done. For a child in the third grade, about 30 minutes of homework a night is recommended. Think of it this way. Sometime between 3 P.M. and 6 P.M. each school night, a 30-minute homework schedule can provide a reasonable routine.

Second, do not allow a child to watch TV until all school assignments are done. Turning off the video box demonstrates that more value is put on homework than the latest "must see TV." The lack of distracting noise and the presence of a clean well-lighted study environment are key to getting work done. Some parents suggest grounding a child on the weekends if he complains during the week about doing his homework. However, this seems a bit extreme. Complaints, however grating, inconvenient, or bothersome, are many times nothing more than honest statements of a person's feelings.

Perhaps a better way to handle this situation is to allow your son a short concise compliant. Once heard, emphasize why your son must do nightly homework on a regular basis. Indicate to him that this short-term "discomfort" (students can seem quite adverse at times to studying!) can lead to long-term success, and more anxiety-free time and relaxation, especially on the weekends when we all need a break.

In the end, you will be allowing your son to have a predictable study routine, while developing a sense of responsibility that can help him now and in the future. ●

How to Cope with At-Risk Students

Q: What can schools do to help the growing number of children who come from broken families or whose parents are neglectful, abusive, or in trouble with the law?

A: Longitudinal studies done over many years have looked at the question of what happens to at-risk children who come from dysfunctional homes. The good news is that these youngsters possess something we are all born with, the innate capacity for resilience. It is this resilience that helps a young person successfully adapt, despite the adversity he or she must face as a child.

In fact, these studies have shown consistently that more than half of the children from such families do indeed turn their lives around. One of the major factors in this transformation is the presence of at least one caring person. According to a 40-year study, it is this caring person who unconditionally provides much needed support for healthy growth and learning development.

Outside of the home, the study indicated one of the most frequently named support people is a favorite teacher. This teacher is more than just an instructor; she is a positive role model, a confidante, someone with whom the child can closely identify.

Certain traditional structures—the home, the church, the neighborhood—for one reason or another appear to be failing to positively affect the lives of at-risk youth. Therefore, it falls on caring teachers to shoulder a special responsibility to build a bond of trust with every student.

When you think of it, educational research has given teachers a winning game plan. Enlightened educators now know what works. When an entire school supports mutual caring and respect, has high expectations for all students, and promotes inclusion by not tracking children, it provides a model in which children can choose to become motivated. A school-wide ethic of unconditional caring among teachers, students, and their parents helps strengthen the natural resilience youngsters already have to help them become caring and successful adults. ●

Negative Thoughts Lead to Poor Self-Image

Q: How much does thinking or talking about yourself in a negative way hurt you in school? Do kids who put themselves down all the time set themselves up for failure in the classroom?

A: To understand the harmful nature of negative thought and speech, first consider the opposite side of the coin. Positive self-esteem has a lot to do with feeling good about yourself. Much of it stems from a youngster's feeling accepted by the important adults in his or her life.

Such a student looks forward to challenges and has the courage to make mistakes. Daily miscues, errors, or imperfections have little effect on the healthy overall belief that continual effort will eventually bring success.

Self-esteem bolstered by positive self-talk, imaging, and visualization contributes to success. Conversely, when youngsters feel that important adults do not accept them, a low opinion of their abilities can be the outcome. Personal doubt—the belief that one does not measure up—becomes a self-fulfilling prophecy.

This erroneous self-appraisal comes into play in the classroom on a daily basis.

Sometimes adults, even a child's parents, forget how unsure a young person can feel in a classroom. Teachers know. Just ask someone to read aloud to the class.

From the third grade to the third year in college, some students will tighten up or even refuse to read a sentence. The problem rarely involves the actual ability to read. Instead, this student has the fear of making an inevitable (embarrassing) mistake. Such an "unforgivable" error would, in the mind of this student, reveal this young learner as an unmitigated fool.

It stands to reason that people—young or old—who are always sending negative messages to or about themselves are clearly harming themselves. Some of the telltale expressions contained in negative self-talk are cliches such as "everything is awful" or the use of absolute terms to put a negative spin on the situation. Especially look out for unqualified negative evaluations that contain the words "must," "always," or "never."

However, not all negative speech or thought is undesirable. Negative ideas can be useful when they lead to a healthy, logical, and constructive conclusion. For example, when a situation is high-risk or even dangerous, negative thoughts can trigger warning signals that lead to positive measures to correct such a situation.

The key is that the negative idea or speech cannot be self-defeating, leaving the thinker or speaker in a cognitive trap. If there is a personal shortcoming, recognize it and plan a corrective solution. This kind of internal problem solving actually leads back to the positive self-image that helps us resolve internal conflict, plan for the future, and make healthy evaluations in life. ●

Behavioral Standards in the Classroom

Q: Is it appropriate for teachers to enforce behavioral standards in class such as sitting up straight and focusing on the lesson?

A: It is absolutely appropriate for teachers to set behavioral standards, even if the prohibited behavior would not be considered disruptive to the class. Teachers need to take direct action to maximize time in class on task (a sleeping student is off task) in order to increase the focus on what is to be learned on a given day at a given time. In other words, teachers have a job to do—teach—and in order to do that, they must be sure that all the students are exhibiting behavior that is conducive to learning.

Granted, advice on sitting up straight may seem like something a parent says to a young child, but that does not mean the teacher should not speak up. If the teacher believes that students are not paying attention, she is within her rights to request that they act responsibly and sit up physically and focus intellectually. After all, attitude affects achievement.

There are many ways to instruct students on appropriate classroom behavior.

Perhaps the best way is for the teacher to model the proper attitude, speech, and overall desired behavior in the classroom. Her modeling should promote the "culture" of a classroom.

School has a serious mission (to educate) and must, at most times, be a serious place. A good teacher must be:

- **Self-confident:** Does the teacher exhibit calm and able leadership?
- **Pragmatic:** Does the teacher act consistently as a problem solver?
- **Friendly:** Does the teacher treat students cheerfully?
- **Sincere:** Is the teacher truthful and objective in the treatment of all students?

A teacher's close attention to appropriate classroom behavior generally demonstrates a sincere attempt to focus all the students in class on learning. If students understand why teachers have rules, it may be easier for them to accept and even support how the rules are implemented. ●

Tackling School Violence

Q: The news is full of stories of guns and knives in school with students and teachers being attacked. What is the best way for schools to address this problem?

A: School violence is a problem that is clearly widespread. During the 2005–2006 school year there were a total of 27 school-associated violent deaths. There were 15 shootings, 4 murder-suicides, 3 stabbings, 1 suicide, and 4 school-associated violent deaths under the category of "other."

There are many causes of this phenomenon, running the gamut from poverty to racism, from substance abuse to easy access to firearms. Not to be overlooked are poor parenting practices and frequent exposure to violence.

One way to help rid a school of this problem is to enforce a zero-tolerance policy (first violent offense means immediate suspension or expulsion), thereby immediately removing the offender from the school population. Such a rule does protect the immediate safety of students and teachers but has been shown to be ineffective in preventing the offending child from later engaging in more serious criminal activity.

Perhaps the most cost-effective and best long-range strategy for all students is a systematic program of preventing violent behavior. Such a program should have the following elements:

- Implement a clear and concise school-violence prevention policy on weapons and violent behavior.

- Develop an ongoing scheduled orientation for teachers, new students, and parents on that policy.

- Enforce school rules on a consistent basis.

- Schedule workshops for students and teachers in nonviolent conflict resolution.

With such a policy in place, schools can focus on their primary mission—to educate. When disruptive behavior is understood to be outside the culture of the classroom, an academic environment arises based on intellectual pursuits and the rewards that come with scholastic achievement. Likewise, when students feel recognized and appreciated, violence is replaced with empathy and cooperation. ●

Which Works Better— Punishment or Reward?

Q: Which works best to motivate kids, the threat of punishment or the promise of rewards?

A: Neither punishment (currently called *consequences*) nor reward truly gets students to take responsibility for their own behavior in the long term. It has been said that punishment and reward are two sides of the same coin.

It is far easier for most people to see how punishment is counterproductive.

When the school punishes a child, one can expect, in some cases, to see manifestations of anger and even revenge on the part of the student being punished. Vandalism, from graffiti on the walls to a rock through the principal's window, can be symptomatic of a vengeful person trying to strike back.

Punishing a student models power over reason. The grudging compliance of a defiant student can be temporary at best. Clearly, negative reinforcement is not a strong model for long-term behavioral modification.

The surprising thing, to many people, is that positive reinforcement also appears not to change long-term behavioral patterns. In short, when the rewards stop, students return to their original patterns of behavior.

In other words, rewards present an incentive for desired student behavior (read three novels a semester) to get a reward (a ticket to an ice cream social). However, after the reward is achieved (make mine chocolate with marshmallows), the incentive (ice cream) no longer exists to continue the activity (outside reading terminates). The ice cream social is an incentive.

Research tells us that incentives simply do not alter our long-term behavior. As a matter of fact, the ice cream social becomes such a short-term focal point, as an incentive, that some students may lose interest in what they were rewarded for doing.

So if both consequences and rewards don't work, what does? The answer lies in setting an environment in which the student makes a choice to engage in the desired behavior.

When parents and teachers unconditionally support the student's intrinsic motivation, they enhance the chance that this genuine motivation will blossom into a long-term personal commitment. Students should not be overly dependent on the teacher's or parent's praise, but allowed and encouraged to be intrinsically motivated to discover and create, and learn from the experience. ●

When a Teacher Should Call a Student's Home

Q: Is it appropriate for a teacher to threaten to call a student's parents to come and sit with the student in class if the student doesn't turn in homework or if he disrupts the class?

A: The use of the word "threatens" in this question is very interesting. In some contexts, this word means to scare, frighten, or even intimidate. If a teacher has said that she would call a student's parents if homework wasn't turned in or behavior was inappropriate in class, should this be considered a threat?

One could argue that it would not be an idle threat if the teacher previously called parents into the classroom under similar circumstances. Still, let's analyze this word "threat" and examine an instance of how positive steps to resolve a problem might be incorrectly interpreted.

For example, if a student suddenly fainted at school and was rushed to the hospital, the examining doctor would naturally try to contact the student's parents. The physician would do this because the parents know more about the student than anyone else. In a very real way, they could help the doctor in reporting the student's medical history or just by being there at the bedside in the hospital for moral support.

Now, if the doctor asked the student who his parents were in order to call them to the hospital, would the student consider that a threat? Of course not. He would presume that the doctor had his best interests at heart, and that calling his parents in would be an aid to the doctor and, more importantly, a help to the student.

Isn't it funny how a teacher trying to do the same thing is seen as threatening? The teacher simply wants the homework in and the class behavior to change. If bringing in a parent once in a while gets the attention of that student (and probably all the other students in that class) so that homework is turned in and conduct improves, who is the winner? It is the student, of course.

If a class feels threatened by a teacher reaching out to parents, that speaks volumes about how student perceptions can be a bit off-base. If the prospect of parents coming to class is disagreeable, the students should simply get their homework done and stay focused in class. However, if a student's parents are asked to come to class, the student should realize that his teacher cares enough about him to get his parents involved so he can succeed in school. ●

There's Lots of Hope for Your Shy Student

Q: How can teachers and parents help a student who is so shy that he rarely speaks, seems to have few friends, and doesn't really accomplish anything in school?

A: When shyness gets in the way of school achievement, certain steps must be taken. However, it's important to realize that being shy is something nearly all of us have experienced at one time or another.

Many children are shy whenever they are put in a situation where the rules of behavior are new or not clearly defined. A good example of this is the temporary nervousness and disorientation felt by children when they switch from elementary school to middle school.

Another common example is a student's first day in class as a high school freshman. Six different subjects in six different classrooms from a half-dozen new teachers can be a bit intimidating for many students.

Shyness becomes a problem in school when it becomes a habitual response to everyday classroom experiences. Students who are afraid of entering common social situations show a general inhibition to join in group activities, are habitually off task due to daydreams, and progressively feel more and more negative about themselves. These students need the intervention of both parents and teachers.

Shy students, as a rule, feel overly self-conscious. Many times it is hard for them to express themselves because of the fear of being singled out and consequently rejected. As a result, a kind of social anxiety develops. The shy child seeks the "comfort" of exclusion from classmates, teachers, and even peers, rather than the "discomfort" of social interaction.

Several solutions exist to the problem of shyness. These solutions rely, to a large degree, on the child's willingness to accept temporary discomfort and practice meaningful social interaction with fellow students, teachers, and parents.

One proven strategy to get the shy student "in the mix" is peer involvement. A cross-age tutoring program can facilitate this. When a shy student is willing to play with or tutor younger children on a consistent basis, his social confidence should show considerable development.

Teachers can utilize some or all of the following ways to respond to the shy student in the classroom:

- Seat the shy student near friendly classmates.

- Engage shy students in nonthreatening special activities.

- Take the shy student aside for private, supportive talks.

- Stand near the daydreaming student, call on this student frequently, and help this student get successfully started on his or her homework.

Speak with parents and advise them that their role is critical for the shy student. Parents, the child's first and most important teachers, can encourage their youngster to join supportive groups (scouting groups, youth soccer teams, and church groups, for example) made up of children of various ages. A parent can use an interest inventory to determine a shy child's interests and then plan trips and other learning activities to stimulate conversations. Parents can also teach phrases to a child to help that youngster

be more assertive. For instance, the ability and confidence to say "May I join the game?" may be all that is needed for a withdrawn child, on the outside looking in, to be included.

One important thing for parents to remember is that children should not be forced to communicate in a frightening circumstance. Demanding a response from a shy child might well lead to a child's embarrassment and thus prove counterproductive.

The journey from shyness to a healthy spontaneity with others ultimately depends on the young person's willingness to accept discomfort and have the courage to interact with others. Children need explanations, encouragement and—most importantly—"practice time" at home to learn social skills.

Opportunities for these socially shaped and engineered interactions at home and school are the responsibilities of caring adults. Teachers and parents should develop a consistent and systematic strategy full of many options and alternatives to develop a confidence and comfort level for the shy child with social groups inside and outside the classroom. ●

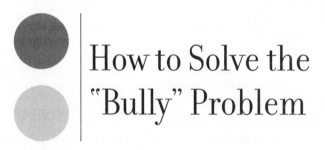

How to Solve the "Bully" Problem

 Q: What can schools do about the problem of children who frighten and bully other children?

 A: Bullying is a problem in schools around the world. It can have profound lifelong negative outcomes for both the bully and the victim alike. When one student threatens, hits, steals, taunts, or even teases another student on a chronic basis, bullying is taking place.

The victim of bullying, who is usually physically weaker, becomes socially isolated. This is, of course, one of the bully's goals—to exclude the victim from the social life of the school. Power and control over the victim (and little empathy) are characteristic of bullying behavior.

Predictably enough, students who bully often come from homes where physical abuse, in one form or another, is practiced. This child has been taught that problems are handled by striking back in defiant, antisocial behavior.

This behavior increases in elementary school, peaks in middle school, and generally decreases in high school. However, chronic bullying behavior in a given individual may endure into adulthood.

The problem is more prevalent than most people imagine. Research indicates that about 15 percent of students are bullied or initiate bullying behavior on a regular basis. As many as 7 percent of eighth-grade students in the United States stay home once a month due to the threat of being bullied. The victim can become depressed and even believe she is partly responsible for bringing the bullying on herself.

How can schools remedy this serious problem? The first step is increased awareness. Because bullying generally occurs when parents and teachers are not present, adults in many cases are not cognizant of the problem. This ignorance on the part of teachers and parents must be counteracted with a consciousness-raising campaign that focuses on the entire school community. Such a campaign should contain strict schoolwide antibullying policies, cooperative education curricular models, conflict resolution counseling, and assertiveness training.

As long as bullying happens in the dark corners and unsupervised hallways of the school, it will continue, essentially unnoticed and unopposed. Bullying can and should be rooted out by awareness of the problem and a supportive inclusion-conscious campus environment. Such a campus establishes an environment in which students empower themselves to regain their school as a safe place where respectful interaction and a fear-free environment are promoted and maintained. ●

Is Spanking Ever a Good Idea?

Q: When it comes to discipline, is spanking a good idea?

A: There is no doubt that spanking continues to be utilized by many in order to discipline children. As a teacher, you will find that parents believe, as their parents probably did, that spanking teaches children not to engage in forbidden behavior.

The problem is, research indicates that spanking does not appear to be effective in stopping undesirable conduct. In 1996, a survey was done on parents who used spanking as a method of discipline. This survey interviewed families that started spanking their child before the child was a year old. The results indicated that these families spanked their children at four years of age just as often as those parents who did not start spanking until their children were four years old.

Therefore, it would seem that as a learning tool, spanking early on is just plain ineffective. The problem with spanking is that it says "no" to something without necessarily telling the child why something is wrong. When a child is hit, he feels resentful, humiliated, physically in pain, and in many cases helpless.

The message that is painfully clear to many children is that bigger people hitting smaller people is a permitted way to solve problems. In fact, routine forms of spanking may well increase the chances of misbehavior, aggression, and depression.

When spanking is the norm, we should not be surprised to see bigger brother hitting smaller brother, or older children bullying younger children in school. After all, the person doing the hitting is only demonstrating learned behavior, modeled by an adult.

There is another way. If a child must be punished, make the punishment related to the offense. For instance, if a child mischievously colors the walls at home with crayons, the parent should take the crayons away for a day, explaining the problem to the child, and why the crayons will be withheld. In this way, the child will come to more fully realize that his favorite activity of coloring can only be done in certain areas (paper on a table). If the child writes on the walls, the privilege of coloring will be withheld.

This is good parenting because it is good pedagogy. Taking away dessert or television, or hitting a child, for scribbling on the walls simply doesn't make the direct connection to what you want the child to learn—the approved use of crayons at home.

Finally, part of disciplining a child is supporting good behavior. Be lavish with hugs—children don't get enough of them. Remember always to ask the children what they think they did wrong and discuss why a privilege must be withheld.

Keep the punishment of short duration and close the chapter on the misdeed. Don't keep bringing up a child's past problems, especially if they are unrelated to present ones.

Communication and consistency are the keys to effective discipline in the home as well as school. Spanking is simply ineffective. ●

Mutual Respect Is Key to Preventing Violence

 Recent shootings at schools make it clear that we aren't doing all we can to stop violence. What are the major causes of school violence, and what can teachers do to stop it in their classes?

 People all around the country feel that school violence is a serious issue that hits them where they live. The causes of school violence include the following:

- Physical parental abuse
- Exposure to violence through the media
- Drug abuse
- Poverty
- Racism
- Easy access to weapons
- Parental neglect

Although it is true that each of these causes can be addressed through better educational programs that can free a child to break through an abusive or otherwise unhappy environment, many schools have an ineffective approach to the problem of school violence. In fact, many schools rely on a one-dimensional tactic of removing the offender by suspension, transfer to another school, or expulsion.

Although this policy can protect the students where the violence originally took place, it has proven ineffective in impeding the offending child from developing a criminal career. A more effective answer to the problem of school violence can be summed up in one word: prevention.

Research indicates that classrooms that focus on scholastic goals, model cultured behavior, and practice immediate nonintrusive intervention discourage the type of behavior that leads to violence. What this comes down to is that teachers must learn to handle classroom problems in the classroom.

For example, when a student uses obscene language, pushes others, or simply acts defiant, a professional educator should not use a knee-jerk confrontational mode. Many times a well-intentioned teacher will reprimand the student with the rest of the class as an audience to a real-life drama. Because kids tend to side with kids, the teacher puts himself in an adversarial relationship with the offending student and perhaps the entire class.

Instead of public confrontation, the teacher should wait for an appropriate time and place to isolate the student, so a one-on-one meeting of the minds can take place. The child must know that while the boorish behavior demonstrated in class is "bad," the child is not "bad." The teacher must make it clear to the student that the teacher's expectation of appropriate classroom behavior applies to all students.

The admonition "You are better than that!" gets the point across effectively. This kind of quick, immediate, and direct counseling states that a student's disruptive behavior must change, while not ripping the child's self-esteem to shreds.

All students should feel appreciated and have meaningful rapport with at least one adult at school. We know what works. Serious violent activity is effectively impeded by mutual respect and understanding. Studies have shown, time and again, that classrooms with a positive climate, where a community feeling is promoted by inclusiveness and nurturance, have the lowest levels of violence. ●

The Gang Problem and a Solution

Q: At many schools, administrators and teachers act as if there is no gang problem. Do gangs exist at all schools, and what can parents do about it?

A: Historically speaking, youth gangs have been around for well over a century. However, they have changed from young boys engaged in organized pickpocketing to a far more threatening force dealing in drug trafficking and drive-by shootings.

Gangs share certain traits. Usually they develop along racial and ethnic identities, are predominately male (90 percent), use distinct styles of dress (colors are important), are loyal to their neighborhood, and attempt—through graffiti—to set clear and defendable boundaries to their home turf.

Gangs appear to be spreading from the inner city to the suburbs and have become a major concern for public schools.

Although gangs have a very high profile in the newspapers and on television, less than two percent of all juvenile crime is gang related. In relative terms, few young people join gangs. Even on their home turf, gang membership rarely exceeds one in ten.

Still, without question, when any organized group that deals in weapons and drug trafficking has a presence on campus, tensions increase. Gang presence can create an atmosphere in which school violence and illegal drug activity can grow. Gang members themselves have their own separate agenda in school. The school is used as a site for recruitment and socializing. The social aspect is so strong that even gang members who have dropped out of school or been expelled return to what is considered "gang turf"—the school.

In order to combat gangs, we must first understand the attraction they have for young males in particular. When young males feel rejected by their family, school, and peers, they have an unmet need. A support group is needed. Gang member-ship, in a twisted way, gives one a sense of belonging. Thus, alienation and powerlessness find an immediate, if unsavory, answer.

Understanding the need "to belong," schools have the resources and personnel to provide youngsters with an alternative to gangs. It is not just saying "no" to gangs which is important. It is also crucial to say "yes" to healthy activities.

Most youth crime, gang or otherwise, takes place between 2 P.M. and 6 P.M. in the afternoon—that critical time between teacher and parent supervision. After-school activities for all students are therefore needed. Clubs, organizations, sports programs, and fun-filled, learning-centered experiences must be available.

We know the problem of gang and youth crime, and now we know one of the solutions. All we need is the will to establish school and community programs for all children. The nickels and dimes required to run these programs will save the heavy dollar and human costs of gangs and youth criminal activity. ●

Changing Student Behavior

Q: How can you get kids to change their behavior in class? Telling them to quit talking and get busy doesn't seem to work for the long haul. Is there a formula any teacher or parent can use?

A: For a real change in behavior to take place, it must be maintained over a long period of time. The key ingredients for behavioral change are desire, effort, and sustained practice. Once a student initially wants to change his classroom attitudes and actions, a step-by-step modification can occur.

There are six different stages in the modification of student behavior:

1. **Denial:** A student simply rejects the idea that his or her behavior is counterproductive to learning.

2. **Acknowledgment:** An individual comes to understand that the behavior demonstrated in class is a problem.

3. **Commitment:** A student expresses the desire to change

4. **Strategy:** After becoming aware of the problem, an individual constructs an

action plan, understanding that the benefits of change are worth the struggle.

5. **Initiation:** The action plan is put into practice and sustained for an extended period of time.

6. **Accomplishment:** The behavioral change has now become a healthy habit.

It is important to remember that just as a student learns in spurts, behavioral change does not follow a strictly linear progression. For every three steps forward, there may be a step or two backward. Lapses, relapses, and even major setbacks predictably occur. However, keeping morale high and gaining insights through experience during the last five stages can actually speed the change.

However, beware of substituting learning about a behavioral problem for acting on that problem. Recall, the day-to-day practice of desirable behavior is imperative if lasting change is to be realized.

In all of this, students need sound advice from a teacher, parent, or therapist. Counterconditioning (substituting healthy behavior for undesirable behavior) is a try–fail, try–fail, try–succeed method that needs a competent and caring mentor. In the end, teachers need the initial desire to change and the firm conviction that with sustained effort, one can eventually accomplish the behavior needed to be successful in the classroom. ●

Dealing with Truancy

Q: How big a problem is truancy? Specifically, what can be done to get youngsters back into school on a daily basis?

A: Truancy is a major problem from coast to coast. The Los Angeles Unified School District has reported one in ten students absent each day. It is telling that only 50 percent of these students return to class with a written excuse. In New York City, a reported 150,000 of the one million enrolled students are absent each day.

Obviously, nonattendance hurts a student's achievement and self-esteem, as well as opportunities for promotion and eventual graduation. Skipping school becomes a habit that inexorably leads many talented, bright, and energetic youngsters to drop out of school altogether. One study that followed African American males who were often truant revealed only 25 percent graduated high school.

Students who fail to attend school report that school is boring, the classes irrelevant, and the teachers uncaring. Schools have been using a variety of approaches, from the courtroom to the classroom, to stem the truancy problem.

Some school districts have taken truants and their parents to court, where they were fined and ordered to attend counseling classes. A reduced dropout rate of 45 percent has been reported using such judicial-based procedures.

Other districts simply draw a line in the sand. If a student misses a certain number of days during a semester (e.g., 5, 10, 20 school days), he or she simply will not get course credit. A district that used ten absences as their base for loss of course credit reported a much-reduced absentee rate of less than 7 percent.

While firm and fair policy decisions are necessary, they are not sufficient. A competent and caring teacher in the classroom is essential to counter the problems of student boredom and frustration. Teachers must show genuine enthusiasm in presenting relevant and challenging course work to all of their students in order to provide an environment that stimulates student effort.

Achievement follows effort. The end result is an achieving student who attains success inside the classroom and ultimately self-efficacy in the world outside the school gates. ●

What Is Sexual Harassment?

Q: Sexual harassment is a hot-button issue on college campuses. Everyone thinks they know what the term means until they hear someone else's definition. What is the generally accepted meaning of sexual harassment, and what is the best solution to this problem?

A: This specific kind of harassment consists of verbal or physical conduct, sexual in nature, which subjugates a person to unfair treatment. Examples may include direct solicitation of sex, physical assault, threats that rejection of a sexual advance may produce a negative effect (e.g., lower grades), or a pattern of conduct to humiliate a subordinate with comments of a sexual nature.

Obviously, some of these activities are clearly illegal; others are unethical. All of the above could end up in a criminal or civil court.

Let's examine how a case of sexual harassment may not be illegal but, according to the policy of many colleges, be clearly unethical. A college instructor and an adult student engage in a consensual sexual relationship. While some may immediately question the morality of this activity, it is not illegal. The instructor, however, may be in peril professionally for unethical conduct.

The reason is simple to understand. The instructor is in a clearly superior and privileged position in regard to power. This instructor's capacity to grade, assess, evaluate, promote, or otherwise make life easier (or more difficult) for the student is precisely why a relationship of this kind is considered unethical.

Solutions to this problem and other forms of sexual harassment begin with a clear college policy. Such an approach has three main components:

- A clear definition of sexual harassment that is effectively communicated to the entire college community

- An unambiguous proclamation that sexual harassment will not be tolerated

- A grievance procedure based on due process and timely resolution

One cannot expect the members of a campus community to change unacceptable behavior if they are not made aware of the existence of such a policy. There is evidence that such a clear statement of campus policy can be beneficial. Recent research indicates that education of an entire college community, in terms of the vigorous enforcement of a sexual harassment policy, can bring about a positive change in the behavior of campus employees. ●

How to Deal with Verbal Abuse in the Classroom

Q: What should a teacher do with a student who always seems to be insulting teachers and other students and has an unacceptable comment for nearly every occasion?

A: Before we can modify the behavior of someone who is verbally rude (this can be oral or written abuse), we must look for the why or the cause of these offensive remarks. Generally, students act in such an inappropriate manner in order to get attention.

A verbally abusive student wants and needs attention, acceptance, and respect because he feels hurt, isolated, and to some degree hateful (toward himself as well as others). In other words, the hurtful language used is an outward sign of someone, most likely unconsciously, asking for help.

Helping these students is simple, but not easy. Here are some ways to help a student who habitually insults others.

- Meet with the verbally abusive student alone. Confronting the student in front of others is a mistake, as it can lead to him trying to play to an audience and have the last insult.

- Gain the student's trust. Never conclude the student's "bad" verbal behavior means the student is a "bad" person. Tell him that insults are unacceptable and that he is "better than that."

- Tell the student to control the speech muscles. Have the student give the "brain" a rest, and simply concentrate on keeping the jaw shut when the urge comes to make a hurtful remark. This simple self-discipline technique works in elementary as well as high school classes.

- Compliment the student's efforts. Breaking a habit is difficult. Long-standing habits are not set in a day, and they tend not to be broken overnight. Learning silence at the appropriate times needs to be actively practiced and openly praised.

Don't forget that any new good habit needs to be reinforced by teachers and parents. The root cause of the student's poor behavior is a need for attention, and continued compliments are the right kind of attention to nurture positive results. ●

Sarcasm Has No Place in School

Q: Is it appropriate for teachers to put kids down by making jokes about them in class?

A: Sarcasm has no place in school—from the students or the teacher. However, humor is very important in class. Sitting in a class without a good laugh each day would be quite dreadful.

We must all—and this includes teachers—learn to laugh with people and never at them. To laugh *with* a person can mean that a joke is centered on a funny situation in which all are basically blameless. We all have a good chuckle and then move on with our day in a positive way.

To laugh *at* a person might indicate that in fact we believe the person guilty of some kind of stupidity. Our laughter is then aimed at ridiculing a specific human being. We may move on with our day in a positive way, but the person mocked is left behind to suffer distress.

For a teacher to make a student the butt of a joke is most unfortunate. A classroom must have an environment of acceptance for optimum learning to take place. There is actual research that the worst fear for many students is not failing a class, but being singled out, laughed at, and held up as an example of stupidity.

Don't think that the situation is not doing harm just because the student being laughed at may laugh himself. There are many students who laugh at themselves in class during the day, only to go home and cry in their bedrooms at night, remembering their embarrassment over that same cruel joke.

This classroom problem would disappear if students and teachers simply demonstrated more understanding and sensitivity. ●

Teaching Children How to Behave

Q: All parents want their children to "be good" in school. How can teachers not only encourage, but teach kids how to behave?

A: Simply talking about good behavior is not enough. Neither is it enough for principals or teachers to make up abstract rules to be hung in classrooms. Likewise, good behavior will not occur if we simply discipline students by keeping them after school or even suspending them when they step out of bounds.

All of these actions may be necessary, but they are not sufficient to teach good behavior. Values need to be learned before they can be lived out in everyday life.

One way is to consistently present stories that inspire youngsters. Of course, the idea of "moral" education through stories goes back to the very beginnings of recorded history. Many of those writings, from the timeless charm of Aesop's *Fables* to the modern enchantment of Dr. Seuss, can have a real impact on how children act.

There are so many wonderful stories with hard-won values. Literature is full of characters who make moral choices only after a real struggle. Take for instance, the insightful wisdom of the children's classic *The Wizard of Oz* (realizing there is no place like home). *Huckleberry Finn*, arguably America's first great novel, is another example of a story with powerful ideas about human dignity and taking a moral stand (following personal conscience to save a friend).

Stories that transcend their particular time and place to make a moral point provide the values of honesty, sincerity, and integrity so needed in today's world. It is important to understand that storytelling should start at a very young age in the home and continue in school and throughout the life of the learner. ●

Habitual Tardiness Is a Symptom, Not the Problem

Q: What can a parent do when he discovers that his child is habitually tardy between classes?

A: First, the problem is not tardiness. Habitual tardiness is a symptom of a deeper dilemma—not wanting to get to class. When a child tries to avoid going to class, he may be saying he fears going to class.

If this is true, what is important is locating precisely what that fear is. Many students fear public embarrassment due to lack of achievement in class. If that is the case, a parent–teacher conference is in order. Here's another strategy you and his teacher might try:

- First, shorten the assignments. Make the "what" and the "how" clear. For example, tell the student that this will be a one-page written assignment on the life of Thomas Edison, mentioning four of his inventions.

- Second, make the assignment achievable. The parent or the teacher should take an initial active role in guiding the student through this kind of straightforward assignment.

- Third, always praise effort. When real effort is given over an extended period of time, a rising level of achievement will occur. Be patient; never lose faith.

One final thought about tardiness: Over the years, many students get into their heads the very questionable notion that they "can make up work missed" because of absence or tardiness. In fact, some work (a teacher's lecture, a student's presentation, a live theater performance), can never be made up. That part of the class is gone forever.

To drive this point home, you might ask your son this question: If you get to the airport one minute after your plane leaves, are they going to call it back? Regular attendance and punctuality practiced in school now have an undeniable application later in life—in the real world. ●

One-Size-Fits-All Dress Code Can Seem Like a Straightjacket

Q: Many high school students feel that there should be no dress code at school. Having administrators tell you what you can and can't wear makes a student feel like a child. For example, some dress codes forbid wearing any kind of hat in the classroom. Doesn't that just set up a faculty versus student situation every time someone walks into the room wearing a hat?

A: One issue that has endured through generations is the dress code. To some adults, it may seem trivial. To many students, however, it is an important question. If school is a place to teach the real meaning of such abstract concepts as the democratic process and freedom of expression, then the controversy surrounding a dress code is a serious topic indeed.

In fact, students do have First Amendments rights in terms of the right to express themselves. The decision in the case of *Tinker* v. *Des Moines* was clear. The court stated: "It can hardly be argued that either students or teachers shed their constitutional rights to freedom of speech or expression at the schoolhouse gate."

School administrators should understand our everyday experiences shape our values. To impose a blanket provision (an inflexible dress code) for all students at all times is poor educational policy.

On the other hand, the school has an obligation to provide an environment of mutual respect, tolerance, and a search for truth. Therefore, hats or T-shirts with hateful messages based on religion, race, or gender have no place on campus.

One of the best ways to make rules at school is for the administration to consult the students and reach a consensus. This calls for give and take, but in the end a workable compromise (and a wonderful learning model for students and administrators alike) can result. The experience of everyone in school becoming involved in a given issue of free and responsible expression can teach a significant lesson about our democratic way of life. ●

SUGGESTED READINGS

Algozzine, B., & Kay, P. (Eds.). (2002). *Preventing problem behaviors: A handbook of successful prevention strategies.* Thousand Oaks, CA: Corwin Press.

Ayers, W., Dohrn, B., & Ayers, R. (Eds.). (2001). *Zero tolerance: Resisting the drive for punishment in our schools: A handbook for parents, students, educators, and citizens.* New York: New Press.

Baker, M. L., Sigman, J. N., & Nugent, M. E. (2001). *Truancy reduction: Keeping students in school.* Washington, DC: U.S. Department of Justice, Office of Juvenile Justice and Delinquency Prevention.

Bergstrom, A., Miller, L. M., & Peacock, T. D. (2003). *The seventh generation: Native students speak about finding the Good Path.* Charleston, WV: ERIC Clearinghouse on Rural Education and Small Schools.

Bireda, M. R. (2002). *Eliminating racial profiling in school discipline: Cultures in conflict.* Lanham, MD: Scarecrow Press.

Blum, P. (2001). *A teacher's guide to anger management.* New York: Routledge-Falmer.

Danforth, S., & Boyle, J. R. (2000). *Cases in behavior management.* Upper Saddle River, NJ: Merrill.

Davis-Johnson, S. P. (2001). *7 essentials for character discipline: Elementary classroom management.* Thousand Oaks, CA: Corwin Press.

Goodman, J. F. (2002, March 20). Teacher authority and moral education. *Education Week, 21*(27), 33, 35.

Howells, K., & Day, A. (2003). Readiness for anger management: Clinical and theoretical issues. *Clinical Psychology Review, 23,* 319–337.

Jacobs, D. T. (2002). Spirituality in education: A matter of significance for American Indian cultures. *Paths of Learning: Options for Families & Communities, 12,* 16–18.

Juvonen, J., & Graham, S. (Eds.). (2001). *Peer harassment in school: The plight of the vulnerable and victimized.* New York: Guilford Press.

Martin, J., Sugarman, J., & McNamara, J. (2000). *Models of classroom management: Principles, practices and critical considerations.* Calgary: Detselig Enterprises.

Mather, N., & Goldstein, S. (2001). *Learning disabilities and challenging behaviors: A guide to intervention and classroom management.* Baltimore, MD: P. H. Brookes.

McEwan, B. (2000). *The art of classroom management: Effective practices for building equitable learning communities.* Upper Saddle River, NJ: Merrill.

McGiboney, G. (2001). Truants welcome here. *American School Board Journal, 188,* 43–45. (EJ 624 727)

McSherry, J. (2001). *Challenging behaviours in mainstream schools: Practical strategies for effective intervention and reintegration.* London: David Fulton.

Mitchell, G. (2001). *Practical strategies for individual behaviour difficulties.* London: David Fulton.

Mogulescu, S., & Segal, H. J. (2002). *Approaches to truancy prevention.* New York: Vera Institute of Justice, Youth Justice Program.

Morrish, R. (2000). *With all due respect: Keys for building effective school discipline.* Fonthill, ON: Woodstream.

Nelsen, J., Lott, L., & Glenn, H. S. (2000). *Positive discipline in the classroom.* Rocklin, CA: Prima.

Newell, S., & Jeffrey, D. (2002). *Behaviour management in the classroom: A transactional analysis approach.* London: David Fulton.

Phifer, S. J. (2002). *Setting up and facilitating student-centered classrooms.* Lanham, MD: Rowman & Littlefield.

Sanchez-Way, R., & Johnson, S. (2000). Cultural practices in American Indian prevention programs. *Juvenile Justice, 7*(2), 20–30.

unit :5

Testing:
Getting It Right

Assessment and Evaluation: Knowing the Score

Q: Schools today seem to be more and more focused on assessing and evaluating students, from report cards to high stakes testing. What is the difference between assessment and evaluation?

A: Whether we are discussing pop quizzes or SAT exams, clearly defined ways of measuring what a student has learned are a necessary part of effective instruction. As you gather and interpret information about what a student has learned, it is critical to understand the difference between assessment and evaluation. Not knowing this distinction can lead to incomplete, inaccurate, and therefore invalid scoring, judgments, and grading.

To begin, assessment and evaluation are not synonymous. Think of it this way—assessment is dynamic and evaluation is static. Assessment can be viewed as a teacher's continual and ever-changing feedback about a student's strengths and weaknesses. The word assessment is derived from the Latin *assidere*, which literally means, "to sit beside."

If you can imagine an examiner sitting alongside a student and providing feedback (based on observing, documenting, and analyzing a learner's work), you might better understand how that learner, over time, comes to appreciate and apply genuine assessment, which is self-assessment. Two things are occurring in a true assessment process: the assessor provides information and quite significantly, the assessed must accept or reject the findings. At this point there are no grades, scores, or rankings. This is because assessment is a process, not an outcome.

Evaluation, unlike assessment, is an inherently static event resulting in a number. It can be a grade, ranking, or score. For example, a student takes a test on a certain day at a certain time and gets a score of 75. The score of 75 does not change over time; it cannot become 74 or 76. It is a snapshot, a glimpse of what that student knew on a particular test on a particular day, which is then converted to a number.

Both assessment (a process) and evaluation (an event) can help a teacher judge how much his or her students have learned. Understanding the difference between evaluation and assessment is critical for teachers. Teachers need to know the difference between these two kinds of appraisal to better make clear day-to-day classroom judgments about what to teach and how to teach it.

Unfortunately, in an age of high stakes exams, standardized tests are commonly misnamed as assessments; they are in fact evaluations producing a certain score on a certain test on a certain day. Too often they are seen as conclusive proof of achievement for purposes of promotion within a system or (as in the case of an admissions test) entry into a school. To compound the problem, too many schools use these tests improperly as an exclusionary tool.

To clearly understand the difference and significance of these two terms you should remember again that an evaluation is essentially a static concept. It is an event that is "about the numbers" so it is summative, closed, quantitative, ranked, objective, competitive, and institutional. On the other hand, assessment is a process and thus dynamic in nature. It is formative (learn as you go), open, qualitative, unranked, subjective, cooperative, and personal.

Assessment and evaluation when properly understood and administered form a relationship that is both complementary and vital to the educational process. The reason for assessing and evaluating, from a teacher's perspective, is to find out how well you have taught based on how much the student has learned.

By continuously assessing and evaluating what a student has learned, both the teacher and the student can better see what has been comprehended in the past and what needs to be studied in the future. ●

Performance Assessment

Q: Old-fashioned multiple choice and true/false tests are being replaced with "performance assessments." What exactly is meant by this term, and do these assessments provide any advantages?

A: Performance assessment is simply a test that requires the learner to create an answer or product that demonstrates the student's skill or knowledge. When the student is an active participant in a project, attention is given to how a solution is found. Such a project also requires that the student show the skills or knowledge required to obtain a correct response on an examination.

For instance, if a student is asked to demonstrate his or her understanding of the piano, a short essay and a brief recital would indicate both knowledge and skill regarding this musical instrument. Such a testing format reveals what the student has learned in a way that is quite distinct from bubbling-in a response on an answer sheet.

Performance assessment isn't really such a new notion. It is quite similar to what used to be called "practical application." An assessment based on performance gives us a different view of the student's knowledge and skill. Simply put, performance assessment enhances our ability to appraise the student's progress and modify our teaching methods to better meet the learner's needs. ●

Best Tests

Q: Which of the following three types of tests—true/false, multiple choice, or essay—is the best way of finding out what a student knows about a subject?

A: Multiple means of evaluation seem logical given the variety of learner goals and tasks to accomplish. When several kinds of tests are given, both teachers and learners have multiple evidence of learner accomplishment. Thus, if there is a "best way" to test, it is probably using many different kinds of evaluation tools to get the most complete picture of what a student knows.

Having said that, the essay test is an especially valuable tool to evaluate learning because it involves such a large repertoire of basic and critical thinking skills. The essay exam is one of the best tests to evaluate critical thinking skills, involve a student's ability to make logical connections, compare and contrast opposing ideas, and support a conclusion.

A student's writing in response to reading is one of the most valid evaluations of a learner's basic comprehension of the text. The ability to write is a main priority of the school experience. Writing should be used to both evaluate and stimulate the learner's higher-order thinking skills. ●

What to Do on the Day of an Exam

Q: What can a student do on the day of an exam to get good grades on the test?

A: There are many things successful students do on the day of an exam that help them maintain good grades. Of course, those strategies will have little effect if the necessary review work hasn't started weeks before the exam.

Research indicates that we can forget 70 percent of what we learn just 24 hours after we have learned it. And yet, with proper review, we can remember up to 80 percent of what we studied six months after we have learned it. Quite a difference.

Here is how you can become part of that "80 Percent Club."

- Be consistent in your daily reviews. Each day remember to "dialogue" with your lecture notes (put your thoughts in the margins) before and after class. This interaction—questioning and evaluating what you have just learned—is a great aid to memory.

- Plan weekly reviews. Go over your subject matter every week for about an hour each weekend.

- Make some personal learning tools for your review. Develop fact sheets, flashcards, chapter outlines, memory hooks, and study checklists.

If you have consistently prepared over the long haul, the following strategies will help you perform your best on exam day. Get to class early and organize your notes. This is not the time to try to reread the entire textbook. Specifically, this is a time to remember all the relevant information you have highlighted and outlined.

When the test is passed out, listen closely to the instructions, and read the directions of the test slowly and carefully. Preview the entire exam. Be sure you know how many points each section is worth, and budget your time accordingly. Before you actually begin to answer the test, write down in the margins any memory aids—formulas, facts and/or equations.

Remember to pace yourself; do not spend too much time on difficult questions. Skip them in order to finish the rest of the questions with the idea of going back to those troublesome items if time permits.

Try to stay positive during the test. Recognize that an examination is a "snapshot" of your knowledge of certain material on a certain day. With proper planning, review, and time management, a successful outcome should be expected. ●

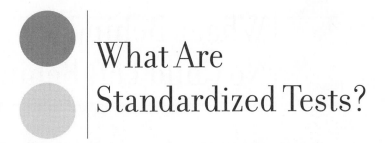

What Are Standardized Tests?

Q: What exactly is meant by the term *standardized tests?* How do schools use them, and what are the advantages and disadvantages?

A: Standardized tests are objective tests, usually produced by private publishers. These tests attempt to give a common measure of students' performances. Think of them as a tape measure to tell how well a certain school is doing, or to get an indication of the skills and abilities of the students being tested. Schools can and do use the results to compare a given student, class, school, or school system to others across the nation who use the same test.

The main advantage of standardized tests is that the school has a measure of what students have learned in math, social science, and other school subjects. These results help teachers develop programs to best meet the needs of individual students.

The primary disadvantage is that many schools use standardized testing to track students (remember the robins and the blue jays—which even children understand to mean the slow learners and the fast learners) by their perceived ability. The problem of splitting students into higher and lower levels is that students in the lower track never seem to catch up. The lower track compensatory and reme-

dial classes never seem to compensate or remediate. Students in the higher track may fall into the lower track, but students in the lower track do not, as a rule, rise to the higher track.

Today, tracking is a largely discredited system. A better solution is not to group students by perceived ability, but to serve the same enriched curriculum to all, using standardized test results to give an indication of which students may need additional individualized assistance.

To avoid the downside of tracking, parents should ask their child's teacher the following questions:

- Which standardized tests will be administered this year?
- How will the teacher or school use the results?
- What other means or methods of evaluation will the school use? Are practice tests and tutoring available to all students?
- What kind of changes in the child's educational program (at school and at home) might the test results indicate?

Standardized tests are a valuable piece of the puzzle to understand a school's or a student's progress. When combined with other tests, evaluated class work, graded homework assignments, and classroom observation, standardized tests can help us better understand a child's strengths and weaknesses. Understanding a child's abilities, at any given point in time, is crucial to developing a successful learning plan. ●

What's Behind No Child Left Behind?

Q: What exactly is the idea and purpose of the No Child Left Behind Act? How are teachers and students affected?

A: Throughout the history of American education there have been many reform movements from the beginnings of the 18th-century common school. The basic idea of No Child Left Behind (NCLB), which became law in 2002, is to reform schools by various rules and regulations that center on the idea of accountability.

Let's look at four of these accountability measures:

- *Highly qualified teachers.* In order to upgrade the expertise of those who instruct, all teachers hired must hold a license with an academic major in the subjects they teach (this was enacted for 2005–2006). Testing in terms of passing various skill evaluation exams at the beginning, during, and after a new teacher's initial licensure (e.g., the Praxis Series produced by the Educational Testing Service) is a fact of life in most states.

- *Public disclosure.* Schools and districts must produce progress reports to the public to indicate whether they are succeeding or not.

- *Adequate Yearly Progress (AYP).* Each state defines the measure of reading and math proficiencies that will be attained by 2013–2014. Each year until that date the state measures the yearly progress to meet those long-range goals. Schools that underperform for five years face closure, reconstitution by the state, or conversion into a charter school.

- *Yearly testing.* Every year each state decides which tests to use in math, reading, and science and what proficiency level is acceptable. To make sure "no child is left behind," schools need to disaggregate the data and report scores by social class, disability, race, limited English proficiency, and ethnicity.

NCLB is controversial to say the least. Those who oppose the law claim that NCLB could better be described as "no child left untested." These opponents posit that high stakes testing is not only time-consuming in terms of instructional days lost, but skews the curriculum toward teaching to the test. Predictably and unwisely, they state, there is a lack of emphasis on subjects like literature, fine arts, and history (not tested under NCLB).

On the other hand, NCLB proponents counter that American education is in serious need of reform. Testing to find out the strengths and weakness of educational programs is imperative if true change is to take place.

Let's look at the *what* and the *how.* NCLB proposes stronger accountability by testing, freedom for states and communities to make decisions on standards and proficiencies, encouraging proven research-based educational methods, and more choices for parents. These are policies that may well strengthen the educational enterprise. How such a mandate is carried out is another question. Since this law's enactment in 2002, there has been a multibillion dollar funding shortfall between promised Congressional appropriations and the dollars and cents schools need to carry out the law's regulations.

There have been many attempts at reforming public schools in the United States in the last half century including racial integration, busing, affirmative action, school-to-work, standards based education, and NCLB. History informs us that the success of national reform depends not only on the merit of the program, but also on the collective will to carry it out. Any reform package systematically underfunded, no matter how enlightened, cannot operate as originally intended. ●

How to Prepare for Standardized Tests

Q: Everyone knows that the SAT is an important test for high school kids wanting to get into college. What exactly is the SAT, and how can classroom teachers help their students prepare for it?

A: The SAT is a standardized test created by commercial publishers, constructed to give a common measure of students' performance. In other words, these examinations are comparative in nature. They match an individual student's performance with other students from a given class, school, school district, or the entire nation.

Standardized tests that measure how much a student has learned are called achievement tests. Other standardized tests purport to measure a student's ability to learn in school. They are called aptitude tests.

What youngsters need to understand is that standardized tests have their limitations. These tests can give a snapshot of a student's performance on the day of the test, but they do not measure intelligence or what a student can or cannot do. Not only is it possible that test scores can vary from day to day, but there are many skills that standardized testing fails to measure.

There are several things that can be done to help students prepare for such a test:

• Explain the purpose of a standardized test, how long it will be until the students know the results, and how the results will be used.

• Tell students the exact time and date of the test and where it will given. Being late can spell disaster.

- Have the students practice timed tests before they take the actual standardized test. Practice booklets are a big help.

- Practice "bubbling in" and even clearly erasing an answer. This sounds mundane, but the tests are scored by machine. A mark outside the lines can turn a correct response into an error.

- Guessing on a test can be hazardous. Check to see if the particular test penalizes guessing.

- There are few absolutes, so be sure to mention that "none of the above" or "all of the above" responses can be traps.

After test results are received, remind the students that major decisions about the future should not be based on a single standardized test. Their previous grades, their interests, and—most importantly—their desire to have a certain career are better predictors of eventual success. While standardized tests can be useful in making future decisions, they were never meant to be a crystal ball. ●

Preparing for Short-Answer and Essay Tests

Q: How can teachers help their students prepare for short-answer and essay tests?

A: Success on objective tests shows that the student is reading the assignments, listening to lectures, and taking good notes. However, a written portion of a test takes a different kind of strategy than an objective section.

The short-answer (or fill-in-the-blank) question is really one in which the student provides a definition or a short description. One strategy to use before an exam is to organize definitions on flashcards (word on one side, definition on the other) of the important terms, people, dates, events, or phrases the student needs to know. Obviously, the more the student practices with these cards, the easier it will be to remember key words and facts.

Answering a question on an essay test demands both knowledge and focus. Sometimes students complain that they read a question and "just go blank." One

remedy is the use of a "memory hook." A memory hook can be a word that helps the student recall a stream of facts.

For example, assume the exam question on an American history test reads, "Who was Harriet Tubman and how did she become a significant historical figure?" The well-prepared student, knowing that Harriet Tubman was a likely subject of the exam, would have prepared a memory hook to help recall pertinent facts about her life. One memory hook a student might have invented would be FURS. The letters represent the first letters of important words regarding the life of Harriet Tubman.

F stands for freedom, the dream this woman had for herself as well as others. Born a slave in the state of Maryland in 1821, this brave heroine escaped from human bondage in 1849.

U stands for underground, and **R** stands for railroad. The Underground Railroad was a secret escape route that stretched from the South to the Free States in the North and to Canada.

S stands for slavery, against which Tubman fought not only by escaping to freedom, but by risking her life—over and over again—by returning to the South to lead more than 300 slaves on dangerous journeys to freedom.

Memory hooks such as this can really get the student into an answer with a torrent of solid facts. By committing 10 or 15 of these self-made acronyms to memory, he will have a ready storehouse of information for a given short-answer or essay question.

However, having the information is not all it takes to do well on an essay test. The student must answer the actual question posed. When writing an essay, he must first read the question carefully to decide what is being queried.

The way the professor wants the question answered is usually contained in a key verb. Here is a list of these commonly used "exam" verbs: analyze, compare, contrast, define, describe, discuss, evaluate, explain, list, prove, and summarize. These verbs give a specific command. Each word calls for a different kind of essay. So follow orders!

After the student has identified the key verb to the exam question and plotted his general approach, he should make a short but specific outline of the answer. This outline will organize his thoughts and allow him to include some of his memory hooks; it should also speed up his writing.

When the student writes that first line, he should artfully use the exam question as part of his answer. For example, if the exam question is, "Discuss the major Supreme Court decisions that have affected women's rights," the first sentence might be, "Women's rights have been affected by six major Supreme Court decisions." As long as the student remembers six key facts, reviews his answers for clarity and accuracy, and writes legibly, he should be quite successful. ●

What Is Test Bias?

 Many people are quick to call a test biased when they don't do well on the exam. What exactly is test bias, and is it really a problem?

 Bias is present when a question on an exam is answered differently by individuals of the same ability who come from different cultural, ethnic, class, gender, or religious groups. Because tests can determine who is considered successful at any level of education, bias can be a real, yet correctable, problem. For an example of bias, let's say that a test examiner wants to evaluate certain math skills that deal with the concept of speed. If a person is asked how fast a yacht could travel with a strong breeze, the word "yacht" may cause the question to be unfair. Quite simply, the word "yacht" might be unfamiliar to a person who doesn't live by a body of water or who never has had the opportunity or need to learn that word.

If that person finds the question more difficult because of the presence of the word "yacht," even though she has mastered the concept (speed and distance) measured by the item, then the question is not fair. It is clearly biased. When an answer to a question tests vocabulary rather than the discrete concept the examiner is trying to evaluate, the test item loses its validity.

A test may also be biased if it contains offensive, demeaning, or emotion-ally charged material. Even if the material does not make the test more difficult for the examinee, it could easily lower the performance of the person taking the test. For instance, some females may feel demeaned by a test that continually uses male job designations: policeman, fireman, or congressman. A rising sense of frustration may lead that particular person to a lower performance than her ability would indicate.

On the other hand, that same person might reach her true potential if the more gender-neutral terms of police officer, firefighter, or member of Congress were used. Remember that the object of the test is to evaluate the performance of a learner in understanding a particular concept, not to stir up the test taker's passions.

Controversial or inflammatory material is clearly unacceptable, because it may lead to an inaccurate evaluation of the person taking the test. Items that favor the performance of one group over another (of the same ability) simply make a test unfair. When a test is devised free of bias, that exam can serve as a fair evaluation. ●

How to Test Children in Lower Grades

Q: What kinds of tests best determine if a young child is doing well in school? How does a parent know the test is accurate? How important are a child's first grades?

A: The best kinds of tests have a clear purpose. Here's a list of valid reasons to test a young student:

- To diagnose learning problems
- To determine level of achievement

- To set up an individualized curriculum
- To serve as a basis to report to parents
- To assist a child in a self-assessment of progress

In testing a young child we are interested in knowledge, skills, dispositions, and feelings. A good time to test is during a child's informal work and play. This way many of the errors of various assessments can be minimized.

However, there are risks involved in assessing young children. For one, young children are known to be poor test takers. Some researchers have concluded that the younger the test taker, the more likely that errors will occur in the assessment. If this is true, a child may be falsely labeled. Experience shows that the longer a child lives under a label (even a false one), the more the child believes the label correctly defines her.

As to the matter of letter grades on report cards, they are generally not considered appropriate until the third grade. Children in kindergarten through the second grade have different developmental timetables. Because of this, their performance is too unpredictable to achieve desired reliability. In addition, there is scant evidence that letter grades contribute to the progress of those most in need of improvement.

Parents should become involved in encouraging their child to assess her own progress. First, in a conference, with or without the teacher, it is a good idea for the young student to discuss work on which she is making good progress.

Second, the child should be encouraged to articulate where she thinks improvement needs to take place. Third, the young student should be asked to request the kind of help needed to achieve future success. Research indicates that most children will be quite realistic in making these early self-assessments. This is also an excellent way for the child to begin to take responsibility for her education. ●

IQ Tests Are Only One Tool in Measuring Intelligence

Q: Do intelligence tests really measure a person's potential?

A: Many teachers, administrators, and psychologists believe that IQ tests do or should measure human potential or some kind of innate capacity. Having said that, there is widespread documented evidence of the failure of IQ tests to actually measure what they are purported to assess.

For example, IQ tests coupled with other diagnostic instruments have repeatedly led to overrepresentation of minority groups in special education. At the same time, IQ tests play a significant role in the underrepresentation of minorities in gifted and talented programs. In order to understand whether IQ tests are valid, one first must ask a simple question: What is intelligence?

One theory of intelligence is akin to what has been called the "law of the jungle"—adapt, migrate, or die. Accordingly, culturally intelligent behavior involves adapting to one's environment, selecting a better environment or, in place of death, reshaping one's current environment. The expression of intelligent behavior is a function of the amount of experience one has with what is being tested.

In fact, there is nearly universal agreement among researchers of the inseparability of experience from intellectual ability. The question then is, Why are IQ tests still used as an evaluation of "innate capability" when one's intellectual abilities rely so heavily on experience? There are probably many reasons: traditional reliance on this test by schools, market forces (the demand of consumers), or even misunderstanding among educators and parents on what is being tested.

Whatever the reason, IQ tests are inappropriate instruments when used to classify individuals according to academic potential. Testing a student's current level of intellectual functioning is important, but it must be accurate and lead to instructional interventions that enhance a learner's intellectual development. ●

Tests Should Measure Development, Not Limit a Student's Opportunities

Q: What kinds of tests are supposed to show a child's aptitude? Don't these tests end up with youngsters being grouped into the "smart" classes and the "dumb" classes?

A: Aptitude tests, in many cases, are claimed to be ability assessments. These tests, which are not assessments but evaluations, measure the level of development attained by the individual in one or more abilities. A child may be given an aptitude or ability test (the terms are often used interchangeably) in any of the following: reading, language, leadership, music, art, or science—just to name a few.

The question of what is being tested is a crucial one. After all, these tests are only a measure of a child's learning experience to that point in the student's life. Some would argue that what is really being tested is the extent of the child's experiences outside of school.

Did you know that the average student, kindergarten through 12th grade, only spends 9 percent of her time in a classroom? A low reading score on an aptitude test may be a reflection of what the child does during the 91 percent of the time spent outside the classroom.

For example, if a child comes from a home in which there are no appropriate reading materials, no time set aside for family reading, and no modeling of reading by the parents—a child will predictably score low in reading ability. This does not mean that the test given to the child is invalid. It does mean that as a "snapshot" in time, the child has not developed a high level of reading ability.

Here is the most important point: A low score on a reading aptitude test does not necessarily mean that the child is not very "intelligent" or has a language-processing problem. If either of these judgments is made, an ability or aptitude test can serve as an unfair gatekeeper—excluding talented, creative, and otherwise wonderful kids from a variety of enriched courses. Research continues to tell us that intelligence is not static (one is simply smart or dumb), but dynamic.

The exciting part of education is watching a person grow in intelligence. Sometimes, a misguided reliance on aptitude tests can shortcircuit a student's opportunity to learn.

Let's be plain about this. The misuse of ability test results has excluded and continues to exclude people from disadvantaged backgrounds from challenging and enriched curriculum. Accordingly, Johnny or Jane is put in the "bluebirds" group rather than the "robins" group, and within a day every kid knows that the bluebirds are the slow group, or as the kids themselves refer to it, "the dummies." Such an

unfortunate grouping is called tracking. It occurs in 80 percent of all U.S. schools. This kind of grouping is unfair and a clear misapplication of aptitude tests.

Aptitude or ability tests have limited predictive value. These tests should be used to clarify a student's strengths and the areas in which a student needs to develop. Correct use of the results of an ability test should tell teachers and parents where a student needs help. For example, in the case of a low score in reading, the student, teacher, and parent should work together to find the appropriate high-interest reading material to boost this child's growing ability to read.

In other words, the whole idea behind these tests should be for students to become aware of their strengths and weaknesses and, with the help of parents and teachers, to develop their talents and enhance their academic achievement. ●

A Formula for Success on Quizzes, Tests, and Exams

Q: Many students dread taking tests, whether it is just a pop quiz, an important test, or a final exam. How can these students improve their performance?

A: This is one of the most frequently asked questions. In answering this question, two things must be kept in mind. First, tests should measure what you learn in a course. Competent teachers know that any test that contains material outside of what has been taught is inherently invalid.

Second, routine success on tests demands habitual student preparation. If your goal is to earn better grades, your method must be routine review.

Better grades start with solid study habits. Following is a checklist of things every conscientious student should do before a quiz, test, or exam:

1. Read all assigned texts.
2. Listen and take notes during lectures.
3. Reread assigned texts (especially difficult passages).
4. Highlight important information to study (but don't overdo it).
5. Meet with the instructor (that's what office hours are for!).
6. Review work regularly.

Reviewing work is critical to success. Rather than waiting until the test date to cram, students should schedule study periods well in advance. Daily reviews can be conducted just before and after the professor's lecture. Weekly reviews should last about an hour per subject. Students should study reading lists and lecture notes. Finally, test reviews should begin about one week before an exam. At least two to five hours of summary study should be allotted for each subject.

One favorite test tool to use for reviews is an "information bank" that can be saved on a computer. Students can write important facts, formulas, or ideas in a condensed and organized format.

Another study tool is a checklist. The student should try to put herself in the teacher's shoes and write down every question and answer that a student should know for the exam.

Reading assignments, major ideas, definitions, and any other material—from equations to historical figures—that could make their way onto an examination should be included. A well-prepared checklist will closely mirror the questions on the actual test.

Organization, time management, and planning ahead are essential in earning better grades. Students who follow these steps will be much better prepared on test day. ●

How to Prepare Students for a Test

Q: What advice can a teacher give to parents to help their child prepare for tests?

A: Parents should make a checklist of things to do to prepare their children for the various kinds of tests, exams, and quizzes they are sure to face day in and day out at school. Here's a short list of actions parents can take on a regular basis:

- Talk to the teacher. Find out on a continual basis what specific curriculum-related activities you can do to help your child.

- Monitor your child's progress at school by reviewing all homework. There is a lot to be said for quality control.

- See that the child is well-nourished and gets to bed on time. Sounds pretty basic, but nutrition and rest play a significant role in how well children perform on tests.

- Have a wide variety of reading materials in your home—books, magazines, newspapers, or online opportunities available to spark your child's curiosity.

- Judge your child by his or her effort, not by a test score. Research shows it is the learner's effort, nurtured by parental involvement, that is the critical element for success in school. ●

Using Portfolios to Assess Math Progress

Q: Is there another way to judge whether or not a child understands what is going on in math class besides tests of rote memory? Remembering a formula and coming up with the right answer on a multiple choice test seems to be all that some math teachers care about.

A: Enlightened math teachers create environments for students to document their reasoning as they problem solve. One way to accomplish and record mathematical progress is to combine instructional and assessment activities in a portfolio.

A math portfolio presents a typical collection of a student's scholastic product (projects, reports, and computational work) that demonstrates an authentic development of higher-order thinking skills. Portfolios present the opportunity to evaluate both process and product. Learning and assessment are thus integrated.

Assessment becomes most effective when it is generated from the core elements of the curriculum. After all, ethical testing rests on the notion that what is taught and only what is taught should be tested when grading a student.

A portfolio should present work that has met a certain explicitly communicated standard. Accordingly, grading systems that score, rate, and rank a student's portfolios must be unambiguous, and the student must always have the opportunity to revise and improve on the core work.

Thus, a portfolio is a representation of a student's best efforts demonstrat-ing the breadth and depth of his or her developing ability in mathematics. The portfolio is an inherently interactive assessment tool, as it can be foundational evidence of academic growth for teacher–student, student–parent, and parent–teacher conferences.

When a student has the opportunity to make a portfolio of the required work, what is created is a type of window where all can see a student's self-directed efforts and growth in the field of mathematics. As students make mathematical connections, they may begin to see themselves as mathematicians and understand their own strengths and weaknesses. This knowledge leads a student to become more responsible about his or her own learning—an insight that is imperative to become a lifelong learner.

Traditional multiple choice testing simply does not afford the more scholastically reflective and authentic evidence of assessed learning present in a teacher and student evaluated mathematics portfolio. In a portfolio, learners of math have the opportunity to process mathematics information, formulate statements about their values, beliefs, understandings, and abilities, and partake in a process that allows them to express their goals and aspirations.

Mathematics portfolios can realize superior educational outcomes, because both the student and teacher take on expanded roles in the learning and assessment process. ●

Types of Math Portfolio Assessment

Q: Evaluating student computational skills by looking at scores on a standardized test really doesn't provide the kind of assessment that lets a teacher know if the student understands how to solve problems or if the student is just using rote mathematical formulas. What kind of assessment would really determine what a student knows about math?

A: It is important that students demonstrate higher-order critical thinking skills that are not to be commonly found in daily assignments or assessment activities. Assessment is most effective when it is an integral part of an instructional format that stems from an enriched core curriculum.

What is called for is a portfolio—a collection of student work that represents a compendium of elaborate and time-consuming projects, reports, and writings demonstrating a student's use of mathematics to solve problems using analysis, synthesis, and evaluation.

There are four kinds of math portfolios a teacher may consider in order to demonstrate both student process and product.

1. **Best Work Portfolio:** This portfolio showcases the student's best work. It is a selection of what the student believes is his or her best work.

2. **Work in Progress Portfolio:** This collection acts as a working folder that may be the basis of a teacher–student conference. Student work can be added or deleted.

3. **Teacher Assessment Portfolio:** This particular portfolio contains all student assignments. The idea here is that there is no disposable work (except for old drafts). These portfolios are used as an assessment tool that can clearly indicate the student's development in terms of the breadth and depth of work over a school year.

4. **Parent–Student Portfolio:** This portfolio is intended to be taken home and is therefore a different kind of learning tool. The Parent–Student Portfolio gives the student the opportunity to explain assignments and review them with his or her parents. This portfolio is a great way to keep parents in the information loop. In addition, this portfolio helps the student realize that he or she has the primary responsibility to develop skills and understanding that will stand up well under a multidimensional form of evaluation.

As students link success to performance through their continual efforts and become self-directed in turning out thoughtful portfolios, they provide the teacher (and parents) many evidentiary examples with which to access global understanding and those all-important higher-order critical thinking skills. ●

Six Steps to Better Grades

Q: What advice can you as a teacher give to parents to help a student who has achieved in the past but is presently struggling in school? How can that student be put on the road to once again achieve higher grades?

A: Let's consider a list of six steps that can be acted on immediately:

- First, the struggling student should talk with teachers from whom they have received high grades in the recent past and have a heart-to-heart talk about what made that experience so successful. Students who have experienced an enjoyable learning atmosphere, while making academic progress, have a way of forgetting that they still had to work in that supportive environment to be successful.

- Second, parents should contact the current teacher and suggest that together with the youngster they might organize a student study package. Such a package could contain readings, helpful Internet sites, written assignments, and study guides for upcoming tests.

- Third, parents should continually praise sincere effort on the part of the struggling student, knowing that

achievement in the form of higher grades will probably follow.

- Fourth, a parent or teacher might help to find a "study-buddy". A peer-tutor can do wonders to ward off the struggling student's feeling of loneliness and marginalization, while learning the value of collaboration on educational tasks.

- Fifth, parents should sit down with their youngster and the current teacher to discuss what is to be studied in the next couple of weeks, how it is to be reviewed, and what kind of learning is expected from the student.

- Sixth, parents can make a simple subject-by-subject form on which the teacher can write daily comments. Close review of this report on a day-to-day basis can be a very effective way to monitor a struggling student's progress.

The fact is, children learn in spurts. It is also true that we learn best in environments in which we not only feel accepted, but also have an idea of what is expected. Indicate to the parents that timely intervention now can recapture the success and better grades the struggling student has experienced in the past. ●

SUGGESTED READINGS

Anderson, L. W., & Bourke, S. F. (2000). *Assessing affective characteristics in the schools.* Mahwah, NJ: Lawrence Erlbaum.

Boston, C. (Ed.). (2002). *Understanding scoring rubrics.* College Park: University of Maryland: ERIC Clearinghouse on Assessment and Evaluation.

Braun, H. I., Jackson, D. N., & Wiley, D. E. (Eds.). (2002). *The role of constructs in psychological and educational measurement.* Mahwah, NJ: Lawrence Erlbaum.

Dombrowski, S. C. (2003). Norm-referenced versus curriculum-based assessment: A balanced perspective. *Communique, 31*(7), 16–20.

Drummond, R. J. (2000). *Appraisal procedures for counselors and helping professionals* (4th ed.). Upper Saddle River, NJ: Merrill Prentice Hall.

Janesick, V. J. (2001). *The assessment debate: A reference handbook.* Santa Barbara, CA: ABC-CLIO.

Jones, M. G., Jones, B. D., & Hargrove, T. Y. (2003). *The unintended consequences of high-stakes testing.* Lanham, MD: Rowman & Littlefield.

Lund, J., & Fortman Kirk, M. (2002). *Performance-based assessment for middle and high school physical education.* Champaign, IL: Human Kinetics.

Martin-Kniep, G. O. (2000). *Becoming a better teacher: Eight innovations that work.* Alexandria, VA: Association for Supervision and Curriculum Development.

McAfee, O., & Leong, D. J. (2002). *Assessing and guiding young children's development and learning.* Boston: Allyn and Bacon.

Moskal, B. (2000). An assessment model for the mathematics classroom. *Mathematics Teaching in the Middle School, 6*(3), 192–194.

Moutoux, M. (2002). Evaluating nature journals. *Green Teacher, 69,* 39–40.

Oosterhof, A. (2003). *Developing and using classroom assessments* (3rd ed.). Upper Saddle River, NJ: Merrill Prentice Hall.

Popham, W. J. (2002). *Classroom assessment: What teachers need to know* (3rd ed.). Boston: Allyn and Bacon.

Rudner, L. M., & Schafer, W. D. (Eds.). (2002). *What teachers need to know about assessment.* Washington, DC: National Education Association.

Stiggins, R. J. (2001). Introduction to the special section. Building a productive assessment future. *NASSP Bulletin, 86*(621), 2–4.

Taylor, R. L. (2000). *Assessment of exceptional students: Educational and psychological procedures.* Boston: Allyn and Bacon.

Thompson, S. J. (2001). *Alternate assessments for students with disabilities.* Thousand Oaks, CA: Corwin Press.

Tindal, G., & Haladyna, T. M. (Eds.). (2002). *Large-scale assessment programs for all students: Validity, technical adequacy, and implementation.* Mahwah, NJ: Lawrence Erlbaum.

Trice, A. D. (2000). *A handbook of classroom assessment.* New York: Addison Wesley Longman.

Wilson, L. W. (2002). *Better instruction through assessment: What your students are trying to tell you.* Larchmont, NY: Eye on Education.

UNIT :6

Curriculum:
What to Teach

Slow Learners Deserve Full Curriculum

Q: Many people believe the biggest problem in school is that kids who are slow to understand what is being taught hold others back. Isn't it time that schools stop teaching to the lowest common denominator? If some youngsters can't cut it, why should that mean that everyone has to stop and wait until they get it? Doesn't that just water down the courses?

A: There is no question that within the average classroom population, some children will learn faster than others. The speed of learning can even differ with each individual student from subject to subject, from year to year. Therefore, in any given class there are almost always "fast" learners and "slow" learners.

It is important to remember two things. First, there are many reasons why a child may be labeled a slow learner. The problem may well be conditional. The child's attitude toward learning, a negative home environment, the lack of language skills, a mismatch between the teacher's teaching style and the child's learning style, or a combination of any of the above may be what is producing the "slow" learner.

Second, the "slow" learner of today is not necessarily the "slow" learner of tomorrow. If any of the above conditions change, a "slow" learner may be able to learn at an average or even an accelerated pace. Past performance under one set of circumstances is generally not an accurate indicator of true potential in a different situation.

Many times, whether a child succeeds in the classroom is directly influenced by poor instruction based on false assumptions. For example, if what is valued is rapid learning of a list of facts and summarized conclusions, "fast" learners will probably meet with success and "slow" learners will most likely meet with failure.

On the other hand, if what is valued is learning, then slower learners are given appropriate learning strategies—more one-on-one instruction, thorough reviews of projects, plus more opportunities to achieve. These approaches could well spell success, because slower learners, after all, are learners.

One other point is absolutely essential to understand. At no time should the curriculum be "dumbed down." All students learn best when the richest possible curriculum is presented and learners are able to work at a pace and using a learning style (e.g., visual, auditory, kinesthetic) appropriate to that student.

Under this format, there is no need to water down what is taught. All classroom learning begins with an enriched core that provides knowledge for all. Every student is expected to master this enriched heart of the curriculum. Within this same class structure, each individual student has the opportunity, under the teacher's tutelage, to accelerate the learning process and investigate the subject matter in greater depth.

With creativity, patience, and an enlightened understanding of learning styles, there is no need to slow down, dumb down, or water down a school's curriculum. ●

An Answer to the Diversity Gap in High Schools

Q: Why is it that so few minority kids take college prep science and math courses in high school? How can these youngsters be reached? Being sensitive to a student's culture might work in language or history class, but how could it possibly work in the math or science classroom?

A: In fact, there is a diversity gap in math and science literacy. There are two fundamental changes a school can make to remedy this seemingly intractable problem.

First, eliminate tracking. In the vast majority of public high schools, non-white students are placed in programs that do not include college preparatory (advanced) math or science courses. These minority students are given a clearly scholastically inferior curriculum throughout their public school education.

This early and rigid grouping is one of the main reasons for mathematics underachievement in the United States. Research reveals that only a small percentage of U.S. students took the advanced math classes necessary to qualify for college math and physical science programs.

Tracking or so-called ability grouping is a product in part of the attitudes of unenlightened educators. Tracking has especially negative implications for African American, Latino, and Native American students.

Low expectations become a self-fulfilling prophecy. The good news is, so do high expectations! Programs that challenge low expectations have had positive results by simply scheduling all students into college preparatory classes—and preparing them all. Other programs put every student in gifted classes while implementing innovative assessment practices that make high expectations explicit to all students, parents, and teachers.

The second basic change a school can make is to incorporate a variety of learning styles and culturally relevant curricula. Just as students bring different languages, space and time interactions, and problem-solving skills to class, teachers must make adaptations in the science and math curricula.

Schools can support varied cultural styles by using culturally relevant materials that best meet the needs of these students. In other words, teachers need to know how the child thinks in math in order to provide proper instruction. Meaning-centered activities that connect science and math to real issues in the students' communities are of great value. These projects can help students master science and mathematics, along with language acquisition skills.

In all of the above, teachers and parents should demand intellectual rigor based on the most enriched curriculum. One way to accomplish high student intellectual achievement is for teachers to provide nurturing, culturally sensitive relationships with students based on high expectations. ●

Where in the World Is Geography?

Q: Many children finishing high school have never had a geography course. Don't the schools think that knowing where countries are is important?

A: According to The National Geographic-Roper Public Affairs 2006 Geographic Literacy Study, only half or fewer of young men and women 18–24 can identify the states of New York (50 percent) or Ohio (43 percent) on a map. In most of the nation's schools, geography is not considered a required course. Only one student in seven takes a high school geography course.

However, geographic knowledge is critical to understanding the world in which we live. Knowledge of geography is basic to the study of other cultures, global ecology and economics. The story of humankind is, in no small part, the study of the global movement of people and products.

Schools and parents can revive the importance of geography by having globes, maps, and atlases available for daily use and discussion. Today, with photography from outer space and up-to-the-moment maps on the Internet, we no longer have to depend on outdated textbooks as our source of knowledge. With new technology, we can elevate geography to its rightful place as one of our schools' basic core courses. ●

What about Science?

Q: With new discoveries every day in so many different fields of science—medicine, biology, astronomy, and physics—you would think most studies should involve some kind of science. Do our schools place enough emphasis on science?

A: About 30 years ago, the often-cited publication reviewing our nation's educational system, "A Nation at Risk," recommended a greater effort on the sciences. Back in 1982, 79 percent of students took biology. A decade later, the number had jumped to 93 percent over the same time period, and chemistry classes rose from 32 percent to 56 percent. Teachers have also joined the call for more science in the classroom.

A recent survey by the Bayer Corp. of 1,000 teachers found that 70 percent of the educators stated schools should put a greater emphasis on science education. Students wish to take more science. Teachers want to teach more science.

What, then, of parental support for science education? As for the always-crucial component of parent involvement, a nearly unanimous 96 percent wanted to help their children with science education.

A start has been made, but it is up to parents and teachers to continue their support of more science in the classroom. ●

Evolution Theory Has Roots in Science

Q: If evolution is just a theory, why can't other theories be taught in science class? Why shouldn't creationism be taught?

A: It is important to understand that not just any theory about a given topic can be considered a "scientific theory." For instance, one may have a theory on whether the New York Yankees will win the World Series. That kind of a theory is usually an educated guess, contingent on many factors, and sprinkled with a fair portion of hope. On the other hand, scientific theory is built over time with a large body of consistent evidence formed within the rigors of the scientific method.

Scientific research is concerned with the "how" of things. The manner of scientific investigation is scrupulously rigorous. The approach must be objective—to observe things as they are, regardless of preconceived views from any quarter. Scientifically speaking, only when observations and experiments can be reproduced are they judged acceptable.

The scientific community has passed judgment on the teaching and learning of evolution. Evolution is the unifying theme of biology. The evidence of evolution can be gleaned from the last 3.5 billion years of organic life on the planet. Fundamentally, the fossil record of ancient life forms and the remarkable molecular similarities among diverse species of organisms form an immense body of consistent evidence.

In terms of the study of biology in the classroom, the very way organisms are classified is based on their evolutionary relationships. That being said, the teaching of evolution remained controversial throughout the 20th century. From the Scopes trial in the 1920s to state laws passed in the 1980s, a battle ranging from the classroom to the courtroom has had a well-documented history.

In the 1980s, both Arkansas and Louisiana passed laws mandating the teaching of creation science alongside of evolutionary theory. In 1987, the United States Supreme Court declared that such laws were an intrusion of religion in the public schools and, therefore, unconstitutional. Science, at its root, is a way to make the world more intelligible for all of us. Evolutionary theory is the road we travel to an ever-greater understanding of the past, present, and future of our environment. ●

Why Is Spelling So Hard?

Q: Why do some students have so much difficulty with spelling, and how can they improve?

A: Spelling is the use of letters to form words. The implication is that the letters are used according to certain rules. Phonics plays a part in spelling. However, there is a problem. English has 40 elementary sounds but it is written with 26 letters.

To understand how confusing a total reliance on phonics can be, consider the sound "ough." The sound changes in words like bough, cough, thorough, thought, through and tough.

There are 14 different spellings of the "sh" sound. Examples can be found in the following words: anxious, mission, fuchsia, and ocean. Unlike Spanish, which is basically spelled as it sounds, about one out of every four English words is spelled differently than it sounds.

There are different ways to becoming a better speller. Students should try some or all of these methods:

- Keep reading. The more familiar you are with words, the more easily they can be recalled.

- Keep writing and proofreading. The more you use words and check your work, the more you practice correct spelling.

- Study with a friend. Research shows that peer group work in spelling creates linkages between reading, writing, and spelling instruction.

- Remember your goal is to become a competent, independent speller. Spelling is a skill. Any skill gets better with practice. ●

Finding Out about the World around You

Q: Many students know very little about the world around them. How can they learn more about other cultures and lands?

A: There are a number of things students (and their families) can do if they really want to learn about faraway places and people who live in other parts of the world. The good news is, you don't need a visa or an around-the-world plane ticket.

- Make a friend from a different country and talk about his or her homeland. Sometimes new friends are as close as your own classroom or neighborhood.

- Use your school or public library and find out how other cultures celebrate holidays. Discuss these findings with friends and family.

- Use maps and make your own maps. Computers are an excellent resource. Try to pinpoint particular cities where your friends may have lived or where current news events are taking place.

- Study political maps. One caution: Be sure the books are up-to-date. Given inevitable political changes—new countries and new boundaries—an old atlas is always outdated. Updated maps on the Internet can be a useful tool.

- Take the opportunity to watch geographic videos. Images of deserts, volcanos, mountain ranges, frozen tundra, and rain forests can introduce you to quite a different world.

- Finally, if you do get the opportunity to travel, take it. It is the most authentic way to experience a new environment. ●

What's the Point of Reading Shakespeare?

Q: Shakespeare's plays don't seem relevant to today's world, and the English is so different that it's almost like reading a foreign language. Why is it important for students to read these plays?

A: Shakespeare's *First Folio* was published in 1623. The English language has gone through many changes since then. At first glance, the casual reader may be put off.

But in that case, the casual reader is making two mistakes.

First, there is nothing "casual" about Shakespeare's drama. He is recognized in much of the world as the greatest of all dramatists. Shakespeare's keen understanding of human behavior in all its varied forms is revealed in his portrayals of an incredibly wide variety of unforgettable characters.

Second, students should not be taking Shakespeare's plays home to read them and think they are truly experiencing the Bard's work. Shakespearean drama is meant to be seen and heard. Shakespeare wasn't writing short stories or short novels.

To have the Shakespearean experience (that is, to be entertained), one must see Shakespeare performed. Students should try to view live performances or videos of Shakespeare's plays, such as either of Kenneth Branagh's films, *Henry V* or *Much Ado About Nothing*, both exquisitely filmed and masterfully played.

Seeing Shakespeare's works will entertain and make follow-up reading assignments more meaningful. Or as Shakespeare wrote, "If this be error and upon me proved, I never writ, nor no man ever loved." ●

The Arts Are Undervalued

Q: Students always seem to consider fine arts classes to be interesting and enjoyable, but not important. Why don't students (or for that matter other teachers and school administrators) understand the value and importance of the arts?

A: Arts are undervalued in the school. The reason for this is that the arts have a dual nature, and many people only see a single side. The art that is experienced by most people in a school setting is the observable curriculum. Everyone has heard the choir sing at an assembly, the band play at a pep rally or the drama classes present a performance. Each of these presentations takes a lot of time, energy, and talent. However, there is another side of the arts that transcends actual artistic performance.

This other side has to do with critical thinking skills based on an appreciation of subtlety, an ability to read between the lines, an understanding of the social implications of art, and a positive attitude toward experimentation.

This is the side of art seldom seen, yet it is crucial to our growth as learners. It is the intellectual side of art that stimulates our minds and opens up new ways to express our culture, our beliefs, and our humanity. ●

What's Going On with Art Programs?

Q: Many parents do not understand the art being produced by their high school students at school. It often looks like the kids take everyday materials and just throw them together. How can one explain the "what" and the "why," not to mention the "how" of it all?

A: To begin with, let's look at the "what." Welcome to postmodernism. Briefly, postmodernist art is constructed out of the everyday society in which we live.

Two terms are essential for understanding postmodernist art: bricolage and eclecticism. Bricolage is simply using whatever materials are convenient to the artist. This could be paint, glue, bricks, or the hood ornament from a 1959 Pontiac. Eclecticism, in this context, means mixing things that don't ordinarily go together—a boxing glove coming out of a TV set, or the Titanic sitting atop the United Nations building.

Now for the "why" part of your question. All true art attempts to leave an ambiguous message. Within that tradition, the postmodernist artist may attempt to surprise the audience with paradoxical statements. Fundamentally, the postmodernist artist displays a personal narrative in which the audience is asked to consider an alternative point of view.

Art then is not premised on "absolutes," but is a platform from which questions are created and considered. Art teachers and their students learn to be open to ideas often ignored, thus providing an inherently more inclusive curriculum.

This should help help parents understand the "what" and the "why" of today's art. As for the "how," the best way to understand that is to sign up for an art class! ●

Does Pronunciation Matter?

Q: Is it fair for people to judge other people because of the way they pronounce words? Do schools really need to place so much emphasis on speech and pronunciation?

A: Although it may not be fair for people to judge others on how they speak, it happens all the time. Sociolinguistics is the study of how language functions in society. Studies have shown that pronunciation has been linked to how others may judge us.

For instance, a New York City study revealed that people hoping to move from the lower middle class to the upper middle class attached prestige to pronouncing the "r" in certain words. The pronounced "r" in the expression "fourth floor" seemed to indicate to many New Yorkers one's socioeconomic status.

George Bernard Shaw's masterpiece, *Pygmalion,* later to become the basis of the musical comedy *My Fair Lady,* has a plot based on the idea of judging a person's social standing on how one speaks.

One final thought: When faulty pronunciation gets in the way of communication, there is a definite problem. We can all think of situations, comical and otherwise, where mispronunciation can lead to miscommunication. Keep in mind that the function of language is to foster human communication and understanding. ●

Are Physical Education Programs Worth the Time, Effort, and Money?

Q: With all the money being spent to upgrade our schools, are there any real benefits to be derived from investing in physical education classes?

A: Here are a trio of reasons why, in the long run, physical education classes are a wise investment. First, from a standpoint of good health, physical activity improves muscle strength, flexibility, and cardiovascular endurance. Second, we know that regular moderate physical activity can substantially reduce the incidence of heart disease, diabetes, colon cancer, and high blood pressure. Third, the most widely available resource for promoting physical activity in the nation is school-based P.E. classes.

Physical education classes don't just happen—as recess might. A solid P.E. program includes enough time in the schedule, functional class size, adequate fields, courts, gymnasiums, safe equipment, a modern curriculum based on the knowledge of exercise physiology, and qualified teachers. These teachers must have content knowledge (kinesiology) and be skillful practitioners in the particular pedagogy needed to make this program meaningful to all students.

Physical education classes have changed over the years from an emphasis on physical training and calisthenics to health-related fitness and behavioral competencies, including the motor skills needed to select lifelong recreational options and healthy lifestyle choices. A quality P.E. program includes experiences that require students to seriously study, plan, and implement their own proper diet and exercise program.

School-based P.E. programs provide an opportunity to improve social and cooperative skills and provide a healthy environment for interaction among every student in the school. It is hard to think of a wiser long-term investment than a first-rate physical education program. ●

Why Is Physical Education Taught in Secondary School?

Q: Why is physical education taught at the high school level? Is it to help students achieve excellence in sports, or is it just an elevated form of "recess"?

A: A good high school physical education program promotes the physical, emotional, and social well-being of the student.

Rather than focus on achieving excellence in sports, it aims at encouraging all students to commit to lifelong health and physical fitness.

In order to do that, students must become physically educated and able to enjoy a variety of physical activities. A good program has a sequence of activities to formulate healthy behavior in both exercise and diet.

All students, not just the few who excel in sports, can become physically educated regardless of their skills, talents, or limitations. Any good P.E. class puts the emphasis on a broad spectrum of learning and personal development.

To be specific, here are some questions a student should be able to answer a resounding "yes" to when judging a high school P.E. program:

- Have you participated in activities you can continue outside of school (e.g., dance, aerobics, swimming, golf, softball)?

- Have you been taught to design and implement a personalized physical fitness and nutrition program?

- Do you understand the ways in which personal characteristics, performance styles, and activity preferences will change as you get older?

- Do you have a knowledge and appreciation of the lifelong recreational opportunities for people at various stages of life?

A good physical education program is of great worth because it teaches the values of health and physical well-being for life. ●

The Jump to Junior High or Middle School

Q: Should elementary school end with fifth grade? Most sixth graders don't seem truly ready emotionally to be with teenagers.

A: Many sixth graders may be over their heads in a junior high school. Although there is no conclusive evidence that sixth graders find the transition to a junior high significantly difficult, there is research supporting this belief.

In 1985, a North Chicago elementary school district, on an experimental basis, dropped junior high school and went back to a kindergarten through eighth-grade format. In the first year of the experiment, average student learning growth nearly doubled.

However, sixth graders in most districts have no alternative but to go to a junior high. One suggestion might prove helpful, and that is to participate in a "shadow" program. This involves a fifth-grade class visiting a junior high and following sixth graders through the school day.

Such a program has had successful results, according to a 1994 Georgia study. Designed to ease elementary students into the next level, fifth graders who participated in the program were found to be socially better adjusted when they reached the sixth grade than those who did not participate in the program.

In any case—and under any format— parents and teachers must continually prepare children with the behaviors necessary to interact in a successful and productive manner with peers and adults. ●

Middle School Selection Is of Crucial Importance

Q: What exactly is a middle school? How is it different from an elementary school or a high school? What should parents look for in a good middle school?

A: Changes in middle level education began in the 1920s when junior high schools became more and more accepted. At that time, junior high schools (serving grades seven through nine) were thought of as an improved way to secure a nurturing education for adolescents.

However, by the 1960s, educators complained that junior high school was being dominated by the senior high schools, and yet another reform movement began. The middle school idea became the focal point of a new approach to teaching young adolescents.

By the 1980s, a strong rationale had been built around the middle school concept. Because it was felt that the extent and variability of change in students between the fifth and eighth grade were so great, middle schools were deemed an educational necessity. Researchers pointed out that young people undergo more rapid and profound changes between the ages of 10 and 15 than at any other period of their life.

With that as a brief background, here are five things teachers can advise parents to look for when selecting a middle school:

- Are the teachers prepared to teach at this level? This is important because educators, who traditionally earn credentials at the elementary or secondary level, need to be specifically trained to successfully teach young adolescents in the 10-to-15-year-old age group.

- Does the faculty share a positive vision concerning student achievement, student-teacher rapport, and parent involvement?

- Does the student receive the richest possible curriculum? High expectations from students, teachers and parents can only be truly fulfilled by an intellectually engaging common core course of study.

- Are family partnerships an integral part of the school plan? The school should be set up to give you continual feedback (telephone, email, etc.) on how well your children are doing.

- Does the school have a positive learning environment? Both the facilities and the human relationships are important factors in establishing the context in which academic achievement and social growth can take place.

Many educators believe that it is the middle school experience that determines a child's future success in high school and college. The importance of selecting a good middle school, with a competent and caring staff, cannot be overemphasized. ●

Are High Schools Getting Tougher?

Q: Many people say that high schools are getting tougher than they used to be. Are they right, and are there any statistics to back them up?

A: There may be more than a grain of truth in what these people are telling you, but so much depends on the particular school. If the school provides all students with the same enriched curriculum and has a competent and enthusiastic faculty, they are probably right. Quality education is "harder," in the sense of more intellectually demanding, but it seems to pay off.

As for hard facts and numbers, it really does appear that more and more students are choosing the most challenging curriculum. For instance, colleges are granting college course credit to high school students at the majority of high schools. More than half of all high schools participate in a college-credit program. More than 200,000 of this year's college freshman entered with college credits they earned last year in high school.

There is also no doubt that there is a greater percentage of students now taking harder courses. Over the last decade, there has been increased enrollment in such courses as physics, world history, precalculus, and chemistry. ●

Oral History Project

Q: Many high school students find history classes very boring. They think that even U.S. history doesn't really teach about them or the world in which they live. What can be done to make history more relevant?

A: More than a few surveys put the social sciences near the bottom of most students' favorite subjects. How unfortunate! History, and U.S. history in particular, can be among the most stimulating classes any student can take.

What is needed is a process to increase a student's involvement and active participation in, and thereby her understanding of, U.S. history. The answer could be an oral history project. Such a project will move the student away from what might seem to be the unconnected dates, names, and events in a textbook. Instead, she will learn "up close and personal" about the life experiences of many Americans just like her.

In an oral history project, one interviews an older person about his or her firsthand memories of relatively recent historical events in United States history. For example, many people over 70 have vivid recollections of World War II, people over 50 of the assassination of President Kennedy, or people over 40 the Watergate scandal.

As the student designs and executes her project, she should remember that she is capturing a historical period as revealed through the memory of a person who actually lived through it. The use of audiotape or videotape in the project is a wonderful tool to record the feelings, emotions, and stories of that time and place.

If the student interviews her grandmother or grandfather, she may well be in for a special bonus—finding something out about herself. Besides increasing her understanding of a specific historical event, she might well encounter the stories, beliefs, and values that have been passed down from her grandparents to her parents. In understanding the life experiences of her grandparents by means of an oral history project, she might better understand her own parents.

As students grasp the stories, beliefs, and values that have been handed down from generation to generation, they will find out the basis of many of their own ways of looking at the world. Not a bad way for anyone to find out about themselves or the world in which they live. ●

Students Learn a Lot on Field Trips

Q: Some people say that field trips provide a fun time, but not as good an education as classroom work. However, many students find it very enjoyable to be outdoors or just to go somewhere different from the classroom. Don't students remember better and as a consequence learn more when they are enjoying the learning experience?

A: There has actually been research done on the effectiveness of field trips, and the results indicate that students do learn more on these outings. In a number of studies, students reported increased interest and enjoyment when participating in a field study, as compared to the more traditional laboratory approach. Whether it is the novelty of the trip or not, students do seem happier and more motivated learning outside the classroom.

Recent research also reveals that students who go on excursions actually learn and retain knowledge better than students who don't. Information appears to be better understood out in the field than inside the confines of a classroom. With this

"one-two punch" of increased motivation and learning, one would think field trips would be a regularly scheduled part of the learning experience.

That is not the case. Surveys of classroom teachers indicate that very few excursions are taken off the school grounds. There are many reasons given for the lack of field trips: travel expenses, insurance, "red tape," and excessive class size are commonly cited.

One factor that can help to overcome these obstacles is a committed teacher. An instructor who uses pretrip instructional materials and focuses on specific course-related activities can establish field trips as a vital part of a school's educational program.

There are those who view the educational value of field trips as self-evident. To others, it may be reassuring to know that research indicates the time, effort, and expense of well-planned field trips can be worth every penny. ●

Television Has a Place in the Classroom

Q: Are there any benefits to be derived from broadcasting television shows into the classroom?

A: Television is a technology that can actually improve one's reading and writing. In order to make this dynamic medium work in the classroom, school districts must develop strategies that make educational sense.

For example, an outstanding Spanish language teacher in Utah interacted with nearly 4,000 students at nine different schools through the use of studio and classroom cameras and televisions. This interactive instruction contained a brainteaser contest in which students could phone in their answers.

In another application of TV in the classroom, a first-year composition course was broadcast over local cable television. The results demonstrated that students improved their writing skills as much as students in traditional classrooms without TV.

What is the benefit? A traditional writing class is bursting at the seams with 35 students. Hundreds, thousands, even millions could take the TV class taught by the same instructor. How's that for cost-effective education?

Finally, let's not forget the breaking-news component of TV. Whether it is the Berlin Wall coming down, the end of apartheid in South Africa, or a landing on Mars, valuable

news summaries are a daily occurrence on the tube. Such broadcasts can lead to meaningful and relevant classroom discussions. The judicious, strategically programmed use of TV means that significant up-to-the-moment events in history or natural science are subjects of immediate knowledge and understanding in today's classroom. ●

Parents Are Right to Limit TV

Q: Should parents set a limit on the amount of time children watch TV? With so many different kinds of things on TV—we get over 100 channels—why should there be any restrictions?

A: It is certainly fair of parents to limit TV time and ask children to plan what programs they want to watch. Let's face it, TV viewing is a habit. Sometimes it is a mindless tendency.

TV viewing can be a good thing when the whole family watches a quality program and discusses it afterward. It is also important, once TV time is limited, to use the extra time productively. For example, increasing the time to read and to participate in athletics, hobbies, and family conversation are all productive alternatives to becoming a TV couch potato.

One last tip: Less TV time may mean more time for homework, and that is not a bad thing. Research indicates that the greater amount of time a student spends on homework, the better the student's grades are in school. Less TV time should equal greater opportunities for study and active diversion. Parents who set effective limits are on the right track. ●

TV or Not TV, That Is the Question

Q: Everyone has an opinion on the effect of TV on the education of our children. What do we really know about TV? Is it good or bad? Should youngsters watch more or less? What's a parent to do?

A: The fact is, 98 percent of all households have at least one TV set. That is a greater percentage of households than have indoor plumbing. In 2004, the average daily TV viewing per family was more than eight hours a day. Given the immense amount of time involved in viewing TV, there is every reason for your concerns.

Research indicates that TV can affect social and emotional behavior. Continuous viewing of violent programs can have a wide range of effects on children, from their exhibiting fear to demonstrating aggressive behavior.

Other studies indicate TV can affect creativity and language skills. Obviously, the more time spent passively watching TV, the less time spent playing, reading, studying, and sharing with parents through meaningful and value-laden discussions.

The problem with TV viewing is that we aren't fully activating all our senses (only sight and hearing), and new and novel multisensory occurrences simply don't happen. The brain is running on autopilot and we find ourselves bored—hence we channel-surf.

Parents have a role to play regarding TV viewing. It's up to parents to determine what is to be seen and when it can be viewed. In order to do this, parents should be aware of the specific programs their children watch and the ideas and values each program presents.

Moreover, parents should allow TV viewing when it does not conflict with other family activities. Recording programs can ease potential conflicts. When possible, watch programs together as a family. This can lead to the kind of language skills best fostered by active family dialogues.

The "good" and "bad" in TV depends on when and how it is used. Did you know that Japanese students watch more TV than American students? There is, however, one critical difference. Japanese parents insist that homework be finished before the TV is turned on. ●

Is PBS a National Treasure?

Q: How much time do school-age youngsters spend watching TV, and how much time do their parents spend in front of the tube? Are there any good effects from watching TV, and if so, what shows are producing those good effects?

A: Young people aged 2 to 17 watch an average of 22 hours of TV each week. They actually watch less TV than those over 18 years of age. For the over-18 crowd, men watch about 29 hours per week. Women view close to 33 hours each week.

As for positive effects of TV, a University of Kansas study had an interesting finding. The research indicated that preschoolers who watched children's educational programming spent more time reading and scored higher than average on verbal and math tests. On the other hand, those who primarily watched non-educational children's shows and adult programming scored lower on those tests than expected.

For more than a generation, the Public Broadcasting System has consistently provided quality children's TV. This wonderful resource costs a family of four about $6.80 in tax money each year. Compared to defense spending, which costs that same family of four about $5,933 a year, PBS appears to be a small part of the national budget that has proved itself to be a national treasure. ●

Economics Is a Vital Element of Citizenship Education

 Many members of the business community are concerned about how economics is taught in the schools. If our kids don't understand our free enterprise system, how are they supposed to run it when it is their turn? Do schools consider the study of economics to be very important?

A: There is no doubt that an understanding of economics is a vital element of one's citizenship education. Some may believe that the great debate over economic philosophy is passé due to the collapse of the Soviet Union. Capitalism has appeared to be the victor over communism—game, set, match.

However, many perennial economic arguments remain that have nothing do with communism. For instance, at issue is a democracy's degree of participatory decision making that extends to every societal activity from cradle to grave. The availability or absence of adequate housing, medical care, or even schooling in a democratic society is, after all, a real dollar-and-cents economic issue.

When schools create content standards for this area of study, they must decide on both the knowledge of economics (e.g., supply and demand, upturns and downturns in the Asian economies, the European Union, international labor issues, etc.), as well as the application of economic skills that students should possess.

As with all quality educational programs, it is not enough to only know about the world's economic systems. Students must be able to demonstrate their knowledge of the world in which they live. Student papers, projects, and oral presentations about running a paper route, managing a student store, or marketing a yearbook can demonstrate the practical meshing of economic theory and practice.

Finally, stressing the importance of a coherent understanding of economics for individual and business decisions is a crucial part of civic education. A quality education must include economics as a fundamental component of citizenship education. ●

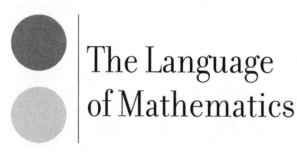

The Language of Mathematics

Q: Why is it that students today do so poorly on "word problems" in mathematics?

A: In short, many students do not understand what we call the language of mathematics. Studies have shown that language minority students (and native speakers of English with inadequate proficiency) have a difficult time at a basic level understanding the math problems they are trying to solve. One institutional deficiency is the traditional lack of articulation between a school's language arts program and its math program. When a math class has few language-based materials and activities, it simply means students have fewer opportunities to hone their skills in the language of mathematics.

Although language minority students are relatively quick to build their basic interpersonal language skills (playground talk, classmate conversational speech), they face a different kind of English in a math class. Within the classroom they confront a cognitive academic language that, in the case of mathematics, presents a terminology and writing style particular to this area of study. Inexperience with the language of mathematics means that these students (and any other student who lacks cognitive academic language proficiency) will be frustrated in developing the higher-order critical thinking skills and performing cognitive tasks required.

Is there a solution to this seemingly intractable problem? The answer is yes, if schools would incorporate instruction that emphasizes language activities across the curriculum—and particularly an interdisciplinary link between language arts and mathematics.

Three basic components are required to implement this solution. First, teachers must be trained to write across the curricula so that they constantly aim toward language objectives that increase communication skills in their classes. Key to this training are workshops and seminars under the guidance of a university that can offer theoretical experts (its professors), a warehouse of courses, and a continuity of instruction.

The joint participation of math and language arts teachers in such a staff development plan is imperative so that the experience and expertise of both disciplines can be melded into cooperative opportunities. An action research model is desirable. In other words, theoretical notions should be integrated with opportunities to apply new interdisciplinary curricula and evaluate instructional strategies in the classroom. Some of the techniques to teach math in the diverse classroom include hands-on problem solving, discovery learning, cooperative group work, and peer tutoring.

Second, new interdisciplinary language-learning-based curricula and materials must be created and made available to staff and eventually to the students. Les-

son plans and activities must be one of the by-products of staff development. It is important for material adaptation to focus on content and language activities in lesson plans across the curricula and be designed with communication activities. The goal is for students to become more and more proficient over time in the language of math through interactive listening, speaking, reading, and writing activities.

Third, assessment needs to be improved. Instruments for measuring content area (math) language proficiency will allow teachers to assess growth in language skills during daily instruction. Accordingly, teachers making those assessments must be ready to use distinct methodological approaches, including reteaching the same material to students who need to raise their proficiency. Thus, the role of the teacher is never to lower standards, but to bring all students up to standard.

Clearly, the cooperation between language arts and math teachers is critical to implement strategies that enhance students' understanding of the language of math. Insights into language and cultural differences can lead to activities that bridge a linguistic and cultural gap which, once crossed, lead to greater language proficiency and mathematical concept mastery. ●

What Is a Portfolio?

Some schools are telling seventh-grade students that they will be making portfolios, and that these portfolios will be with the students through seventh and eighth grades and all the way through high school. What exactly is a portfolio, and what are the benefits of making one?

A: Making a portfolio is a lot of work, but it is interesting work that celebrates a student's best efforts and demonstrates his or her continuing development as a learner. Portfolios are more than just writing assignments. They can include photographs (of projects or original art), audiotapes, videotapes, and computer disks. Portfolios can also include notes from teachers and parents on how well the student is doing, along with self-evaluations. A portfolio is just another way of demonstrating what the student knows, and it should be an accurate reflection of what the student is learning.

There are three different types of portfolios, each serving a different purpose:

- Showcase portfolios: a celebration of the student's best work
- Descriptive portfolios: a nongraded demonstration of work
- Evaluative portfolios: a graded demonstration of work

The most important point is that portfolios should be full of typical assignments so that from year to year, students can see what progress they have made. When students notice the improved quality of their work over time, they will really appreciate their portfolios.

The Evolution of Literacy

Q: With all the rapid changes in technology, what does a student need to know in order to keep up? In other words, what traditional learning experiences have to change in order for a student to succeed in the 21st century?

A: The very core of your question deals with literacy. Due to computer access to the Internet, what is needed is an expanded definition of literacy. In the 21st century, a literate person must not only be able to read and write, but understand what information is needed to solve a problem and have the ability to find, judge, and use that information.

Thus, it becomes a major mission of the school to be sure that all students and faculty have the ability to use new technologies to find, judge, and apply the material they need in an ever-expanding universe of ideas and information. Since literacy is a process, information literacy skills must be at the heart of the school's curriculum.

The uses of information literacy skills are decidedly decentralized—much different from the traditional 20th-century centralized lecture model. Typically, 21st-century students, through the use of information technology, will be learning different things from different sources at different times. Significantly, these new literacy skills will enable students to build their own knowledge and construct their own ways of comprehending the universe around them.

How will students be able to demonstrate this new knowledge? Instead of 20th-century staples (e.g., true/false or multiple choice tests), 21st-century "tests" will consist of portfolios, learning logs, and other multimedia productions, which highlight the student's higher-order critical thinking skills of analysis, synthesis, and evaluation.

The great enabler in all of this is information literacy. With it, a student can increase manyfold his or her critical thinking powers. Curricular activities, whether in mathematics, music, literature, or science, all stem from comprehending the messages and knowing how to access, evaluate, and use more information.

Given the plethora of information available through an ever-growing knowledge base, there can be little doubt that the student of the 21st century will, though the use of information literacy, encounter more and more information to evaluate and apply. The richer the knowledge base, the greater the learning potential. ●

SUGGESTED READINGS

Alber, S. R., & Foil, C. R. (2003). Drama activities that promote and extend your students' vocabulary proficiency. *Intervention in School & Clinic, 39*(1), 22–29.

Brown, S. W., & Hansen, T. M. (2000). Connecting middle school, oceanography, and the real world. *Science Scope, 24*(3), 16–19.

Cox, T. (Ed.). (2000). *Combating educational disadvantage: Meeting the needs of vulnerable children.* New York: Falmer Press.

Crumpler, T., & Schneider, J. J. (2002). Writing with their whole being: A cross study analysis of children's writing from five classrooms using process drama. *Research in Drama Education, 7*(1), 61–79.

Fisher, N. (2002). Teaching accuracy and reliability for student projects. *Physics Education, 37*(5), 371–375.

Fry, R. (2003). *Hispanic youth dropping out of U.S. schools: Measuring the challenge.* Washington, DC: Pew Hispanic Center.

Furman, L. (2000). In support of drama in early childhood education, again. *Early Childhood Education Journal, 27*(3), 173–178. (EJ 610 229)

Long, K., & Kamii, C. (2001, March). The measurement of time: Children's construction of transitivity, unit iteration, and conservation of speed. *School Science and Mathematics, 101*(3), 125–131.

Midgley, C. (Ed.). (2002). *Goals, goal structures, and patterns of adaptive learning.* Mahwah, NJ: Lawrence Erlbaum.

Minke, K. M., & Bear, G. G. (2000). *Preventing school problems, promoting school success: Strategies and programs that work.* Bethesda, MD: National Association of School Psychologists.

Naparstek, N. (2002). *Successful educators: A practical guide for understanding children's learning problems and mental health issues.* Westport, CT: Bergin & Garvey.

Newman, M. (2002). *The designs of academic literacy: A multiliteracies examination of academic achievement.* Westport, CT: Bergin & Garvey.

Ogbu, J. U. (2003). *Black American students in an affluent suburb: A study of academic disengagement.* New Jersey: Lawrence Erlbaum. (ED 476 118)

Pope, D. C. (2001). *"Doing school": How we are creating a generation of stressed out, materialistic, and miseducated students.* New Haven, CT: Yale University Press.

Reeves, D. B. (2002). *Holistic accountability: Serving students, schools, and community.* Thousand Oaks, CA: Corwin Press.

Schmnidt, W. H., McKnight, C. C., Houang, R. R., Wang, H., Wiley, D. E., Cogan, L. S., & Wolfe, R. G. (2001). *Why schools matter: A cross-national comparison of curriculum and learning.* San Francisco: Jossey-Bass.

Stan, S. (2002). *The world through children's books.* Lanham, MD: Scarecrow Press.

Tomlinson, C. M. (2002). An overview of international children's literature. In S. Stan (Ed.), *The world through children's books.* Lanham, MD: Scarecrow Press.

Whitley, M. D. (2001). *Bright minds, poor grades.* New York: Perigee.

Zimmerman, B. J., & Schunk, D. H. (Eds.). (2001). *Self-regulated learning and academic achievement: Theoretical perspectives.* Mahwah, NJ: Lawrence Erlbaum.

unit :7

Methodology:
How to Teach

Collaboration Is a Formula for Better Education

Q: What is the best way for parents and teachers to help a student learn?

A: Each new school year, a fresh cycle of studies begins. Students return from the summer months to sit with a new class, a different teacher, and perhaps an unfamiliar school. If they are making that difficult transition from elementary school to middle school, or from middle school to high school, those first days can be harrowing.

What is crucial for students to know is that they are part of a learning team. It is a team that boasts a pretty powerful lineup.

Leading off are the student's parents. In many ways, Mom and Dad are the most important teachers a child will ever have.

Next up are the child's classroom teachers. Although only 9 percent of a student's time between kindergarten and high school is actually spent in the classroom, much is—and should be—expected from these professional educators.

Finally, batting third, is the student. Although the responsibility to learn is clearly on their shoulders, students are dependent, to a great extent, on the guidance, teaching skill, and nurturing of the first two groups of team members.

In analyzing some of the ways each member of the team can coordinate with the other members, we can uncover a winning combination in that annual September-to-June drive for academic success.

PARENTS

The role of parents in education is crucial to the success of their children. The research is clear on this question. Parental involvement makes a positive difference in student achievement and self-esteem. In addition, parental involvement in a child's schooling improves the parent–child relationship at home.

Here are four ways for a parent to get involved:

- **Exercising your choices:** Parents have choices in recommending coursework, selecting programs, and even choosing schools for their children. Become informed on the alternatives and take an active role in these critical decisions.

- **Visiting the campus:** A parent's periodic physical presence on campus is important because it indicates to the students and the teachers that this mom or dad cares enough to make an on-site inspection of the learning process.

- **Opening lines of communication:** Far more important than reading the school's newsletter is direct communication with your child's teachers. Use the phone. Although underutilized, the phone provides an up-to-the-minute "report card" of your child's daily challenges and successes.

- **Reading aloud to your children:** Research has shown that reading aloud increases both a child's ability to read and interest in reading. Also encourage your child to read to you.

Remember, be proactive. Don't wait for the school to make the initial contact. Make the effort to get involved. The time and energy spent will add up to the child earning better grades, having an improved attitude toward school, and demonstrating acceptable behavior in class. Getting involved is worth the time and energy, because the positive results can be experienced and enjoyed with your own children.

TEACHERS

A superior teacher approaches his or her task as a good coach would. A good coach knows that it is not enough if just some members of the team are successful; everyone needs to work hard for the team to be a winner. A teacher must have a definite approach to working with students and be able to articulate that method to students and parents alike.

Basic to any specific teaching approach are four fundamental factors:

- **Enriched curriculum:** A rich curriculum must be administered to all students. The lecture and readings given to students must be challenging and of the highest quality. A good teacher always teaches to the highest level of the class and has the highest expectations for all students. At the same time the teacher must be dedicated to the proposition that all students can learn. Standards are not lowered—instead, students are pulled up to meet the standards.

- **Peer review:** A peer-review component must be established. Students should be put in a position to give positive input to fellow students. This student-to-student help creates a win–win situation. The student who is in most need of help can access it, whereas the student giving the help reinforces what he or she already knows.

- **Individualized education:** A teacher should make time to sit down and review essays and other projects with students face to face, line by line, idea by idea. Some may think of a professional educator as a math teacher, a history teacher, or a science teacher, but that adult in front of the class is really a teacher

of human beings. Individualized education provides the opportunity to establish that personal rapport, so necessary in the learning process, between student and teacher.

- **Feedback:** Continual student updates communicated to both student and parents are indispensable. A teacher who makes it a habit every two weeks or so to phone the homes of all of his or her students, makes it easier for the learning team of parent/teacher/student to function. Information about behavior and homework assignments, along with the success and challenges of everyday school experiences, should be communicated on a regular basis to the parents.

STUDENTS

With parents and teachers doing their part, there is only one team member left. The student is the most important person in the lineup.

The mighty efforts of parents and teachers will mean little unless the student meets each day with a "can do" attitude. Although this positive spirit is necessary, it is nevertheless not sufficient to guarantee success in school.

Here is a checklist that can help every student serious about learning:

- **Be prepared:** Don't get caught short-handed. Having an organized binder, an assignment calendar, pencils, pens, and a calculator may seem pretty basic, but having the necessary school supplies on hand can make a positive difference in how much and how fast one learns and achieves.

- **A "study" room:** Less than 10 percent of a student's time from age 5 to 18 is spent in the classroom. Having a clean, well-lighted, quiet place to study is essential.

- **Ask questions:** There are times in school when a student becomes "lost" or confused with an assignment or a test.

Who can help? There are three human resources immediately at hand. Ask another student, ask the teacher, or ask your parent. Don't forget, these people will find it difficult, if not impossible, to help a student who doesn't ask questions.

One goal every student should have is to "take control" of his or her education and become a self-directed learner. After all, the one ultimately responsible for growing socially and achieving academically is the student. To students go the rewards, grades, diplomas, and eventually the vocation or profession of their dreams.

In order to be a self-directed learner, a student must first master the basic skills and then develop his or her critical thinking skills. A motivated student constantly focuses on the daily thinking process, which involves many activities such as observing, judging, memorizing, and just wondering.

As this process moves from thought to action, the student will give oral reports, write essays, paint pictures, sing songs, and even make videos about his or her ideas and opinions. In all of this, the student will be expressing what she knows and how she feels about what is learned.

The self-directed learner realizes that sharing information is a wonderful way of reinforcing knowledge. Collaborating with others (parents, teachers, and other students) to review one's knowledge or learn new materials is a sign of intellectual maturity. Such a learner accepts the personal responsibility to learn the most challenging material, and has the courage to make mistakes.

Finally, the self-directed learner can complete a course of studies but, as a lifelong learner, never stops seeking knowledge.

As the new school year begins, it is important to remember that a student's success is premised on the teamwork that only dedicated parents, teachers, and—that most crucial of all team members—the student can provide. ●

Working in Groups Can Yield Positive Results

Q: What do you think of students in school doing more and more group work? There are always groups where a few people do the most work, if not all the work. Do students really know that this so-called cooperative group idea can deliver a big payoff for all students?

A: Many research studies done at the kindergarten through high school level indicate that students completing cooperative group assignments tend to score higher on academic tests. Furthermore, these students had higher self-esteem, more positive social skills, increased racial tolerance, and a better understanding of what they were studying.

Still, your example of groups where some people did most of the work is an important observation. The truth is, just because students work in so-called cooperative groups doesn't mean they are cooperating to ensure that they or other members of the group are learning.

A successful cooperative learning experience has an essential framework. To measure if the assigned work fits into the successful mold of a cooperative group, use the following checklist as a guide.

- Is there a precise description of objectives, namely, what the students are expected to learn and be able to do on their own at the end of the unit?

- Do students perceive the objectives as their own? Do they realize that everyone in the group needs to master a common core of information and skills?

- Are the instructions clear and concise? Are such instructions given before students engage in group efforts?

- Are the three-, four- or five-member groups mixed as heterogeneously as possible? Are students tolerant of diverse viewpoints and considerate of a wide range of thoughts and feelings?

- Does every student have an equal opportunity for success? Do all groups and students have equal access to the richest curriculum and materials?

- Are all students engaged in interactive activities such as trust-building, conflict-management and constructive criticism? Are they given time to reflect on how they worked together as a team?

- Do the students have sufficient time to learn the specifically targeted content and skills?

- Is each student formally and individually tested to see if he or she mastered the targeted knowledge and skills?

Unless these elements of a cooperative group learning experience are implemented, one cannot expect the research-based positive effects of this type of mutual group instruction. Time invested in teamwork, where everyone does his or her fair share, can pay big dividends. Remember, many of the positive affects of cooperative learning, demonstrated over years of research, only emerge after four weeks or more of group work. ●

Cooperative Learning Leads to Results

Q: Is there a best way for teachers to work with their classes?

A: This question has been asked by students, parents, and educators ever since formal schooling started many thousands of years ago. This doesn't mean that the question is unanswerable. As a matter of fact, today we have a large body of research to confirm what are the best ways to teach school.

One method that consistently has proved successful is cooperative learning. This is a teaching strategy that uses small student teams with learners of different levels of educational experience.

Cooperative learning employs a variety of learning activities to improve the understanding of each subject. The idea is that each team member is responsible not only to learn what is being taught, but also for assisting his teammates in the learning process. Cooperative learning methods create a scholastic atmosphere where increased student achievement and an improved relation among ethnically diverse students have long been documented.

To give you a clearer picture of how cooperative learning works, let's look at STAD (Student Teams Achievement Divisions). Instead of traditionally tracking students into high or low perceived ability groups, students with varying academic experiences are assigned to a four-

or five-member team in order to study material that the teacher has previously presented. Teams complete a unit of study and then are tested individually. Teams earn recognition based on how well all team members have progressed over past examinations.

Such a heterogeneous grouping of students develops and uses critical thinking skills and teamwork. In addition, cooperative learning groups implement peer coaching, establish a scholastic environment where achievement is valued, and promote positive relations among an ethnically diverse student body.

There are more than 70 major studies in cooperative learning that have confirmed that when the two necessary key elements of this strategy are present—group goals and group accountability—the effects on academic achievement are consistently positive. One other finding that should be of importance to educational planners is that students who cooperate with each other tend to like each other.

High achievement and improved student relations are two consistent outcomes of cooperative learning, making this teaching strategy one of the most effective. ●

The Essay Menu

Q: Many students have difficulty writing essays. They may have a lot of good ideas, but just not know where to start. Then, when they get to the end of the paper, they often feel like they have more to say. What advice can you give these students?

A: This problem is one that occurs from early elementary school classes to postgraduate studies. However, the solution can be summed up in one word—organization.

Of course, you have probably heard about the concept of organization from more than one teacher. The trouble is, most people can figure out "what to do"—it is the "how to" part that keeps a lot of students making the same kinds of organizational mistakes.

So, here is a formula for writing essays (complete with a fast-food memory hook!) that has been used by many students, elementary school through college, with great success. First, set up a memory hook by thinking of placing an order at your favorite fast-food restaurant.

Let's say you order a hamburger, a chocolate shake, and French fries. By deciding on what you would like to eat, you have just written an introduction. By naming specific items, the scope of the essay has been narrowed. Accordingly, simply state what your essay is about (burger, shake, and fries), and then decide the order in which you will write about them.

The sequence is important. Your strongest item should be last. A reader recalls best what was last read. Let's say the burger is the most important item on the menu. Next in importance is the chocolate shake (designate it the first item mentioned). Last in significance would be the French fries (make it the second item mentioned).

Now you are ready to write a coherently sequenced essay (in five parts if you count the introduction and the conclusion) where you know where you are going, where you have been, and where you need to end up. Your introduction (first paragraph) speaks of a mouth-watering trek to a fast-food haven. There you select (pay attention to the order) a chocolate shake, French fries, and a burger.

Next (second paragraph), you speak of a cold creamy chocolate shake, the kind that is too thick to sip through a straw. Mention every aspect of what it looks like, how cold it feels on your tongue, and how wonderfully sweet the chocolate is. Do not mention anything but the shake itself.

Then (third paragraph), reveal the wonders of French fries. Describe how you munch and crunch these slender fried potatoes. Describe dipping them into the catsup, adding a little more salt, and how the fries seem to disappear from your paper carton all too fast. Confine your comments to the fries.

Now (fourth paragraph), it is time to mention the main course, the hamburger. Describe the size of the meat patty, how it was grilled, the warm bun with a sesame seed top that surrounds it, the mustard, catsup, pickles, and onions—even a slice of cheese that you added at the last second. Remember, this is the most important part of the essay, so while you are explicitly describing the burger (and only the burger), bring your reader to a crescendo of detail about the magnificent sight, smell, feel, and taste of this particular American sandwich.

All that is left is the conclusion (paragraph five). Simply, without bringing in any new information, point out that you have fulfilled the mandate of the introduction, to describe your favorite meal in three distinct parts.

Some might say, "Great, the next time my teacher asks for an essay or oral report on McDonalds or Burger King—I'll be ready, but the likelihood of that happening is only slightly smaller than the nutritional value of such a meal." Not to worry.

Recall that this is only an analogy of how to write an essay in five parts. The subject matter can by any topic at all. For a science report on the solar system, simply pick three planets. For a history report, just choose three presidents. For a math report, select three formulas. Got the idea?

Speaking of formulas, that is what you now have—a way to organize your thoughts that can lead to successful essays or oral reports. Let's review:

- Part one: Mention the three items under consideration.

- Part two: Choose only one item to discuss in depth.
- Part three: Choose another item to thoroughly discuss.
- Part four: Mention the last and most significant item and give an in-depth analysis.
- Part five: Simply restate the introduction, mentioning that you have fulfilled your task (do not bring in any new information here), and make a summary concluding statement.

There you have it. A lot of disorganized essays have been transformed into coherent dissertations once students followed this formula. For converting your thoughts into essays that are sequenced and coherent, adopt "the essay menu." ●

A High School Design Flaw: Six Classes a Day, Five Days a Week

Q: If a high school was being started from scratch, how should it be scheduled? Isn't there a better way than one hour of this course and one hour of that course?

A: Unfortunately most schools are organized on the assumption that all students can learn on the same schedule. Due to this belief, the standard "six classes a day, five days a week" schedule is quite common.

Because the assumption about students learning in lockstep is incorrect, the rigid traditional six-period-a-day format is an easily observable design flaw. This archaic schedule can put a student in eight different places (under eight distinct sets of rules and expected behavioral patterns) a day. Think about it. A student gets off the bus, goes to first, second, third, and fourth periods, eats lunch, returns for fifth and sixth period, and then gets back on the bus. This kind of frantic schedule is particularly hard on students with a fragmented home life. It can be a hurried, impersonal, and disorienting experience for any student looking to build a rapport with a teacher, needing individualized instruction, or desiring to study a subject in depth.

The traditional inflexible schedule exists, at least in part, due to administrative and institutional expediency. In short, the "why, we've always done it this way," attitude is common among administrative nonpractitioners.

So, what is the answer to the problems inherent in the traditional format? One solution may be to simply allow larger blocks of time to be spent by the student and teacher to produce a more flexible and productive classroom environment.

Researchers have found that when a school adopts a block scheduling format (there are many variations—e.g., four 90-minute blocks per day; school year divided into two semesters, and former year-long courses completed in one semester) some significant pedagogical improvements occur. Under block scheduling, more course credits were completed, equal or better mastery of material was accomplished, and an improved rapport between teachers and students was observed. In addition to all this good news, there was an impressive reduction in suspensions and dropout rates.

Because a block schedule allows students more time to be coached by their instructors, a mentoring relationship between teacher and student can take hold. The increased time for teachers to build rapport with students leads to enhanced student achievement, and hence greater satisfaction with the learning process among all concerned.

One note of caution should be mentioned. In order to make this change in a school's schedule work; teachers must be trained to teach in the larger block. Specifically, they have to revise their methodological approach to include not only explanation, but also application and synthesis.

Merely offering an explanation in a class session (a typical strategy in the tra-

ditional 50-minute class) is not enough. Two additional elements are needed. First, an action plan based on the application of concrete strategies (writing the essay, conducting the experiment, rehearsing the music) is necessary. Second, a synthesis segment (combining the new information with what the student already knows) should be part of each class to confront ambiguity and/or understand nuance.

Thus, the design flaw known as the traditional schedule can be corrected through the reallocation of time during the school day. ●

Replacing the Six-Period School Day

Q: Most schools are run on a six-classes-a-day, five-days-a-week schedule. Is this schedule really best for the students?

A: There are major problems with the traditional concurrent six-period school day. Here's a short list of the downsides to traditional scheduling:

• **Fragmented:** During a typical school day, the student is in eight different locations, with many different teachers, learning different subjects. The teacher sees between 125 to 225 students a day, and must make multiple curricular preparations.

• **Impersonal:** There is inadequate time for probing ideas in depth, and certain learning activities cannot be squeezed into the 55 minutes of time allowed per class. Individualized education becomes highly improbable.

• **Ineffective:** One easily noted design flaw can be seen in the case of the chronically absent student. In practice, students can be absent for any reason for almost any length of time, and the school keeps the door open for their eventual return. Sadly, because of the immense amount of work to do in an 18-week semester, the chronically absent student (who misses 20, 30, 40 percent or more of his or her classes) reenters the school just in time to fail or, worse yet, to be socially promoted.

The six-period school day exists partly because of administrative inertia. I think many principals are caught in the "we have always done it that way" syndrome.

There is a solution that can help remedy the fragmented, impersonal, and ineffective concurrent format. It is called "block scheduling." Research in evaluating schools using block scheduling indicates more course credits completed, equal or better mastery and retention of material, and an impressive reduction in suspension and dropout rates.

There are endless variations to this kind of flexible block scheduling. Here are three of them:

- Four 90-minute blocks per day: the school year is divided into two semesters; former year-long courses are completed in one semester.

- Alternate day block schedule: six to eight courses are spread out over two days; teachers meet with half of their students each day.

- Intensive education: three-week sessions of five hours of instruction on a single subject; the sixth hour is spent in an elective field.

Now take a closer look at the third option: intensive education. If we carefully analyze the three problem areas of the fragmented, impersonal, and ineffective traditional format, the intensive education solution might seem quite reasonable:

- **From fragmented to unified:** Students, gathered into a single five-hour class, would not suffer through the constant bell ringing, class changing, and attendance-taking routine of the six-period school day. They would be able to have more allocated time for study. As for teachers, they would have time to mentor and to provide the richest curriculum to all students by being able to handle ideas in depth. Moreover, a teacher is virtually guaranteed a "homeroom," where that educator can establish the proper learning environment for the subject being taught.

- **From impersonal to personal:** The educator, who works with the same class for five hours, has time to set and reinforce the boundaries of student behavior. Imagine knowing each student's name by the end of the first class! Most significantly, the instructor, who now has time to build rapport with each student, can take on an essential responsibility for the success of each student.

- **From ineffective to effective:** The rotating door of chronic absenteeism is closed. With three-week sessions (and staggered starting times for each course), a student can miss no more than two five-day sessions in order to get credit. If a student does miss more than twice in a three-week period, the course must be repeated.

This gives multiple chances to the at-risk student, while enhancing the value of constant attendance as a requirement to earning a passing grade.

Traditional structures, like the concurrent six-period day, are hard to change. But students are changing. Families are changing. The school of tomorrow must adapt to a new set of circumstances.

If the school is to fulfill its societal role, it must be ready to make fundamental operational changes that allow more time for enhanced student–teacher relationships by providing an environment that nurtures collaboration and mutual trust among students and teachers in this changing society in which we live. Block scheduling in general, and intensive education in particular, may well be operational formats that advance these goals. ●

A Game Plan to Enhance Student Achievement

Q: I have read that "enhanced student achievement" is a major goal in the classroom. How can we inspire students to learn more in school each day?

A: Intellectual, social, and emotional processes in a given student are inextricably connected. Recent research in cognitive development clearly established a link between social ties and intellectual growth. In other words, friends play a part in our learning!

Furthermore, it is known that learning can be facilitated or mitigated by one's emotions. In fact, emotions drive learning and memory.

Understanding the link among cognitive, social, and emotional processes helps in developing a game plan that can enhance student achievement.

The courses students take day in and day out need to be different from the traditional models of teaching and learning (e.g., instructor lectures, students take notes). One way to reshape the learning environment, while realizing the power of stimulating the social and affective side of a student, is to bring the personal experiences of students to bear on a topic.

Teachers should always provide a scholastic atmosphere in which students use their critical thinking skills (analysis, synthesis, and evaluation). Students should search for meaning, expect and even appreciate ambiguity, and be proactive in their inquiries.

Too often, traditional curricula have an overemphasis on performance and "getting the right answer." This misconceived formula promotes short-term retention and sacrifices long-term understanding and the ability to use knowledge and concepts outside the classroom.

In order for students to take responsibility for their own learning and become autonomous thinkers, teachers must model the kind of enthusiasm for the curriculum that inspires students. Creating and acquiring knowledge is a collaborative process incorporating social and affective relationships among students, teachers, and parents.

Professional educators must take the leadership role in promoting student and parent involvement in learning by transforming the school into a learning community. A true learning community respects all its constituents' and delegates' responsibility with commensurate authority. Student participation can be promoted by expanding the number of student leadership roles on campus.

Finally, collaborative strategies that ensure all learners receive the most enriched curriculum, reward student activities, and provide social, emotional, and intellectual support for faculty and students, set an atmosphere in which increased student involvement leads to enhanced student achievement. ●

What Is Andragogy?

Q: What is the best way for an old dog to learn new tricks? In other words, is there a way adults can take classes and not feel the pangs of embarrassment they still remember from the days when they were kids in grammar school?

A: This is a most interesting question, because many adults avoid furthering their education because of memories of anxious moments from their younger days as students in elementary school or even high school. There is a specific theory geared toward teaching adults. That adult education model is called *andragogy.*

As a methodological approach, andragogy understands that the adult learner has had different life experiences as compared to a child—and that different teaching and learning techniques must be utilized to educate this "different" kind of student. Learning for the adult should become increasingly self-directed. The adult learner is not seen as a sponge but as a rich resource due to his or her authentic personal experience.

Life's tasks and challenges in many ways can lead to a readiness to learn. Life experiences can stimulate questions about the "why" and "how" of an adult's surrounding environment and perhaps the interest to seek out new living and/ or work options. Correspondingly, an adult's motivation comes from within. Indigenous curiosity and a striving to "problem-solve" are the ingredients for empowerment.

The learning environment for an adult should be a warm, trusting, relaxed, informal setting. The classroom atmosphere should be free from the all-too-frequent (and unenlightened) autocratic decrees of the kindergarten through high school teacher. Instead the school's climate is mutually respectful, the support collaborative. Under this kind of setting the teacher acts as a facilitator.

Accordingly, the teacher typically carries out the planning, the diagnosis of needs, and the setting of objectives, whereas assessment can be handled through negotiated learning contracts based on the adult learner's readiness. Learning activities can be based on experimental techniques such as online education rooted in inquiry projects and independent study.

Evaluation is based on evidence that is learner-collected, validated by both peers and facilitators (e.g., online threaded discussions), and applied by the facilitator to criterion-referenced norms. The outcome of the andragogical approach is to transform the adult into a self-directed lifelong learner. ●

Experiences Affect How and What We Learn

Q: Young people today seem so very different in attitudes and even what they know than previous generations. Should schools change the way they teach these children?

A: To be sure, the experiences we have in life shape our knowledge. On this information we base our opinions, our values, and even the way we learn. Clearly the life of a child in the 21st century is far different than it was for children in the 1950s and 1960s.

For example, many children today have both parents working, or come from a single-parent family where the parent spends much of his or her day at school or work. There are more than a few negative outcomes from the increased workload of both two-parent and single-parent families. As a result, many youngsters grow up as "latchkey" children. Afternoons and sometimes evenings for these youngsters go unsupervised.

Learning from watching TV goes on as it has since the 1950s; it is just that instead of watching "Mr. Wizard" or "American Bandstand," youngsters are tuned into "Next" or "Degrassi." Moreover, these children's apparently ever-shorter attention span has been conditioned to the omnipresent TV remote control. This device is used to instantly transport them from channel to channel until some kind of immediate gratification can be found.

Youngsters today also live in a fast-food world. Eating alone or on the run with a frozen dinner, piping hot from the microwave, appears to have become an accepted part of the culture.

Nevertheless, even among all of these regrettable consequences, there are yet some positives of which parents and teachers should be aware. Because parents aren't around as much as in former generations, youngsters tend to be more self-directed in solving problems.

Given all the new information tools from pagers to email, children today are the most technologically literate youngsters in the history of humankind. They have access to, as other generations couldn't have, an incredible amount of information on the Internet.

How do schools, which is to say teachers, reach such different youngsters? Every effective teacher—or parent—must at some point enter (intellectually and by experience) the world of the young learner.

It is in understanding the young student (his or her prior knowledge, expectations, and values) that the teacher can best present educational alternatives to that learner. These new learners don't like to be grouped or pigeonholed. They want options, flexibility, and a variety of ways to learn (video, DVDs, the Internet, self-paced modules, graphics, and even cartoons). For learning to occur, a student must have the opportunity to interpret new knowledge so he or she can use the critical thinking skills (analysis, synthesis, and evaluation) so necessary in a quality educational experience.

People are and have always been, to one extent or another, products of their generation's collective experience. Teachers who understand the diverse life experiences of each new generation will do what all good educators have always done—continue to adapt their teaching to the unique characteristics of the contemporary learner. ●

Critical Thinking Skills in the Classroom

Q: What do educators mean when they talk about critical thinking skills, and how are these skills taught in the classroom?

A: Critical thinking skills (e.g., analysis, synthesis, and evaluation) stress the ability to collect, judge, and ultimately use information in an effective manner. In the classroom, there are any number of ways the teacher can present a curriculum in order to stimulate critical thinking. Here are four examples:

• **Ask open-ended questions.** Instead of searching for "the right answer," encourage students to respond creatively, without fear of giving "the wrong answer." In the real world, most complex problems do not yield to a singular solution. Encourage a range of acceptable answers based on reflective thought.

• **Develop the use of analogies.** For instance, the measurement of an acre is very commonly used to describe an area. Yet many students have no real idea how large an acre is. However, if you tell students that the area of an acre is quite close to the size of a football field (120 yards by 52 yards), nearly everyone will have a concrete idea of the size of an acre.

• **Allow sufficient time for reflective thought** based on new information. One of the best methods for stimulating this kind of critical thinking is the reflective essay. When students make explicit connections with their reading or lecture notes, along with their authentic personal experiences, a powerful learning paradigm can result. Adequate time to ponder and conduct research avoids the all too common snap judgments or the simple parroting of the opinions of others. A well-written reflective essay affords the opportunity to confront our ambiguities about what we have learned, and express new ideas and beliefs.

• **Transfer critical thinking skills.** There is no curriculum in which critical thinking skills cannot be used. It is up to the instructor to provide students the opportunities to realize how their developing critical thinking skills can be applied both inside and outside the classroom.

Learning should be an adventure where higher-order critical thinking is taught and valued. Open-ended questions, analogy, reflective thought, and transfer of those critical thinking skills are all excellent ways to enhance the learning process in the classroom. ●

Children Learn Best from Self-Initiated Activities

Q: Why is it that some youngsters learn so much more from certain teachers, especially in elementary school classes, than others? Every teacher seems to give different kinds of assignments. Are some assignments better for learning than others?

A: As every competent and caring teacher knows, schoolwork assigned in class must illuminate the mind in not only what one learns but how one learns. Children advance at an accelerated rate when they are assigned work that helps them master a unit of study and teaches how to learn new material. Teachers should present assignments that allow a child to develop into a self-directed learner.

We know every teacher is assigned a certain course load—math, reading, science, and so on—but a competent and caring teacher delivers much more than the written or stated (explicit) curriculum. An implicit curriculum based on a child's opportunity to problem-solve is at the very core of every professional educator's daily classroom approach. When a curriculum is based on problem solving, students become active, not passive. In short, the learner has a chance to use his or her higher-order critical thinking skills of analysis, synthesis, and evaluation.

With the right kind of open-ended assignments, students are encouraged to become self-starters rather than mere "sponges" waiting to be told what and how to learn something. This leads to one important factor that should be present in every class: child-initiated activities.

Classrooms characterized by child-initiated tasks can enhance a child's creative development. Research indicates that young children in child-initiated classrooms have better verbal skills and appear more confident about their own cognitive skills. One area often neglected in assessing quality education is the classroom environment that encourages student-initiated assignments guided by the teacher. Children who are given opportunities by the teacher to self-initiate learning create a positive classroom climate.

Again, the research is clear, children's emotions and their participation are inextricably linked. Simply put, kids learn more from activities they create and enjoy. When a child is taught to be a self-directed learner, he or she not only seeks "the right answer," but a special insight.

In evaluating a teacher, parents (and schools) should look for evidence of child-initiated activities when they visit the classroom, and observe the way the teacher assigns classwork and homework as well as the kind of work the children are doing. Remember, it is this "hidden" curriculum (child-initiated activities) which encourages children to learn on their own, producing a powerful lifelong learning skill. ●

Students Balk at Assignments

Q: What do you do with a student who just won't study? He won't even start his homework, let alone finish it, and when he has different assignments, he can't decide which one to start first. He has said many times that no matter what he tries, it always ends in failure. What can be done to help this student?

A: When a student has an assignment, there is a choice to be made. The learner can face the work with a secure thought or an insecure thought.

Once a habit of insecure interpretation begins ("I just know I'll screw it up"), a succession of wrong opinions, false conclusions, and inept decisions will surely follow. This fear of making a mistake blocks the kind of enthusiasm, energy, and commitment it takes to succeed academically.

There is an answer to this problem. If the mind has accepted insecure thoughts, the same mind can reject them. The imagination must now make a conscious effort to focus on the "can do" aspects of learning. With a secure thought, the student can now dream, anticipate, plan, and act.

Habits are hard to break. Nearly everyone, however, has the power—with practice and over time—to change thoughts from insecure notions to secure ideas. It is a change parents must encourage by requesting prompt attention to homework, monitoring by checking the assigned work, and rewarding by praising sincere effort. ●

Getting Homework Done on Time

Q: Many students have a major problem getting homework done on time, and sometimes don't turn it in at all. What can these youngsters to do get their work completed in a timely fashion?

A: When we put important things off, sooner or later we can expect to get "messed up" results. These kids are part of a very large club, to which every member of the human race belongs at one time or another.

Here are five ways students can effectively tackle homework assignments:

- Keep an up-to-the-moment checklist of all assignments with due dates. Don't be afraid to ask your teachers for clarification.

- Use your checklist to divide your work into smaller tasks. Think in terms of little chunks when organizing what you will do first.

- Enlist the help of your parents to provide you with a well-lighted, quiet study area, and to monitor your progress. Research shows this really helps.

- Establish a routine time for homework, one you can live with. For instance, pick out a block of time (an hour or so a day) in the late afternoon or early evening that is dedicated to schoolwork.

- Accept initial discomfort. Remember, you are starting a new habit. The idea is simple (organize and get to it), but in the beginning it's not easy.

With the help of parents and teachers, students can make those deadlines. More and more, they will be able to trust their own routines and become more self-reliant. ●

Mixed-Age Activities

Q: Some school districts are starting to use a "cluster" approach to education. For example, two preschools, two elementary schools, one middle school, and a senior high school would all work together as a unit or, as they call it, a cluster. Has this approach been shown to be of any benefit to the students?

A: Here's an example of educational cooperation that uses a cluster to really build a link between preschool and middle school. Students at one middle school have written children's stories and then told those stories to local preschoolers. Here are some steps that made the program work:

- First, middle schoolers participated in activities to develop a sense of what was of interest to the preschool audience.

- Next, the middle school students wrote their stories and met in small groups to discuss their ideas.

- Finally, the middle schoolers visited the preschoolers and related their written stories to them.

The results were quite positive. Surveys of the preschool children after these visits indicated that they read more books, maintained a desire to read, and told more of their own stories. When an adolescent in a school cluster presents an interesting written story to a preschooler, both students can be expected to have an improved awareness of and a better appreciation for the written language. ●

How to Get Students to Turn In Their Homework

Q: In some high schools, particularly those in "tough" neighborhoods, most of the time only a small minority of the youngsters even turn in homework. How can teachers help?

A: Let us assume that the teacher is presenting a rich curriculum and challenging everyone to get involved in learning, but still is not getting results. The best thing to do is to turn to the people who can help the most.

Open the lines of communication on a continuing basis with parents. They are in a unique position to help the classroom teacher. One of the best ways to do that is to use the telephone and call every parent at least once every two weeks. Phoning parents and giving them updates on students' work due and work completed will make a dramatic change in the class.

First, when parents know what assignment is due, they can steer their child in the direction of completing the homework. Second, students tend to be on their best behavior when their parents are receiving continuous updates. If a teacher tries phoning each parent twice in one month, by the following month he might see a significant rise in the number of students turning in assignments. ●

The Self-Directed Student

Q: What is one of the most important goals for high school students?

A: One goal every student should have is to become a self-directed learner. In order to be a self-directed learner, a student must first master the basic skills and then develop his or her critical thinking skills.

A self-directed learner is one who consistently focuses on the daily thinking process. This thinking process involves many activities, including observing, judging, memorizing, or just wondering. As this process moves from thought to action, the student will find himself giving oral reports, writing essays, painting pictures, singing songs, or perhaps even making videos about his ideas and opinions.

In all of this, the student will be expressing what he knows and how he feels about what he has learned. The self-directed learner realizes that sharing information with others is a wonderful way of reinforcing knowledge.

Collaborating with others to review knowledge or learn new material is a sign of intellectual maturity. The self-directed learner accepts the personal responsibility to learn the most challenging material and to have the courage to make mistakes.

Finally, the self-directed student may graduate from school, but he never stops the quest for knowledge. ●

Teachers Should Distribute Lecture Notes

Q: Many students have trouble listening to a lecture and taking down notes. There are just too many important ideas to write down in too short a time. Why don't teachers give a copy of their lecture notes to students?

A: It would be quite helpful for instructors to reproduce a class set of notes to their lectures. Some may object, saying that this might keep students from learning how to take notes, but there are ways to solve that problem without keeping the teacher's notes a "state secret" from the students.

One format that allows the distribution of lecture notes and gives students an opportunity to enhance their note-taking ability is the skeletal guide. This three-part model divides a lecture accordingly: the main ideas, the relationships between ideas (e.g., general to specific), and spaces left for students to fill in relevant information.

Students then can use part three of this model to further develop their note-taking skills while fleshing out ideas by writing down definitions, logical extensions and analogies as they actively follow the lecture. There is research that demonstrates that students with skeletal notes are more attentive during lecture and have higher scores on items related to information presented in lecture.

Being able to encode the important ideas of a lecture for subsequent review is essential for accurate recall. The skeletal guide seems to be an effective tool for students to gather more information while improving the quality of their own notes. ●

Real World Thinking and Problem Solving

Q: Education sometimes seems concerned only with teaching facts to students. People say that the more a student knows, the more he can use what he knows. Is

that why teachers hand out long lists of vocabulary in English classes or pages of famous dates in history classes?

A: Teachers should be doing more than simply handing out lists of words or dates to stimulate their students. Trying to learn definitions or facts out of context is like trying to memorize the phone book. This kind of education seems to put little importance on the role of the learning activity.

Learning is a process of building knowledge in a real world environment, not just acquiring it. Simply put, learning (a list of vocabulary words, historical dates, or any other learning task) should take place in context.

When a student solves problems and constructs ideas and opinions, he or she can use the lists of words or dates as necessary links to better comprehend what he or she is learning. It is necessary for a student to be constantly practicing higher-order critical thinking skills (analysis, synthesis, and evaluation). These, of course, are the same set of skills he or she uses to solve problems in the classroom and in real life.

The problem-solving method of learning rejects the structured, linear, out-of-context approach. Those supporting the notion of teaching through problem solving argue that studying just a list of words is unacceptable. They reason a learner who studied such a list would know about the words on the list but not necessarily how to use them. It would be like a mechanic who knows every part of an automobile but can't repair a car.

On the other hand, if the vocabulary words were learned in context (e.g., a story reflecting the complexity of the real world where certain vocabulary words were critical to understanding the author's message), a form of the problem-solving method would be taking place. For instance, if the phrase, "Racism is insidious," was a part of a reading selection, obviously the meaning of "insidious" would be critical to understanding the text.

Significantly, "what" we learn, both in quality and quantity, is shaped by "how" we learn. Therefore, it would not be enough to instruct the students that the word *insidious* means a seemingly harmless event that can be extremely harmful. Nor would it be sufficient to pose a true/false or multiple choice question about the meaning of the word.

Instead of asking the "right-wrong" questions so common in many classrooms, teachers might say, "What do you mean, 'racism is insidious'?" or "What proof do you have that racism is insidious?" The idea is to challenge the students to use the same kind of critical thinking we want them to use outside the school—in real life.

When learning becomes a process of inquiry, those lists of vocabulary words or historical dates may well become important in the context of intelligent discussion. In sharing information, positing ideas, and making explicit connections to what the students have read, the learner has an opportunity to practice all the language skills (listening, speaking, reading, writing) as well as their higher-order critical thinking skills.

Language and critical thinking skills are transferable to environments outside the school. As much as students and their parents may want success inside the walls of the classroom, the true payoff is knowing not only "what" to learn, but "how" to learn in the real world. ●

Collaborative Skills: Teamwork That Lasts a Lifetime

Q: Besides the "3 Rs," what other kinds of things should youngsters be learning in school? Can you really teach a child something in elementary school that they can use later as an adult?

A: One of the most important obligations of a school is not just to present information to a student but also to communicate ways in which a learner can team with others to solve real world problems. Teamwork is a skill that can be learned at a very young age and should be practiced for a lifetime.

Fundamentally, teamwork uses a collaborative model in which a fully participating team member goes through six transformative actions. A team member should be ready to:

1. **Commence:** A decision is made on what to study and what questions need to be answered.

2. **Investigate:** Learners organize and analyze the material, defining and clarifying key concepts.

3. **Blend:** Students combine new knowledge from their investigation with previous knowledge as they communicate with one another.

4. **Alter:** New ideas confronting old ideas will eventually produce innovative thought and enhance knowledge. The search for the truth is dynamic, not static.

5. **Expound:** Learners present their authentic findings to an audience that interacts with the ideas.

6. **Revise:** Facts and opinions are interchanged. Members of the group not only amend and reshape their new knowledge, they also reflect on how the cooperative sharing process can be improved.

The collaborative model can produce the kind of environment where "right answers" are not hoarded before a quiz or exam in order for a student to score highest on a bell curve. Instead, information is freely shared, and many solutions sets are considered, as the entire class gains new insights. Thus, the critical interchange of ideas occurs as students (and teachers) all gain new knowledge and a better understanding of how the collaborative approach works.

The teamwork ethic provides a durable working model that can be implemented in a wide variety of environments. In short, the collaborative model is an effective learning paradigm, highly recommended for the classroom as well as the workplace. ●

How to Teach Conventional Math Classes in a Short Period of Time

Q: How can a math teacher speed up the learning process in class for older students, especially students who are learning English? So many concepts—so little time.

A: One strategy is to bunch similar learning objectives, regardless of the grade level at which they are taught. With the older student, a teacher has an advantage that these particular learners do not require as much time to master objectives usually taught in the lower grades. Briefly, the trick is to integrate a variety of math strands into one lesson.

For example, in calculating the area of a soccer field, students can demonstrate:

- Measurement of the lengths of objects in customary units
- Multiplication of whole numbers
- Multiplication of whole numbers by decimal units

During these kinds of mathematical tasks, teachers can assess a learner's mastery of previously presented material, while continually presenting new concepts. Of course, at any given point in the process, the teacher must be ready to reteach previously presented content that has not been completely mastered.

As in most instructional designs, the teacher is the primary model of both the expected work and appropriate class behavior. Revision of work not up to standard can become a learning opportunity for the teacher as well as the student.

At this critical point in a student's learning, the teacher must realize the student's need to better understand a concept. Correspondingly, the teacher needs to have an array of different methodological approaches to the curriculum to fit the student's particular learning style.

Although mathematical concepts can relate to the daily life of a student, it is also helpful to relate mathematics to other curricular areas. Here are some interdisciplinary examples:

- Language arts students can solve a math problem and then write a convincing defense of the solution they reached. Students could also apply math concepts within a narrative to demonstrate how well they understand the concepts.

- Social studies students can study the most recent U.S. Census to practice decimals, rounding, and graphing some of the most pertinent demographic data about immigration and ethnic composition.

- Fine arts students can study the impact of math on music, patterns, and shapes, and the conversion of mathematical concepts into aesthetic forms.

- Science students can gather, use, and interpret data with special emphasis on mathematical skills that permit them to understand patterns, classification, and logical reasoning. The focus is "hands-on math" to understand science.

In all of this, it is important to take into account the age, English proficiency, and developmental level of each student. What must not be done is to "water down" or "dumb down" the curriculum. The essential math objectives in the core curriculum must remain the same for all students.

Thus, what is being recommended is that the math objectives be condensed and grouped so as to modify their scope and sequence for the older student. In addition, an older student, in particular, can benefit from math problems that reflect a previous cultural experience. Of course, the target language (English) continues to remain in focus. Math tasks that involve concrete previous experiences build a bridge between math skills and English language learning skills.

Thus, in order to assist the older students in math who are still developing their English language skills, lesson plans should incorporate the following features:

1. The teacher must model both the expected work and class behavior.
2. The curricula should contain streamlined objectives using previously learned math concepts and English vocabulary.
3. Lessons should adopt a wide variety of teaching approaches utilizing students' experiences to reach each learner and provide every class member with the richest possible math curriculum.

By clustering math objectives across grade boundaries, teachers can accelerate the academic growth of older students who are learning English as a second language. ●

Teaching Mathematics to Children

Q: Many youngsters end up so frustrated with math at an early age that they never take the more challenging courses in high school or college. What is the best way to teach math to kids?

A: First, let's make one thing very clear—everyone, to some extent, struggles or becomes frustrated with mathematics. Sometimes when we struggle with something, we tend to devalue it. The idea that, "This is difficult and it is more bother than it is worth," is a most unproductive thought when it comes to math.

Mathematics is an essential tool to understanding the world in which we live. Once we accept the "struggle" as a part of learning math, we can begin to make progress in our studies.

As a parent or teacher approaching the teaching of mathematics, there are certain student objectives to keep in mind. The student must:

- Know what math principles are being presented
- Be shown how to solve distinct math problems
- Understand the value of learning math
- Grow in confidence in his or her math abilities
- Learn to reason and communicate mathematically
- Understand that math grades are not given, but earned

In all of this, parents have a major role. It is no secret that the amount of parent involvement affects to a great degree the level of student success in school. Obviously, partnerships between the parents and the school can go a long way in promoting the social, emotional, and academic development of children. When parents exhibit attitudes and values that are supportive of learning, they are setting their children on a pathway to success.

Specific to mathematics, parents need to be patient when their children come up with "wrong" answers. After all, wrong answers can be helpful. An incorrect response means further understanding and work is necessary.

One way to attack a wrong answer is to see if the assigned question was misunderstood. Another way to handle a wrong answer is to ask the child to explain how he or she solved the problem. His or her response might well clarify if the wrong formula was used or a concept was not understood.

Don't forget, problems can be solved in different ways. Though a problem may have only one "right" answer, there are often many ways to reach a solution!

Encourage your children to do math "in their heads" at times. The exclusive use of calculators and computers can lead students to accept unreasonable answers.

It is also important that parents keep themselves in the information loop by sending notes or telephoning the teacher to stay updated on all new concepts and assignments given in class. Think of math as a "family affair." A parent's interest in a child's work is an inherently profound value statement, informing the child that math is important to the demands of daily life. ●

Four Requisites to Academic Accomplishment

Q: Why is it that some youngsters, depending on what teacher they have, either work hard and complete their class work, or simply do next to nothing and fail a class? These are the same students, so why do they act so differently? An example is a good English student who becomes a bad English student almost overnight as soon as he changes teachers. It seems like the youngster loses all forms of concentration. What can parents do to get their child back on track?

A: Of course, there may be many reasons why a student does well, then loses focus and begins an academic slide to failure. However, there is an answer that can solve a very common problem that many students have as they go through emotional hills and valleys.

Consider four requisites that you as a teacher can advise parents to review with a student—especially a student who appears turned off to giving a consistent effort to achieve academically.

1. Students must be clear on what it is they are being asked to accomplish. Parents should have a checklist of all assignments and help their children budget their time so as to move expeditiously through one assignment after another. There should be multiple copies of the checklist. Parents

should stick one on the refrigerator! This way the teacher, student, and parent are all in the loop as to what is to be done by the student.

2. Students must know how an assignment can be successfully completed. Sometimes this means that the teachers should begin homework assignments in class or parents should help their children get started. In any case, a model must be presented so that the youngsters don't have to wonder, "Is this what the teacher wants?" Parents, when viewing the model, can help monitor their children's work.

3. Students must see value in doing the assigned tasks. So often in a rush to get through certain curricula, teachers fail to impress upon youngsters the important concepts being taught. If a student can see the value of writing an essay (confronting hazy thoughts and transforming them into coherent ideas), there is a much better chance that the student will perform the task.

4. Students must see themselves as capable of doing the assignment successfully. Many students give up before they even attempt an assignment because they believe they "aren't smart enough" to do the project. Sometimes this is nothing more than protecting their ego. The rationale goes something like this, "If I don't try, then I really can't fail." Parents should tell their children that if an assignment is not up to standard, what is called for is revision, not rejection. The revised "up to standards" assignment should be viewed as a complete success.

By using these four requisites, parents can help their children achieve a broad array of academic subjects under a wide range of teachers. All four requisites demand that parents get involved in the "what" and "how" of a task, explaining the value of classwork and homework and telling their children that with consistent effort, they can be successful on school assignments. ●

Struggling Students Aren't Bad Students

Q: How can parents help children who are bad students become good students? As a teacher you might wish to give the following advice.

A: First, it is better to talk about students who are "strong" or "struggling" in some school subjects, rather than "good" and "bad" students. Good and bad are moral terms. Some children who aren't successful think of themselves as bad students,

hence bad people. Obviously, this kind of distorted thinking can lead a young person to false and even lifelong conclusions about his or her worth as an individual.

Following are three basic objectives parents and teachers should set up as program goals to help the unsuccessful student.

• Give students a sense of belonging, identification, and membership. The school community should act as an extended family. The rapport between student and teacher must be built and nurtured on mutual respect.

- Give students the skills they need to take on personal responsibility. School rules should be written with a positive emphasis, so that good behavior is rewarded with greater student freedom. The all too common "Mickey Mouse" rules regarding seat assignment or restroom passes should be phased out as youngsters exhibit increasingly mature behavior. Otherwise, how are they to exercise a sense of personal responsibility?

- Give all students the most enriched curriculum in such a manner that every learner comes to understand the key principles of what is being studied. For the struggling student, this means using varied learning options, including the instructor's commitment to reteach concepts. This means everyone has to learn to expect success.

The most direct route to student failure is a lack of faith in the abilities of a child—by the parent, teacher, and the impressionable student. Belief in one's abilities and hard work equals enhanced student achievement and higher grades.

When a student's studies become more personalized, they become more focused. Learning takes place within social relationships in an environment where the student has a sense of well-being.

When parents and teachers give the student a sense of belonging, a step-by-step opportunity to demonstrate personal responsibility, and an enriched and varied curriculum, those parents and teachers are saying that they value the student as a person. Such a unified statement by home and school promotes the best in all of us. ●

Not All Students Work at the Same Pace

Q: Giving all students the same kind of enriched coursework is a good idea, but how can you make the class interesting to everybody when the class is so diverse? Won't some students be bored waiting for other students to catch up?

A: Students should not get bored if the instructor knows how to adapt instruction to respond to the diverse needs of a heterogeneous class. To better understand the kinds of adaptations a teacher can make, we should first be clear on what a teacher should not do.

A teacher should not grade some students harder than others. Neither should the teacher let students who finish ahead of time play games or get an early recess or lunch. Even extra math problems or extra reading assignments are not appropriate for the quicker students, because these students will see it as an extra burden—a penalty for being the first to finish the regular assignment.

After a review of undesirable education practices, we can delineate what a teacher should do. If the goal is to foster continual student growth, the methods must include a variety of ways for students to explore what it is they are to learn and a variety of ways to demonstrate their mastery of the curriculum content.

This kind of learning is student centered. This means that students are active explorers. The teacher is a guide, not the fount of all knowledge. Educators should be more interested in concepts than simply "covering" the curriculum.

The problem with a coverage-based curriculum is that the teacher feels the need to see all students do the same work. That is what bores students. Because students come from different backgrounds, work at different speeds, and do not all finish at the same time, a coverage-based curriculum is inherently flawed.

In a concept-based curricular design, it is the student who, instead of fighting boredom, grows as a self-directed learner.

Teachers should share goal setting in a concept-based curriculum with a student predicated on that student's readiness, interest, and learning style. The student's earned grade should be based on the student's academic growth and goal attainment. In all of this, the teacher must remain flexible and make ongoing assessments of the student's ever-changing readiness and academic development.

We know all students' academic development and social growth are best served in a heterogeneous classroom. It is up to the teacher to deliver the most enriched curriculum to all students and provide for a student-centered approach. The concept-based formula allows all learners to expand their understanding of the key curricular ideas and cancels boredom by providing a dynamic scholastic environment for the self-directed learner. ●

What Are Critical Thinking Skills?

Q: What is meant by the term *critical thinking skills,* and how can parents and teachers help children develop these skills?

A: Critical thinking is the ability to effectively gather, consider, and apply information. Developing critical thinking skills depends on how well a learning situation encourages student discovery. The important point is that students are given a learning experience in which they can detect ideas rather than memorize them. Here are some ways to enhance that "spirit of discovery" needed to stimulate critical thinking skills:

• **Look for analogies.** One way to better understand a concept is to construct a parallel idea based on the learner's ex-

perience. Explicit connections between thoughts open up new ideas.

• **Search for alternative solutions.** Problems that stimulate critical thinking should not assume a single absolute answer. Open-ended questions are best if you wish the student to think and come up with a creative solution.

• **Allow sufficient time to ponder.** School is not a quiz show! Critical thinking skills are not usually developed through rapid replies or snap judgments. Permitting a reasonable amount of time for an answer lets the student know that he or she is expected to make a deliberate effort to contemplate before coming to a solution set.

Critical thinking skills are at the core of learning. These higher-order skills will provide the means to answer questions in new and different situations, giving the learner the ability to collect, judge, and implement information to solve problems. ●

SUGGESTED READINGS

Bennion, J., & Olsen, B. (2002). Wilderness writing: Using personal narrative to enhance outdoor experience. *Journal of Experiential Education, 25*(1), 239–246.

Brandt, R. S. (Ed.). (2000). *Education in a new era.* Alexandria, VA: Association for Supervision and Curriculum Development.

Broek, P. V. D. (2001). *The role of television viewing in the development of reading comprehension.* Ann Arbor, MI: Center for the Improvement of Early Reading Achievement.

Conchas, G. Q., & Clark, P. A. (2002). Career academies and urban minority schooling: Forging optimism despite limited opportunity. *Journal of Education for Students Placed at Risk, 7*(3), 287–311.

Dyment, J. E., & O'Connell, T. S. (2003). Getting the most out of journaling: Strategies for outdoor educators. *Pathways: The Ontario Journal of Outdoor Education, 15*(2), 31–34.

Ferree, A. M. (2001). Soaps and suspicious activities: Dramatic experiences in British classroom. *Journal of Adolescent & Adult Literacy, 45*(1), 16–23.

Fullan, M. (2001). *Leading in a culture of change.* San Francisco: Jossey-Bass.

Garmston, R., & Wellman, B. (1999). *The adaptive school: A sourcebook for developing collaborative groups.* Norwood, MA: Christopher-Gordon.

Greenwald, N. L. (2000). Learning from problems. *The Science Teacher, 67*(4), 28–32.

Hammond, W. F. (2002). The creative journal: A power tool for learning. *Green Teacher, 69,* 34–38.

Jester, R. (2002). If I had a hammer: Technology in the language arts classroom. *English Journal, 91*(4), 85–88.

Morrison, T. G., Bryan, G., & Chilcoat, G. W. (2002). Using student-generated comic books in the classroom. *Journal of Adolescent & Adult Literacy, 45*(8), 758–767.

O'Day, S. (2001). Creative drama through scaffolded plays in the language arts classroom. *Primary Voices K–6, 9*(4), 20–25.

Raywid, M. A. (2001). What to do with students who are not succeeding. *Phi Delta Kappan, 82*(8), 582–584.

Rossi, P. J. (2000). Young children's opera: Having a multiple literacy experience from the inside-out. *Youth Theatre Journal, 14,* 26–39.

Sanders, M. G. (Ed.). (2000). *Schooling Students Placed at Risk.* Mahwah, NJ: Erlbaum.

Strickland, D., & Rath, L. K. (2000). *Between the lions: Public television promotes early literacy.* Newark, DE: International Reading Association. (ED 444 118)

Wagner, T. (2002). *Making the grade: Reinventing America's schools.* New York: RoutledgeFalmer.

White, H. B. (2001). Problem based learning. *Biochemistry and Molecular Biology Education, 29*(1), 24–25.

unit :8

Learning to Read, Reading to Learn

Encourage Young Readers by Reading Aloud

Q: Everyone knows how important reading is. How can a teacher, parent, or another family member help a young reader who won't pick up a book on her own and doesn't appear to like to read very much?

A: Language is made up of patterns and rhythms. Those who read little may become frustrated because they don't recognize the patterns or appreciate the rhythms. What this young reader may need is a role model, such as a parent or older sibling. The following method will encourage a love of reading.

Introduce books to a young reader by reading them aloud to her. Your skills in understanding language patterns and rhythms can bring the written language to life and increase her reading comprehension.

At present, when she picks up a book and reads silently, she uses the single sense of sight. For the inexperienced reader, silent reading of some material can be difficult. She may become easily frustrated, distracted, or simply not focused on what she is reading.

However, when you read aloud, you are using at least three different senses. First, of course, is the sense of sight. The second one is called the auditory sense—your engaging voice is heard. The third is known as the kinesthetic sense—your facial expression and gestures are involved.

What you are really doing with your oral interpretive skills is giving her a multisensory experience. These three senses can combine to breathe life into a story. Your acting skills should make the story more understandable and thus increase the child's reading comprehension. In turn, this might make picking up a book on her own more attractive to her.

In short, what you are trying to do is have the reader visualize what is taking place in a story, kind of like running a movie in your head. Reading out loud gives her the opportunity to connect the spoken and the written word.

Be sure to have two copies of the same text so that while you are reading orally, the child is both hearing and sight-reading the words—making those vital connections with the spoken word, the printed word, and the meaning.

Your modeling is critical. It is up to you to be interesting, engaging, and entertaining. After you have begun a story, let the child share the experience of rereading the same passage out loud to you. Soon you may find yourselves reading passages back and forth, and later discussing their meaning.

Recall that reading is a skill, and any skill gets better with practice. Reading aloud is a time-tested skill-builder. ●

Language Skills Are Key to Intellectual Development

Q: Although schools emphasize the importance of reading and writing in the classroom, it seems that people outside the classroom do more speaking than anything else. What can be done to improve a young person's speaking skills?

A: Oral language is used to communicate with other people. It is considered a natural process. However, speech can be defined as more than simple oral communication. Speech involves thinking and knowledge. Speech is also a skill that, as with any skill, can be improved with practice.

When youngsters have the opportunity to talk about their experiences, they provide themselves with the foundation for the development of other language skills. It has been argued that speech gives us the first opportunity, as children, to organize our thoughts so that they make sense to

others. This is not just a language issue; it is also an issue of early intellectual development. Children who are encouraged early on to speak seem to develop a better capacity to reason and forecast.

Unfortunately, some research indicates that oral language development has been overlooked for too long in the classroom. In most classrooms, this should be no surprise—teachers do most of the talking. Students in this kind of class tend to be passive listeners, and more significantly, may develop a passive attitude toward learning.

Teachers need to encourage a child to speak more frequently in class and to form independent opinions based on his or her own ideas and background. Moreover, the teacher should provide a suitable model of oral language.

There can be no doubt that speech is a skill that requires ongoing practice to develop ever higher levels of oral proficiency. The opportunity to express relevant ideas about a subject under discussion should occur for every student, every day, in every classroom. ●

Taking Steps toward Writing Effective Essays

Q: What can a high school student do if she has problems writing required essays? Her teachers write that her work is too short and goes off the point.

A: Writing that is clear, concise, coherent, and on point is a goal that all students should strive to attain. With diligence and practice, anyone's writing can improve dramatically. Here's a plan of action for high school students:

- Read to understand, not just finish, the material you are asked to write about. That "lost in space" feeling when you write can perhaps be traced to a lack of comprehension of what you just read. Try reading aloud. This gives you the chance to use your imagination by employing oral interpretive skills. Although reading aloud is slower than sight reading and may no longer be "fashionable" for high school students, it can be a real help to truly

understanding and interacting with what you are reading.

- Write a thesis statement that answers the teacher's question and that you can support with evidence from the text you have read. Let's say the idea be-

ESSAY DISMISSED — LACK OF EVIDENCE!!

hind your thesis statement is "Taxes are robbery" or "Taxes are necessary," and your job is to confirm your point. Like a lawyer in court trying to prove his or her case, your essay must have hard evidence. This "evidence" is located in the reading you have done to prepare to answer the question. It is this very evidence that permits you to write with conviction and even passion. By judicious use of quotations and coherent analysis, you are well on your way to writing a successful essay.

- Make a brief outline of the essay, and stick to it. People who get lost need road maps. A one-page outline should include three things: an introductory thesis statement (what you are going to prove), three to five major points you are going to support with evidence (save your best point until last!), and a conclusion based on what you promised to deliver in your introduction to sum up the argument.

- Finish the writing assignment by reading. Read carefully what you have written and, if possible, share it with other students or teachers before turning it in. Presenting your work to others is an indication that you have done your best to craft an essay and would appreciate feedback to make the paper even stronger.

Getting a handle on written assignments is most important because the writing process is a wonderful opportunity to use your reading, writing and critical thinking skills to reinforce and amplify all that you have learned. ●

Revision Is an Important Part of an Assignment

Q: Why do teachers make students rewrite their work so much? Even when papers don't have many spelling errors, some students almost always have to do their papers a second time.

A: Many students see a rewrite of their papers as an indication that they didn't do a very good job, or even that they failed the assignment. They view rewriting as an exercise in correcting errors in order to get eventual credit for their papers.

Students need to understand that when they revise their work, they are doing much more than checking the spelling, grammar, or word choice. Revision is something that extends beyond simple mechanics; it is at the very core of the entire writing process.

Fundamentally, revision means a re-thinking of ideas and a clarification of meanings. The writer further explores his or her words and sentences to better express their meaning. Revision or a rewrite is mostly about meaning. It is a lot more than mere editing or proofreading. Think of revision as the third part of the writing process (prewriting, writing, and revision)—not as a failure to get the assignment right the first time.

Teachers who request revisions are doing their job. They are after quality in fluency, word choice, grammar, and most importantly, meaning. Students should approach a rewrite as the final stage of a process to reshape thoughts and elucidate ideas. As they re-explore their convictions and improve their written expression, students will enhance communication with a very important person—the reader. ●

Learn to Read, Then Read to Learn

Q: Some of the worst students in high school are also the poorest readers. How does a poor reader ever become a good student?

A: This question, in one form or another, is probably the most frequent query of parents, teachers, and students. High school students who struggle with reading at their own grade level are at a tremendous disadvantage in class. At this level, high school students should be reading to learn, and yet they really have not learned to read.

The struggling reader typically does not realize that reading communicates personal meaning. These unsuccessful readers typically believe reading is a process of merely getting the word right rather than comprehending the meaning of a sentence, passage, or book. Some of the insights successful readers have (hearing a voice on the page, skipping words, or scanning certain types of materials) are unknown to the struggling reader.

A poor reader can become a successful student by becoming a successful reader. In order for that to occur, caring attention by a knowledgeable teacher is essential. This teacher must realize that incomprehension has three causes: self-centeredness, inexperience, and inadequate motivation.

Self-centered readers are likely to make irrelevant associations based on their own overly subjective thought. This student needs to hear other ideas and analysis. Discussion groups provide an answer. In such a group, the struggling reader realizes other interpretations of the text may eventually make more sense.

Inexperience comes into play when a student simply has no familiarity with certain concrete things or abstract ideas presented in the text. Television and movies can play a role in introducing new ideas. A teacher's oral interpretative skills (reading aloud from the story and enthusiastically explaining fresh concepts) can also play a key instructional role.

The lack of motivation is evident in a student who either does not even bring the text to class or simply is ready to give up before he or she has started a reading task. A teacher must set up situations where students can find reasons to make consistent efforts to comprehend their reading assignments. By assigning a project at the end of the reading assignment (a writing task, a mural, or an oral report), reading and comprehending the text now has a practical purpose. In a nutshell, the teacher needs to create contexts for success, be unconditional in the support of student effort, and allow students the freedom to select some of the materials, books, and topics to be explored.

After all is said and done, reading is a skill. The better we understand the unsuccessful reader, the better we can devise solutions to get that student to practice reading. A student who consistently practices reading can learn to read and then transition to the ultimate goal of reading to learn. ●

Integrated Approach to Language Arts Pays Off

Q: Reading and writing skills are probably the two most important abilities to learn in school, yet youngsters don't seem to read as much as they used to. Are there any programs parents and teachers should know about to help improve children's reading and writing? If such programs exist, why aren't schools using them?

A: There are such programs. They are contained in curricula that integrate the language arts. More than 60 years ago, John Dewey, the great American educational reformer, described the learner as an explorer. In other words, he believed the student should be an inquisitive person who is in constant search of answers to personal questions.

An integrated language arts program operates on principles to encourage the themes and activities that stimulate Dewey's curious learner. In short, an integrated language arts program lets the learner explore issues by using, among others, the skills of listening, speaking, reading, and writing.

In Britain during the 1960s and 1970s, an integrated approach was implemented when students were encouraged to write and then dialogue with others about their written work. In the United States, although many teachers favor an integrated approach, research indicates that only sporadic language arts integration actually occurs on a typical class day.

There are reasons for this discrepancy between what is advocated and what is practiced. First, teachers are not adequately trained to teach integrated language arts. Changing the traditional curriculum of teaching skills in isolation (word lists, grammar rules, and "busy work" handouts) has proven difficult.

Public schools in the United States are quite structured as to time, perceived ability grouping, and curricular content. These factors have a chilling effect on the acceptance of new ideas on how to teach reading and writing.

Sometimes it seems that school curricula are designed to be "teacherproof." What is to be taught and how it is to be taught can be quite prescriptive, leaving little room for teacher creativity. It takes a teacher with a good understanding of educational research, solid training, and great confidence in his or her ability to teach to implement an integrated arts curriculum.

When you think about it, language, thinking, and learning are naturally inseparable—until teachers are trained to split them up into various proficiencies. It is this artificial separation of writing from spelling, of literature from grammar, this almost obsessive desire to dissect the language—that can make the study of language so dry.

The focus should be on using language as a tool to learn desirable content—something you want to know. In order for this to happen, an environment must be shaped in order to allow students to embark on a genuine pursuit of knowledge.

Following is an example of an integrated language arts curriculum that has been successful with a wide variety of students from diverse backgrounds and skill levels. Nearly 100 students in a 10th-grade English class were tested at the start of the school year to determine their reading level. The norm-referenced standardized test revealed that the average student had a 9.2 rating in reading comprehension. This meant that the average student in class was eight months behind other 10th graders across the nation in comprehending what they read. They had experienced a traditional language curricular approach for a decade, and they were clearly behind.

The following integrated language approach was used, emphasizing a common learning experience based on a consistent use of listening, speaking, reading, and writing skills on a daily basis:

- **Daily oral reading:** The teacher read a literary selection to the class, using his oral interpretive skills to bring drama, humor, and a sense of excitement to the text where appropriate. After this "vibrant" model was set, every student would be expected to read orally to the class at each session.

- **Daily dialogue:** As the oral reading progressed and every student contributed by reading a sentence, a paragraph, or a page, the class would stop to dialogue about the text. At this point, teacher enthusiasm was crucial. Students cannot be expected to want to learn something the teacher does not enjoy teaching.

- **Daily writing:** Using the reading selection as the basis, a daily visit to the computer lab to put thoughts into words was essential. This made students organize their thinking and confront their fuzzy notions, turning them into coherent thoughts.

- **Daily editing:** Students were required to edit other students' written work. This peer-tutoring model encompassed reading, writing, and conversational activities.

- **Daily outside reading:** Parents were notified by letter and telephone to monitor one hour of pleasure reading by their youngster each night. Learners acquire cognitive competence through experience. Parents were asked to provide a clean, well-lighted, quiet place in their homes for student pleasure reading.

These five approaches introduced an integrated language arts approach to learning. The proof of the efficacy of this particular model was made evident in a posttest on reading comprehension for these students at the end of the academic year. The difference between the September score (9.2) and the May score (12.2) indicated that in one academic year, these students went from the beginning 9th-grade level in reading comprehension to the beginning 12th-grade level.

Although the results were most impressive, they should not be surprising. The teacher simply combined educational theory with a solid integrated language arts classroom approach. Listening, speaking, reading, and writing are skills, and like all skills, they improve with practice. An integrated approach ensures those skills are practiced on a consistent basis. ●

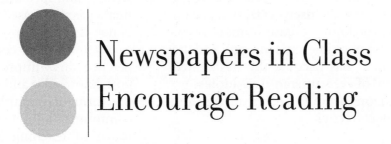

Newspapers in Class Encourage Reading

Q: What is being done outside the schools to encourage youngsters to read? Does anyone besides the schools really care about the growing number of functionally illiterate people in our society?

A: There is at least one group of people who truly do care—newspaper publishers. Let's face it, people who can't read have very little reason to use newspapers—printed or online.

Newspaper in Education spearheads literacy drives in many communities by providing reading material to millions of students. NIE staff members, employed by local newspapers, provide free or low-cost teacher guides to facilitate instruction in the classroom. Teachers receive programs such as "The Stock Market Game," "Quest for Science," and math-based ways of following a hometown professional sports team.

To a large degree, free newspapers are supplied to the schools by subscribers who donate the cost of their unused newspapers as part of a vacation donation program. The core idea is a simple win–win proposition. For schools, a newspaper is a tool that helps students develop reading ability and enhance their skills and knowledge. The newspaper business ben-efits by cultivating a new generation of readers.

As to the educational merit of having a daily journal of current events in the classroom, there are a number of specific advantages:

- Newspapers are enjoyable to read. What better motivator to read is there than fun?

- Newspapers have continually updated news. There are many times when a newspaper has more accurate information (such as contemporary scientific discoveries) than any textbook.

- Newspapers demonstrate the necessity of developing reading skills. Informed students will see the explicit connections between the skills and concepts they are being taught in the classroom and the up-to-the-moment material presented to them by a print or online newspaper.

By promoting literacy and expanding the curriculum to important and relevant current events, newspapers (in the traditional print or online edition) are very special educational resources indeed. ●

Like, How Come Kids, You Know, Can't Communicate?

Q: Why is it that high school students aren't able to express themselves clearly? The incessant "you know" phrase seems to occur more than once in every sentence, and the word "like" has become the designated first word of every utterance an adolescent makes. Don't schools teach students how to speak correctly?

A: Fundamentally, oral language is used to communicate with others. In fact, almost all children come to a school with some oral ability. The school's job is to improve this ability (fluency, clarity, and sensitivity) and teach the child to communicate more effectively. It is clear that schools simply aren't doing the job they could do in oral language development.

Most of the time when oral language is used in the classroom, it is the teacher doing the talking. The problem with the "teacher-talk-and-student-listen" model is that the student becomes a passive listener. This means the opportunity for student practice, necessary to develop oral language, simply does not occur.

Another problem is that children may carry this listening passivity over to their entire attitude about learning, producing the all too common uninterested, "bored" student. What educators should realize is that literacy learning (listening, reading, writing, and speaking) is a continuum. All literacy is skill-based and, for a skill to get better, it must be practiced.

A child's basic communications competence can be improved, but this involves both knowledge and skills. Knowledge (in the form of examples) of effective oral communication must be taught. We know much of teaching is modeling. Therefore, the teacher must routinely model appropriate speech. Skills can only improve with practice. Every student must be given continual opportunities, as part of the regular school curriculum, to speak one-to-one as well as to small and large groups.

By the way, not only will the student's oral communication improve, but his or her higher-order critical thinking skills will also develop. How valuable is "thinking on your feet"? Without a doubt, delivering an articulate impromptu or extemporaneous answer to a question requires both linguistic and critical thinking skills. The more time spent on oral communication skills, the more developed critical thinking and reasoning abilities will become.

When students have an opportunity to orally bring their ideas and knowledge into classroom learning activities, they not only learn to speak, they speak to learn. ●

The First Lesson in Reading Can Be an Experience

Q: Many parents have heard that they are the most important educators in the lives of their children, but they don't always have the tools to be the best teachers. How can parents make reading a habit at an early age?

A: This is an important task on which volumes could be written. Teachers need to let parents know there are three activities that have proved quite successful. The first two are pretty standard. The third may surprise you; many people are amazed the first time they see the approach used with a youngster.

The first activity that helps create an enjoyable habit of reading is to read bedtime stories aloud to children each evening. Second, talk about these stories and check for comprehension by asking children to retell the reading selections to you as best they can.

The third activity can be used with a "prereader," and has been successful with very young children who "could not read." Here's how it works. Ask the child what he has done the previous week, and as the child speaks, write the child's experience (a day at the beach) on the board.

After writing six or seven simple sentences such as "I went swimming at the beach" or "I made sand castles," ask the child to read the sentences that the child has just dictated. You will be amazed to hear the child read his dictated composition on a day at the beach as you point to each word.

This activity demonstrates that experiences precede interest in what we are about to read. And here is the important point: If we are interested enough in the experience, we can muster the ability to read about it.

In other words, effort creates ability when we care enough about the outcome. Try this activity and you will be amazed and gratified by the results. ●

Helping Beginning Readers

Q: There is a lot of information out there for parents about how to help children who are beginning to read, including ways to teach children to read whole words and ways to emphasize phonics. But once the child gets past that phase of learning to read, what advice should teachers give parents on continuing to help their child?

A: At about the mid-elementary and middle school years, there is a shift from reading stories of familiar knowledge to reading that introduces new opinions and concepts. This shift reflects the difference between learning to read (beginning reading) and reading to learn (developing skills). In reading to learn, silent reading in different subjects (for example, history or science) becomes more prevalent.

Some educators teach reading comprehension as a series of subskills. There are as many as 350 subskills that can be singled out, taught, and tested at this level. Other educators do not see reading comprehension as a product of learned subskills. Instead, they recommend extensive reading of interesting literature. In this approach, the understanding of word meanings and the development of critical thinking abilities are stressed.

Although at this next reading-to-learn step there is no single consensus approach, we know one thing: reading is a skill. The more we practice a skill (any skill), the better we get. Having a reading hour in the home each evening can only benefit a child's progress as an independent reader and a self-directed learner. ●

Reading Starts with Identifying Sounds

Q: Is there a nuts-and-bolts way to go about teaching reading at home? Do parents have to buy expensive phonics programs, or is there a way to get a preschooler started in reading without the expense?

A: Teachers should advise parents that there are many ways to get started in reading, but first we must understand the concept of phonological awareness, which is your child's growing ability to identify different sounds and associate these sounds with written words. A phoneme is the smallest unit of sound. For example, "fat" contains three distinctly different sounds. Including the letter combinations such as "th," there are 44 phonemes in the English language.

The idea is to have a child identify and manipulate these sounds. By segmenting, rhyming, and blending sounds,

a child is getting ready to read. There is a double dose of skill-building going on here—phonological awareness affects early reading ability and the ability to read increases phonological awareness.

Here are some helpful activities from researcher K. E. Stanovich to increase phonological awareness:

- **Phoneme deletion:** What word would be left if the *k* sound were taken away from "cat"?

- **Word-to-word matching:** Do "pen" and "mile" begin with the same sound?

- **Blending:** What word would we have if we blended these sounds together: *m, o, p?*

- **Phoneme segmentation:** What sounds do you hear in the word "hot"?

- **Phoneme counting:** How many sounds do you hear in the word "cake"?

- **Rhyming:** Tell me all of the words that you know that rhyme with "cat."

There are dozens of variations for each phonological awareness question.

Of course, as you go through these tasks, remember it is very important to model the correct sounds. When these and other fun reading readiness activities are done frequently, they can be a powerful way to introduce reading. ●

Finding That Inner Voice to Make Reading Enjoyable

Q: Some students have trouble reading novels or even short stories. It's not just the words. They have trouble just getting interested enough to keep reading after they open a book. It's hard for these students to concentrate because they always get the characters mixed up, and then they just lose interest. How can they solve this problem?

A: Here is some advice for students who are having trouble getting interested in reading. First, slow down. Read at a pace that lets the story open up to you. Picture yourself as the narrator. A good storyteller reads and becomes involved in a story. As a listener, you may have had such an experience. Perhaps when you were younger, your parents or your teacher piqued your interest by reading a story aloud to you.

Find that inner voice in your head and become the narrator. A good storyteller always gives an interpretive reading—finding the right tone and pace to set an appropriate mood. With an entertaining narration, you will become more focused. You will find that a good story will more than keep your interest.

After a certain number of pages, you'll automatically begin to reflect on what you have read and start guessing what will happen next. This is when the fun of reading really kicks in. The more fun, the "easier" it is to read even the thickest novels. Whatever you do, keep reading. Remember that reading is a skill, and it will only get better with practice. ●

Help a Child Love to Read

Q: Everyone knows the importance of reading to get good grades. What can parents do when their eight-year-old would rather watch TV than read?

A: Advise the parents that in grades one through three, children are still learning how to read. The process of reading is quite complex. Not everyone reacts to this skill with the same degree of success. To put it plainly, some children find reading easy, others find it difficult. Care must be used not to overemphasize the learning-to-read aspects of this process.

We tend to do better at things that intrigue, excite, or otherwise provide us with enjoyment. That being the case, involved parents should provide reading materials for a child that stimulates her curiosity. In other words, they should consult with the child, then go to a library or bookstore and together find a book that is just fun to read.

This may sound like a "spoonful-of-sugar" method, but if it gets a child to read, we have solved a problem. Remember, the more a child reads, the better he or she will become at reading. Reading is a skill, and any skill gets better with practice. ●

Mix of Teaching Strategies Is Key to Reading Success

Q: What is the best way to teach reading in school—the whole-language method or phonics?

A: Neither approach by itself serves all children adequately. Phonics is the study of sounds represented by individual letters and the development of independent word-recognition skills. For more than half a century, research has shown that systematic phonics instruction produces high reading achievement in terms of word identification, to at least the third-grade level.

A shift from learning to read to reading to learn occurs in the mid-elementary to junior high school years. The emphasis changes from reading stories with a controlled vocabulary and known content to more difficult materials that teach the child new information.

Proponents of the whole-language approach argue for high quality literature that meets the child's need for meaningful content. Studies indicate that the whole-language approach produces high reading comprehension scores.

Thus, a combination of reading strategies is necessary. In order to improve our reading, we must have a solid foundation (phonics) and be exposed to high quality literature (the whole-language approach).

In addition to these fundamental tools, modeling is important. When a parent or teacher models reading as a way to get information and enjoyment, it sends a powerful message to children to join in the fun. Reading aloud at home or in school is the kind of inclusive reading strategy that can make a real contribution to spur the student's interest in reading.

The goal of reading is not merely understanding individual sounds or even words. It is comprehending written material, evaluating it, and using it. The issue is not an either-or debate, but rather a challenge to find a judicious mix of reading theories while closely monitoring each student's growth in the ability to read. ●

Ways "Poor Students" Can Learn to Read

Q: How do you get poor high school readers to do better? Most of these youngsters have been doing so badly for so long that the answer seems to escape everyone.

A: A lot of these low-achieving students are products of or have been studying unsuccessfully in a "skills" program. In order to make a breakthrough with these poor readers, we must ask the fundamental question: Why does one read? The answer is that a person reads print in order to find personal meaning. Unless the printed page gives us meaning, it will not serve as a tool for learning.

A solution to the problem may start with the introduction of high-interest, appropriate-level readings. These readings can come from newspapers, magazines, books, or even the Internet.

Another crucial element is that the student must find the reading relevant. Comprehension is the key. The lack of comprehension can be based on the lack of motivation or the lack of experience. Here is a specific approach to change a low-performing adolescent into a more successful reader.

First, the reading must be compelling if it is to be successfully accomplished. Make the reading relevant by constructing an inventory of the particular student's interests. Once this task is accomplished, you have begun to attack the poor reader's motivational problem. You now know what material is of expressed student interest.

Second, understand that reading is a broadening experience in language, and then provide activities that lead to a variety of language experiences. Some of those

experiences may include listening to oral and recorded reading (books on tape are great), asking questions, dictating stories, and reading in small groups.

Once the meanings and the passion of the readings begin to flow into conversations, students should write about what they have read. The standard format of prewrite, write, and revision is, after all, inherently a reading experience.

Writing can clearly reinforce a crucial skill needed for reading proficiency—basic reading comprehension, understanding the meaning not just of isolated words but of sentences and paragraphs. Increased comprehension leads to detecting the main idea, relating facts, drawing conclusions, and even identifying transcendent themes applicable to one's own life.

Language is clearly a path to enhanced understanding when reading leads us to construct personal meaning. By using high-interest and appropriate-level reading relevant to a given student, a launching pad is readied for a journey to a universe of knowledge based on an ever-increasing comprehension of what one reads. ●

Learn Grammar without Drills

Q: Why do students have to spend so much time doing grammar drills and studying vocabulary lists? Students have claimed that an hour after writing out grammar patterns, they have forgotten the material. The same is true of vocabulary lists. Every week there are twenty new words, and they are not words that they ever otherwise read or write. Isn't there a better way to learn this material?

A: For some students, drills must make grammar seem like a collection of unidimensional rules about never-changing structures in the English language. In fact, grammar has more than one dimension. It contains form, meaning, and use. Combining these three into a living, breathing language can express our deepest fears or our noblest dreams.

However, memorizing rules and repeating models can be downright boring. When we are bored, we can easily use more and more effort to learn less and less.

The problem with simple memorization is that it treats grammar and vocabulary lists as if they are static areas of knowledge. This is the wrong approach; in order to be learned, grammar and vocabulary must be part of a communications process.

For example, you could conceivably learn every grammatical rule, but that in itself would not give the ability to effectively use grammar to communicate your thoughts. It would be like the mechanic who knows every part of the car but can't repair it.

The goal of learning grammar and vocabulary is to be able to use it to express personal meaning. One of the best ways to learn grammar and vocabulary is to read. When we continually read, we are literally bombarded with standard English grammar and an ever-widening vocabulary. If you read enough, you can't help "painlessly" internalizing many of the forms, meanings, and uses of standard grammar, as well as a host of vocabulary words in context.

After extensive reading, you are ready to write. It is in writing that the sense of the language you have acquired through reading pays off in your uses of both grammar and vocabulary.

A teachable moment arises when the teacher confers with the student face to face and goes over the grammar—in context—line by line. It is in a student's own written composition that the knowledge (and power) of grammar is critical to the student writer. The chance that the student will internalize grammatical rules that are of personal and immediate need for self-expression is high.

Here is just one final note about vocabulary: using just the right word is critical. I am reminded of what Mark Twain said about word choice: "The difference between the almost right word and the right word is really a large matter—it's the difference between the lightning bug and the lightning."

Remember that grammar and vocabulary must be understood and practiced to be retained. In order to remember your grammar and vocabulary, put it to work in your speaking and writing. ●

Five Ways to Become an Exemplary Listener

Q: Most people know that the best way to introduce reading to a child is by reading to him or her. However, how do you help a child to become a good listener?

A: This is a most important question, because between 50 and 75 percent of students' classroom time is spent listening to someone (the teacher or another student) or something (a video or audiotape). To be a good listener, one must focus attention on a given message and review the significant information.

Parents can model good listening behavior by demonstrating to their children these five traits of an exemplary listener:

1. **Be interested and attentive.** One can tell if another is listening by the way the person spoken to reacts. For example, if the parent pushes the "mute" button on the TV's remote control when a child asks a question, this is a positive sign of the kind of undivided attention needed to be a good listener.

2. **Make eye contact.** Making and maintaining eye contact with the speaker indicates focus on the person speaking, and should be conscientiously modeled by the parent.

3. **Be patient.** People (not just children) think faster than they speak. Due to a child's limited vocabulary, it may take a child more time to find the right words to express an idea. Parents and teachers must give children that time.

4. **Do not interrupt.** It might be difficult not to cut a child off when you believe you "know where they are going." However, letting a child express his or her opinion models the same respect you would want your child to show you and other people.

5. **Sense the nonverbal messages.** Children send messages through the tone of their voice, the expressions on their face, eye contact (or lack of it), and their overall behavior. How something is said may be more important than what is said.

It is a fact that children attending kindergarten through twelfth grade only spend 9 percent of their time in school. That means that parents are responsible for the other 91 percent of the time and have a fundamental role in building language skills. Listening is no exception.

Remember that the parent is a child's first and most important teacher. The parent is continually setting powerful examples (enlightened or unenlightened) of how to listen, speak, read, and write.

Parents that model attention, interest, and patience when spoken to produce exemplary listeners. ●

Q&A Sessions Need the Right Kind of Questions

Q: Why is it that some teachers get so much more of a response from their questions to students than other teachers do? Some question and answer classes are really interesting with students voicing different opinions. Class time seems to go quickly. Other classes seem dull, and the questions the teacher asks are about one fact or another and appear to be from a script.

A: Teachers have been conducting question and answer sessions ever since instruction began. It is estimated that teachers ask their students questions eight of every ten class minutes. Other studies have estimated that teachers ask about 300 to 400 questions per day. By the way, Q&A sessions have been a constant activity in U.S. schools dating back at least to the beginning of the 20th century.

Even though the Q&A approach is so prolific, it still must be done correctly if the transfer of basic knowledge and advanced conceptual thinking are to occur. In short, it has been said that to instruct well, a teacher must question well. Good questions keep students involved, lead to open expressions of thought, and facilitate teacher evaluation of the breadth and depth of an individual student's understanding of what is being taught.

So what is a good question? The best question is one that asks the student to use his or her knowledge to solve a problem—analyze, synthesize, and finally evaluate. Questions that call upon higher-order critical thinking skills seem to activate academically invigorating classes. Low-level-knowledge questions (e.g., When was George Washington born?) can lead to memorized answers that don't contain the kind of higher-order critical thinking skills that lead to intellectual stimulation.

To be most effective in asking higher-order critical thinking questions, a teacher should phrase each query clearly and give the student adequate time to respond. It is important for teachers to request that students state their opinions based on explicit connections to the text or other objective evidence.

In addition to asking a good question, a teacher must listen closely to a student's response in order to formulate the next question. Such a nonscripted approach directed toward learning and evaluative thinking leads to a more spontaneous and logically sequenced Q&A flow.

In summary, it is critical that a teacher, in each class, pose open-ended questions that lead to creative thought and self-directed learning. Good questions should lead to good answers. ●

Understanding the Textbook

Q: The problem with too many textbooks is that they are so dry and dull it is hard to concentrate on a subject and almost impossible for students to recall anything that they have read. What can be done to make textbooks more readable?

A: We have all experienced textbooks, for example in science or history, that just seem to drone on and on as we fight through page after page of lexical density. It is a very familiar predicament and a very significant problem. If the expository text becomes "boring," we simply will learn less.

Here are some of the many factors at play with the "reading the textbook" challenge. First, the text itself may present difficulties in its format. Second, students may lack the reading competency, background experience, or motivation to read. Third, the instructor may not be laying the groundwork for presenting the text in a way that helps students understand the material.

Understanding these factors, we can now zero in on the text itself. What can be done to improve the book? The following list may help authors, publishers, and those who assign readings (teachers and parents) to make the textbook a more effective learning tool:

• **Present a structured overview.** It is important that students get a gestalt (the big picture) on what the textbook is attempting to communicate.

• **Include chapter summaries.** A shortened form of each chapter that summarizes the major points helps the student embed new knowledge. Students learn best when material is presented in "bite-size chunks."

• **Incorporate multimedia.** Audio- and videotapes can go a long way in stimulating the combined student senses of seeing and hearing in order to highlight knowledge communicated in the text. Internet sites and other computer software can also be incorporated to appeal to the visual and aural senses.

• **Use graphics.** A simple graph, a funny cartoon, a memorable photograph, or a timely illustration can provide comprehensible input in order to make the accompanying text understandable.

• **Read aloud.** This is an old technique, but one that can be most effective—especially with an enthusiastic teacher who immediately checks for textual comprehension.

As long as schools exist there will be textbooks and/or text files to read. The challenge is to bring the textbook to life with a variety of text-based, sensory-based, and media-based approaches so that students with a variety of learning styles get the most out of their education. ●

How to Encourage Reading

Q: What should parents be doing at home to help their preschooler become a good reader in the future?

A: Inform parents of research indicating that children learn about reading before they enter the classroom door for the first time. Here are some ways to introduce reading to a child:

- Start by reading short stories to the child. It is essential that reading be an enjoyable experience.

- Point to everyday informational writing (stop signs) and other written signs around the neighborhood. Discuss the letters and what they mean.

- Whether it is a sign or a book, use your finger under the line of print to go from left to right. This will help the child gain an understanding of certain conventions of reading.

- Vocabulary enrichment can come from the different reading selections a parent reads to the child.

- Provide a varied reading experience. Information about hobbies (constructing a toy), value-laden stories (such as fables), or even reading the comics will provide many distinct kinds of reading experiences.

- Write short notes to the child as he becomes more familiar with reading in school, and encourage short notes from him.

- Finally, remember it is important to make the initial experiences of reading as enjoyable and supportive as possible. A positive initial attitude can build a lifelong reader—and a lifelong learner. ●

Use This Trick to Get a Child to Read

Q: How can you help a child who doesn't read well? A boy has an active imagination and expresses himself well verbally. He says he is not interested in the stories in the children's section of the library. How can you make reading fun while introducing him to written words?

A: Let parents know that one of the best activities for introducing reading is based on the notion of making the activity fun and relevant. Here is a step-by-step procedure for a not-so-secret formula.

- Ask the child to retell a favorite thing he has done—where he went, what he did, who was there, and why he enjoyed himself.

- As he tells his story, neatly print out on a piece of paper (or the keyboard on your computer) his story in his own words.

- Now here comes the fun (and amazing) part. Ask him to read the story back to you. Many students who "couldn't read" do an amazing job at actually reading the story back with little prompting, pointing to the words as they read them.

A lot of "can't read" kids are really "won't read" kids because what they are reading is of little or no interest to them.

Try this method and repeat it with new stories as the child's reading ability and vocabulary grow. ●

Helping a Child Read at Home

Q: How can parents help young children to read? Although all parents want their children to read, seeing kids read certainly doesn't happen as often as we would like.

A: Inform parents that a tremendous amount of educational research has been done on learning to read. There are a number of things the research shows time and again:

- Children who read widely get better and better as readers.

- Good writers were good readers first.

- Parents are crucial to the task of reading, both as model readers and in cheering along their child's efforts in reading.

With those three ideas in mind, here are some specifics on making reading happen consistently at home. First, you must model the desired behavior. Whether it is a read-aloud story or a silent time for reading, it should take place regularly.

Next, provide a wide variety of reading materials in the home. Your most cost-effective resource is as close as your neighborhood public library or the Internet on your home computer.

Finally, always praise effort. Whether the reading task involves a hobby (instructions on building a model airplane) or doing a book report, repeated encouragement of reading raises it to a family value.

Success in reading has much to do with the opportunities and home environments that we provide to children. ●

Questions to Ask about School Reading Programs

Q: What kinds of reading activities should children be doing at school?

A: The goal of a reading program must be to produce a successful reader who reads to learn; you should be concerned if your child fails to adequately progress. Here are four questions to ask of a reading program:

- Are students required to read outside of school every day?

- Do teachers read aloud to students on a consistent basis?

- Do students come into contact with reading that is challenging?

- Are students constantly assessed in terms of their reading progress?

Besides classwork, part of the answers to the questions on this list can be found in a home environment in which reading is a valued part of family life. Question four deals with quizzes, exams, and standardized tests. Parents should have clear and up-to-date assessments in order to monitor their child's progress.

If these four questions are answered, and an appropriate home reading program is also in place, students will soon discover what a rich, adventurous, and interesting world awaits them as avid readers. ●

Early Reading Builds a Lifetime Habit

Q: Although children are able to learn at a very young age, isn't it rushing things to read to an infant? When is the best time to start reading to children?

A: Let parents know it actually would not be rushing things to read to an infant, because we know that when you speak to a baby, you set a model of behavior that

the infant will eventually attempt to replicate. If we model speech for an infant, why not reading?

There are many ways to introduce reading early on in a child's life. For example, try reading with vocal variety and rhythm. Children's literature and songs usually combine rhyme and rhythm that depend on the reader's inflection. Reading and

singing the songs in a book should be done with enthusiasm and wonder.

Use books that have simple concepts and bright, bold pictures. Pop-up books are wonderful. Textured books become tactile experiences. Hearing, seeing, and feeling the story make reading a multisensory experience for the child.

Permit the child to interact as much as possible when you are reading aloud.

Sometimes the child will wish to talk about the pictures or repeat part of the story. Such interactions are more important than immediately continuing the story. In a sense, these "interruptions" are a gauge of how successful your initial attempts at introducing reading are.

Use more than your voice to tell a story. Here, digital communications (your fingers) become important. A big part of introducing a book to a child is literally pointing out pictures and involving the child in identifying the illustration by seeing and touching it.

Have a certain time of the day for reading. Children function best with a routine. On the other hand, remember that books are portable and can go anywhere. You may find that having one handy will give your child another set of experiences with books at different times during the day as well as in varied places.

A child's first encounter with reading should indicate to him or her that books are full of fun and interesting ideas. The interest and pleasure you model in the process will help form your child's initial perception of reading.

These efforts will be well worth the time. Research indicates that children who are read to at an early age become successful readers, do better in school, and retain the reading habit for a lifetime. ●

Story Time Helps
Children Learn to Read

Q: How does a parent teach reading at home to a preschooler? Where do you start? Are there steps to follow?

A: Advise parents that learning to read should begin at home, well before the first day a

child arrives at the classroom door. When a parent recites a rhyme, sings a song, or tells a story to their baby, a reading readiness program has begun. These poems, songs, and stories help the child hear the similarities and differences in the sounds of words. When children hear rhymes, they normally begin to repeat them and then make up rhymes of their own.

Next to be taught are the names of the letters and the sounds different letters represent. Then, as the child's motor skills increase, parents can teach their child to trace and write letters and numbers—the child by now should already recognize the shapes. The child then learns to associate the sounds of words he or she speaks with the different letters of the alphabet.

During this entire process, the parent continues to point out words found in our day-to-day environment (stop signs, business signs, words on cereal boxes, etc.) while still reading aloud to the child. Research says that reading aloud is the best way to introduce the fun and enjoyment of reading to a child.

After a parent has modeled the reading habit, it is very common for a child to try to tell part of the story and actually attempt to read books either with parents or on his or her own. The child will re-member parts of favorite stories and try to sound out unfamiliar words. The more the child practices, the more adept the child will become in recognizing familiar words quickly and easily.

It is at this time that a child will pick up what linguists have described as a "sense of the language," which is recognition of the patterns of spelling and the patterns of words as they appear in sentences. It is also at this point that attention will be given less and less to the letters and isolated words and more and more to the meaning of words, sentences, and the entire text.

Key to the process of reading is the child's ability to identify specific oral word sounds and associate those sounds with the squiggles we call written words. Practice makes perfect. As the word and sentence patterns are seen, recognized, and recalled, the child begins to read with relative ease and confidence. This should not be surprising. Reading, after all, is a skill. Any skill can, and will, only improve with practice. ●

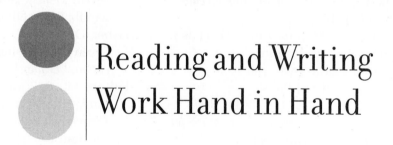

Reading and Writing Work Hand in Hand

Q: How can parents discover if their youngster is becoming a better reader?

A: Let parents know that reading and writing are two sides of the same coin. They are both skills that presuppose the other. Reading is to writing as listening is to speaking. You can think of these two skills as interdependent pairs.

It is important to be aware of this relationship because a person's writing provides an insight into his or her reading. Assessing a child's writing is an effective way to check reading comprehension by studying the child's written responses to what that child reads.

According to researchers, reading is taught as a succession of individual skills learned one at a time. There are two main analytic approaches to teaching reading. In the phonics approach, isolated letter sounds or letter clusters are studied in sequence and blended to form words. In the linguistic approach, patterns of letters are studied and combined into words.

The problem with both approaches (which teach discreet skills outside of meaningful context) is that many students adopt an analytic reading style based on information retrieval. Unfortunately, such reading may be very ineffective because the reader might miss many of the implied ideas in a textbook, magazine, or newspaper article.

A solution to this dilemma is writing in response to reading. When students have the opportunity to write about what they read, they learn to organize, clarify, and refine their thoughts. A short written composition is a helpful way to confront a fuzzy idea one has read and crystallize it through writing into a coherent thought.

One concrete suggestion is to have a child keep a reading log. In such a log, perceptions originating from one's read-ings are duly recorded and thoughts clarified in a written response.

If your students are reading nonfiction, they could respond in their reading logs by stating their opinions on a controversial topic. Likewise, if they are reading fiction, they can log in their views about an interesting character or how the theme of a novel may apply to their own lives.

When students respond to reading by writing, they engage the critical thinking skills of analyzing, synthesizing, and evaluating. The reading log gives the student a chance to improve both reading and writing skills, and it gives the parent and teacher an opportunity to evaluate a child's growth as both a reader and a writer. ●

SUGGESTED READINGS

Allington, R. (2002). You can't learn from books you can't read. *Educational Leadership, 60*(3), 16–19.

Allington, R. L., & Johnston, P. H. (Eds.). (2002). *Reading to learn: Lessons from exemplary fourth grade classrooms.* New York: The Guilford Press.

Brown, J. C., & Oates, L. (2001). *Books to grow on: African American literature for young children.* Washington, DC: National Association for the Education of Young Children.

Brozo, W. G., & Hargis, C. H. (2003). Taking seriously the idea of reform: One high school's efforts to make reading more responsive to all students. *Journal of Adolescent & Adult Literacy, 47,* 14–23.

Coley, R. J. (2002). *An uneven start: Indicators of inequality in school readiness.* Princeton: Educational Testing Service.

D'Arcangelo, M. (2002). The challenge of content-area reading: A conversation with Donna Ogle. *Educational Leadership, 60*(3), 12–15.

Fisher, D., & Frey, N. (2004). *Improving adolescent literacy: Strategies at work.* Upper Saddle River, NJ: Merrill Prentice Hall.

Fisher, D., Frey, N., & Williams, D. (2002). Seven literacy strategies that work. *Educational Leadership, 60*(3), 70–73.

Fulton, M., & Porter, M. (2001). *Common state strategies to improve student reading.* Denver, CO: Education Commission of the States.

Ivey, G., & Broaddus, K. (2001). "Just plain reading": A survey of what makes students want to read in middle school classrooms. *Reading Research Quarterly, 36,* 350–377.

Jacobs, V. (2002). Reading, writing, and understanding. *Educational Leadership, 60*(3), 58–61.

Lester, J. H. (2000). Secondary instruction: Does literacy fit in? *The High School Journal, 83,* 10–16.

Lin, C.-H. (2001). *Put reading first: The research building blocks for teaching children to read: Kindergarten through grade*

3. Washington, DC: National Institute for Literacy.

Smith, M. W., & Wilhelm, J. D. (2002). *Reading don't fix no Chevys: Literacy in the lives of young men.* Portsmouth, NH: Heinemann.

Sunderman, G., Amoa, M., & Meyers, T. (2001). California's reading initiative: Constraints on implementation in middle and high schools. *Educational Policy, 15,* 674–698.

Teale, W., & Yokota, J. (2000). Beginning reading and writing: Perspectives on instruction. In D. S. Strickland & L. M. Morrow (Eds.), *Beginning reading and writing. Language and literacy series* (pp. 3–21). Newark, DE: International Reading Association.

U.S. Department of Education, Office of Communications and Outreach. (2005). *Helping your child become a reader.* Washington, DC. Retrieved September 24, 2006, from www.ed.gov/parents/academic/help/reader/index.html.

Vacca, R. (2002). From effective decoders to strategic readers. *Educational Leadership, 60*(3), 6–11.

Worthy, J., Moorman, M., & Turner, M. (1999). What Johnny likes to read is hard to find in school. *Reading Research Quarterly, 34,* 12–27.

Zipperer, F., Worley, M., Sission, M., & Said, R. (2002). Literacy education and reading programs in the secondary school: Status, problems, and solutions. *NASSP Bulletin, 86,* 3–17.

UNIT :9

Inclusion and Service: Yes, That Means Everyone

Decisions That Concern Students with Disabilities

Q: Is it appropriate to place students with disabilities in regular classes? Who makes the decision about who goes to what school and which class?

A: In terms of the policy for where students with disabilities go for their education, the federal government's position is quite reasonable. Back in 1994, the U.S. Department of Education stated that the regular classroom in a neighborhood school should be the first placement option considered for the disabled student.

Another federal policy is that all children with disabilities be provided a free appropriate public education in the least restrictive environment. Many times, this turns out to be the regular classroom.

Some research indicates that when students with severe disabilities are put into general education classrooms, they show better social development, their presence gives their classmates more positive attitudes toward disabled students, and their attendance results in higher academic achievement. Key to providing the best educational environment for the student with disabilities is proper placement. The family and the teachers should review the goals, objectives, related services, and technology needed to make the placement work. In other words, placement should be made after considering which program or class would be of the greatest benefit to the student on a case-by-case basis.

Having a student with disabilities in the class should not be disruptive if the school administration provides:

- A school atmosphere that both welcomes and accommodates diversity
- Time available for teacher planning and collaborating with the child's family
- A curriculum that fosters student interaction with and mutual support from peers
- Specialized support personnel available to the school program

In order to implement a successful inclusion program, the school must focus on the philosophy that all students can learn. Early and continuing decision making about student placements should involve regular teachers, special support personnel, and the family of the child. ●

Ways to Test Students with Disabilities

Q: What is the best way to test a student with disabilities? How can a parent or teacher know if the test given is suitable for a particular student?

A: First, a working definition of "students with disabilities" is needed. A student with a documented physical or mental impairment that significantly limits his or her activities is generally considered disabled. Working from this premise, assessing the abilities of a student with (or without) disability should be at the core of a school's program to diagnose levels of achievement and academic development.

However, testing students with disabilities must be done in a manner that ensures that the results are valid. A teacher needs to know if there are special procedures for giving a particular test. For example, written instructions for students with hearing loss, large-type tests for students with vision loss, or untimed tests for a student with learning disabilities—all may be appropriate to effectively test a student's current ability in a specific area.

Even if this is done, we are still not out of the woods. If any of these kinds of adaptations in test administration are made, parallel interpretive guides for proper assessment, if available, must be used. In other words, standardized tests should only be given when the student can be meaningfully assessed under the same conditions in which the test was standardized.

On the bright side, there are tests that offer specialized administrations for students with common disabilities. College admission tests frequently have such options. Some tests may be given in groups or one on one. Other tests of every variety are given in Braille, sign language, with a reader, or on audiocassette.

As for the factor of time, it can be extended or waived. For example, a test to assess a visually-impaired student's knowledge of music history could be converted from a straight paper-and-pencil test based on written questions to an oral examination. In such an oral exam, questions are asked of the student and the student's oral answers are recorded on audiotape for scoring.

Remember the goal of any modified assessment is to determine how a disabled student would have performed if the student were free of the disability and could have taken the test under standard conditions. ●

Does Your Student Have a Learning Disability?

Q: Some children do better than others in school. How do teachers know when a child isn't doing well because he's lazy, or if he really has a learning problem? What are the solutions?

A: The cure for laziness is work. Many books and articles have been written over the years regarding positive reinforcement, parent involvement, and nurturing the student's will to succeed. These are invaluable steps in the learning process of any child.

The second part of the question, regarding a learning problem, is more difficult to answer. To begin, we must try to define what a learning disability is. A learning disability (LD) can be viewed as a disorder in the process of using language. This may be manifested in the imperfect ability to think, listen, speak, read, write, spell, or do math.

Not to be included under LD are students who have problems that primarily result from vision or hearing loss, motor disabilities, mental retardation, emotional disturbance, or environmental, cultural, or economic disadvantage.

Now you can better appreciate the difficulty in identifying who has a learning disability and who does not. In fact, virtually everyone has learning difficulties at some time during his or her life. Consider the math professor who has difficulty spelling or the brain surgeon who has trouble following a map to his grandmother's house. Depending on the specific task, we may be able learners or struggle mightily in order to complete the job.

For a student to be considered to have a learning disability, learning difficulties must be so severe that they chronically interfere with learning on a daily basis. Depending on the severity of the learning disability, different school services are not only available but also legally required.

Free public education from birth to age 21 is federally mandated. Different kinds of programs, including regular classrooms, self-contained classrooms, or residential settings, may be deemed appropriate depending on the needs of the student with a learning disability.

Many programs for LD students find the students "mainstreamed" into regular classrooms, but taking advantage of a specialized resource room where the homeroom teacher and resource-room teacher collaborate to provide the child with an appropriate learning plan.

Critical to helping the LD student is to locate the precise nature of the disability, and then to make the necessary adaptation. For instance, if a student has difficulty spelling, a spellchecker may be the solution. If a student has trouble reading, audiotapes or videotapes may provide the same information in a way that can be better assimilated.

These simple accommodations should be available not only in school, but as the LD student enters the workplace. In understanding and meeting the needs of particular individuals with learning disabilities, we open up a new productive world of opportunities for them, and a better world for all. ●

Teaching Special Education Students in the Regular Classroom—A Team Approach

Q: Parents with special education children want the best for their children. They usually want their youngsters with special needs to be mainstreamed in a regular classroom for at least part of the day.

How are teachers supposed to cope when they have an ever-growing number of special education students in their room? Many teachers were not trained to handle these kinds of students. This is a real problem that just seems to be growing and growing. What can be done?

A: As more and more special education students are channeled into the regular classroom, new teaching approaches are necessary. One such instructional arrangement to handle the mainstreaming of these students is called cooperative teaching. A teaching team made up of a general education and a special education teacher work together to set the goals, make the decisions, instruct the class, assess the learning, and comanage the class.

In our ever more diverse society, a heterogeneous (mixed) group of students can perform successfully in the same classroom when a regular teacher and a special education teacher are simultaneously present. Both of these teachers take joint responsibility and make coactive decisions with curricula (what is taught) and methodologies (how something is taught). Although responsibility and commensurate authority are shared, the roles these teachers play can, at times, be mutually exclusive.

For instance, a general education teacher follows state guidelines and district policy in presenting a specific curriculum. On the other hand, a special education teacher typically provides instruction by understanding the learning styles, strengths, and particular needs of individual students, and adapts instruction to best meet those needs. Although both teachers bring training and experience into the classroom, usually general practitioners (regular teachers) bring content specialization, whereas special education teachers bring diagnostic assessment and instructional adaptation expertise.

When a school district is willing to provide these teachers with the time to plan, develop, and evaluate their ongoing collaborative activities, the resultant teaching model has great possibilities for enhancing student achievement. Teacher preparation and in-service (professional development) programs are imperative. These programs permit teachers to access and perform action (in-class) research concerning the actual effectiveness of cooperative teaching, diversity training, and mixed grouping.

We know today that research indicates that this kind of cooperative teaching benefits both regular students and their special education counterparts. To what can this improvement be attributed? All students received more meaningful attention and more opportunities for individual assistance.

In such an atmosphere, all students can enhance their social (greater knowledge and acceptance of others) and cognitive (tests scores and grades) strengths. Pairing special education and regular classroom teachers may furnish an answer to meet the needs of all learners, by combining teaching expertise and thereby providing a quality learning environment for all. ●

Setting Up Learning Environments for Students with Attention Deficit Disorder

Q: How can a parent and a teacher work with a child who has ADD without making the youngster feel he is being singled out? When you single out a kid by doing things differently just for him, how do you keep from embarrassing the child?

A: First, let's spell out what we mean by ADD (attention deficit disorder) or ADHD (attention deficit hyperactivity disorder). The areas of concern for these chronic disorders can be characterized as a limited attention span, a persistent problem with impulse control, and hyperactivity (in the case of ADHD). ADD and ADHD can extend from childhood to old age and can have obvious negative consequences in the home, in school, or at work.

The American Psychiatric Association lists a number of attention span and hyperactivity criteria for diagnostic purposes (e.g., does not listen when spoken to directly, loses things, is easily distracted, etc.). Two-thirds of the criteria must be noted by a clinician before a student is categorized as having either disorder.

Once a student has been diagnosed with ADD or ADHD, the teacher or parent can introduce individualized instruction, while still having the classroom learning experience occur in an inclusive environment. For example, the teacher can make sure the ADD or ADHD student sits close to the teacher's desk to optimize focus on academic tasks. The teacher can also surround this child with students who are good role models and can engage in peer tutoring.

Classroom routine is critical; too many changes or disruptions are to be avoided. A quiet, stimuli-reduced area for study is also a good idea. In addition, testing should not be strictly timed. After all, a teacher should be testing knowledge, not attention span.

With all these adaptations, one may ask whether the ADD/ADHD student would feel stigmatized by this kind of special treatment? The answer is no. All of the above-mentioned pedagogical strategies can also be quite helpful to the typical student. Therefore, the entire class can be given many of the same kinds of learning environment opportunities. Although not every student can sit next to the teacher's desk, all can take part in peer tutoring, experience a routine, be shielded from disruptions, and be given a clean, well-lighted, quiet place to study.

Parents should receive a signed daily portfolio of activities and confer daily with their son or daughter about schoolwork (what a great way to extend the learning day). Parents should also remember, when monitoring a child's homework, that the child should be told to focus on one task at a time. Finally, a supportive attitude that consistently praises effort is essential for all students, and that includes ADD/ADHD learners. ●

Will All Non-Gifted Students Please Raise Their Hands?

Q: What exactly are the criteria for a child to be termed "gifted"?

A: This is an important question that seems to pop up all the time. One definition, which the House of Representatives used about twenty years ago, may be useful. According to a resolution on education, gifted students were defined as children "who are identified at the preschool, elementary or secondary level as possessing demonstrated potential abilities that give evidence of high performance capability in areas such as intellectual, creative, specific academic or leadership ability, or in the performing or visual arts."

Congress was trying to make the definition quite encompassing, but in light of what we have learned about education in the last two decades, even such a broad definition is inadequate.

School districts, individual schools, principals, and teachers make "decisions" about who can (and cannot) attend so-called gifted classes using grade point averages and IQ scores to cull the gifted/talented students from other students. Here's the problem: Although IQ tests can measure linguistic intelligence and logical mathematical intelligence, we now know that there are many different kinds of intelligences.

Noted neuropsychologist Howard Gardner has written about other intelligences. Gardner, a Harvard professor, lists the following types of intelligence: the kinesthetic, the musical, the spatial, the interpersonal and the intrapersonal—just for starters. Who could argue that these "new" intelligences do not also indicate giftedness in a child?

Depending on the course of study a student is taking, his or her talents may not be easily observable. In a classroom situation, a student who speaks, reads, and writes fluently may be considered obviously gifted, whereas a student demonstrating disruptive behavior may not be. Yet the disruptive student may be simply bored or unchallenged. His behavior is judged rather than his intellect, resulting in a flawed diagnosis of that student's current or potential abilities.

Even more disturbing is the fact that there has been an obvious and historic underselection of certain minority children to gifted programs. In the United States in 2006 33 percent of all students are African American or Latino. Although there is no basis to contend that these children, as a group, are less gifted than other children, these two minority populations only comprise 18 percent of gifted classes. The problem is even more striking when you realize that every gifted program has different criteria administered by different people and yet practices a form of structured inequality by barring many historically underrepresented students from gifted programs.

This does not mean that gifted programs should be discontinued. Sound educational theory and an immense body of consistent evidence on student achievement demonstrate that gifted programs are beneficial, but they should be inclusive.

If you address a group of students at the elementary, secondary, college, or graduate level, you will always get the same answer to this question: "Will all those people who aren't gifted please raise a hand?" It is a rare occasion when a hand is raised at any level.

This and other evidence suggests that all students should get the richest possible curriculum and that we should do much more to discover every child's special gifts.

Nurture the giftedness your child possesses, and demand that schools present all children with the most enriched curriculum possible. ●

An Inclusive Educational Strategy: Specially Designed Academic Instruction in English

Q: With so many different kinds of youngsters with different abilities sitting in the same classroom, it is no wonder that lots of them get discouraged and sooner or later end up as dropouts. In the same class, you have sharp students who speak, read, and write English well, and others who never pick up a book, as well as a growing number of children to whom English is a foreign language. How can a teacher hope to reach them all?

A: What is called for under these circumstances is a specially designed methodological approach to present the most enriched curriculum to all students. One example of this pedagogical tactic is called Specially Designed Academic Instruction in English (SDAIE). SDAIE can help when an enriched content course (e.g., history) is taught to a group as diverse as the class mentioned in the question. SDAIE should not supplant a two-way bilingual program, but like an effective English as a Second Language format, ought to support it.

One reason SDAIE can help is that it is geared toward teaching the language of instruction in a content course through a system called scaffolding. In other words, core subjects are best taught to a heterogeneous class by developing support mechanisms (scaffolds) to help students better understand the language of instruction (e.g., English), which leads to understanding of the content course being taught (e.g., biology).

How does this occur? A teacher or a parent can use the following instructional scaffolds:

1. **Model:** This can be as easy as simply showing a sample of what the final project should look like, or demonstrating how to do something by taking a student through the steps. It is said that 80 percent of learning takes place through modeling.

2. **Synthesize:** Simply refer to the students' previous knowledge and build an analogy to new knowledge. All knowledge is associative and therefore is interconnected.

3. **Develop metacognitive skills:** This means teaching students to think about how they think. By understanding one's own learning styles, a student can best approach the process of learning new knowledge.

4. **Utilize a multisensory approach:** Present students with verbal, written, and illustrative examples so the material is articulated and reiterated through as many of the five senses as possible.

By embedding contextualized English, language skills are amplified by the multiplicity of methodological approaches that explain new words and concepts. Diverse students with a wide variety of out-of-school experiences can best learn when the curriculum is both enriched and associated with prior learning experiences.

Every student deserves access to an enhanced core curriculum. SDAIE is a tool that can help. When utilized skillfully, it can give all students the best opportunity to be successful in their studies. ●

Having Friends at School

Q: How can an older student help her 8-year-old brother learn how to make friends at school?

A: This kind of interest from an older sibling would benefit young children everywhere. To begin, "well-liked" children seem to have better communication skills than those who are less popular. Research reveals that well-liked children call other children by their names, make eye contact, and touch the other children to whom they are talking.

An older sibling should practice these techniques with her brother, letting him know how to act and react to other children. She should try to set up play activities with other kids a little younger than her brother so that he can feel more at ease and build up his confidence.

If he has a conflict with another child, be sure and listen to your younger brother's point of view. Then ask him for a solution. Children can come up with excellent solutions to their problems when they are allowed to think them through. The key to a good solution is that it is fair and the child feels good about himself in making the solution.

Children who feel good about themselves and have the love and support of their families tend to have high self-esteem and make friends easily. ●

Dealing with Dyslexia

Q: Dyslexia is a term that a lot of people have heard, but practically no one can define. What is it, and what can be done to overcome it?

A: Dyslexia is defined as a developmental reading disorder which is not due to a defect in vision or hearing, nor to a neurological disorder. Unfortunately, that definition is rather vague. When a student is not achieving academically and has a reading ability markedly below grade level, what is called for is more precise information. Once we can better define the problem, we can then attempt to generate a precise answer.

Let's think of dyslexia as a neurocognitive deficit that shows up in classroom reading and spelling tasks. It is important to remember that dyslexic children (3 to 6 percent of all school-age children) are bright youngsters quite capable at other academic tasks.

A dyslexic child has what are called phonological core deficits. These phonological deficiencies occur when a child struggles in identifying the sound structure of language. Children with dyslexia may not recall the pronunciation of letters, word segments, or entire words. Dyslexia may involve confusion in memory, auditory perception, visual perception, oral language, and thinking.

Now that we have better identified the problem, here are five ways a parent or teacher can intervene to help dyslexic children:

1. Teach the similarities and differences between the speech sounds they hear and the visual patterns across words they see.

2. Instruct on the segmenting and blending of sounds, moving to progressively larger chunks of sounds and then words.

3. Expose them to decodable words on a regular basis. Challenge them to sound out new words and guess their meaning. A good reader is someone who makes good guesses.

4. Provide positive—if corrective—feedback. Remember, as with anyone who is struggling to learn, always praise effort.

5. Model oral interpretative skills. Reading an entertaining story aloud makes a narrative contextual and more meaningful.

As with many adaptive educational methodologies, all students can benefit by using techniques that involve more than one sense. For instance, all students, dyslexic or not, can utilize a multisensory approach to reading (combining the visual with the auditory) by using books on tape or CDs. Focusing on the written word of a particular text while listening to a professional narrator read with oral interpretive skills provides a wonderful opportunity for every learner to build reading skills. ●

Dealing with ADD

Q: What homework practices should a teacher follow to assist a student with ADD?

A: There are three basic recommendations regarding homework:

• Tell your student to be sure that he or she writes down his or her homework in a notebook each day.

• Sign the book, verifying that all assignments have been correctly recorded.

• Try to simplify; avoid multiple tasks. Help your student complete the assignments by introducing one task at a time.

It is important to monitor your student frequently, while showing an interested attitude. Your student may need extra time for certain tasks, so be patient and supportive. Encourage positive "self-talk" when your student has a successful accomplishment. A phrase you would like the student to repeat, such as "I'm doing better," can be helpful.

Of course, the eventual goal of all tutoring is that the student will become more and more self-directed. So when appropriate, ease off and let your student do as much as possible on his or her own. Always encourage and compliment the effort your student gives to various homework tasks. ●

What Is Service Learning?

Q: How can we get the students and the community, made up of people from different backgrounds, to feel more connected to their schools?

A: In order to do this, students (and teachers) have to understand the nature of democracy (from the Greek *demos* meaning "people" and *kratos* meaning "to govern") and the notion of civic responsibility.

From this foundation, grass roots social action in a school's community can get an ever more culturally and linguistically diverse group of students and citizens to fulfill the collective goals of a democratic society.

The base philosophy can be found in writings from Sophocles and Plato to Locke and Freire. Service learning proposes to strike a healthy balance between our civic rights and obligations, while bringing everyone under the big tent of civic responsibility.

Unfortunately, many times the community and/or the school can still be socially segregated—even when people are living in the same neighborhoods or attending the same institution. In other words, geographical proximity does not equal social integration. However, when people are working together toward a common goal (e.g., literacy campaigns, voter registration, or other community issues), the opportunity for people of diverse backgrounds to appreciate the efforts of all can become a reality.

Service learning proposes to reach out and build bridges to the community by integrating into the school's academic curriculum projects designed to provide a service that is mutually rewarding. Specifically, service learning can occur within a wide range of curricular activities:

- Ecology students cleaning litter from storm drains in order to restore streams, rivers, and/or oceans

- High school English class students tutoring elementary and middle school students in reading and writing

- Auto shop students providing free oil changes to low-income families in the neighborhood

- Biology students growing food in school gardens to provide fresh produce to needy members of the community

- Music students touring local hospitals and senior centers to bring song and dance to those socially shut out from their surrounding community.

These and a host of other activities benefit the school, the community, and the young people involved. There are other values to service learning programs. Because the community sees that the school is responsive to its needs, vital community support for education can result. Significantly, research evidence indicates that service learning curricula lead to a decrease in truancy and vandalism, while demonstrating an increase in student achievement.

As the community and the students, in particular, become more aware of the balance between rights and responsibilities, they become more attentive to the reasons for a quality educational experience. Service learning is a scholarly encounter that embraces civic commitment to our local community, while strengthening the democratic traditions of our nation. ●

Linking Students in the Classroom with Their Communities through Service Learning

Q: How is service learning different from community service or internships? Aren't there already a number of volunteer programs in schools that do the same thing?

A: Service learning is different from a school's volunteer programs. In essence, service learning is both a philosophy of education and an instructional method with direct ties to a school's curriculum.

Philosophically, service learning promotes the idea that education should put a high value on social responsibility in preparing students to live in a democratic society. As a methodological approach, service learning is a blend of service activities stemming from the academic curriculum, which get students actively involved in meeting genuine and indigenous community needs.

There is another difference among service learning, community service, and internships. In volunteer community service (e.g., working in a soup kitchen), the primary beneficiary is the individual being served. In an internship (e.g., student teaching), the service provider is the one who primarily benefits. In service learning, we get the best of both worlds. True service learning requires that both the service providers and the service recipients derive a benefit.

Seen from the vantage point of school curriculum, service learning contextualizes student academic achievement and social growth. It provides an atmosphere in which students can develop problem-solving, organizational, and team skills to help them in future work and learning. In other words, service learning is geared to connect students to their communities by actively engaging them in the learning process as they meet human needs.

Correspondingly, service learning exposes students to diverse groups of people from different backgrounds, ages, and cultures, while making the students aware of community issues rooted in the school's curriculum. Another way to define service learning is through the worthwhile activities in which the students are actively engaged.

Let's look at a concrete example of service learning.

- In a high school class, English-speaking students are given English as a Second Language (ESL) texts to review.

- Under faculty supervision, these high school students administer a pretest to a group of ESL middle school students to determine the younger students' comprehension level.

- Next, following a brief training period, the high school students offer one-on-one lessons in English geared to the ESL middle school students' individual language needs.

- Then, the high school students administer a posttest to determine how effective their lessons were and what kind of language learning occurred.

- A mirror image of this program can be accomplished by using high school students who speak a language other than English (e.g., Spanish) and having them extend their abilities and talents to English-speaking Spanish as a Second Language (SSL) middle school students.

- The results of both programs would be a more biliterate school and society.

U.S. students want to do better in school, but they also want and need a better understanding of the ever more culturally and linguistically diverse communities in which they live. Service learning can actively help students learn, develop, and apply academic skills to address the real-life needs of their specific communities. ●

Nurturing Children of Mixed Heritage

Q: There is a lot going on in schools these days to make sure that everyone's culture is respected. Should schools do anything special to help out children from mixed backgrounds?

A: More than 100,000 multiracial children are born each year in the United States, according to the U.S. Bureau of the Census. If the parents and the schools give a positive social message of inclusion to these children, they will have an enhanced sense of self-esteem and greater intergroup tolerance. In addition, depending on what tongue is spoken at home, these children have the opportunity to increase their linguistic facility in more than one language.

However, given that racism is still a sad fact of life in many parts of the nation, developing a positive identity can be a real challenge for a multiracial child. When a child comes from a background of mixed racial, ethnic, or cultural ancestry, it is important that the youngster develop a multiracial identity that promotes pride in the richness of his or her heritage.

In the school, children from mixed heritages need to be exposed to models of all ethnicities, and also to specific multiracial models. These role models can range from Jennifer Lopez to Tiger Woods to community members who understand the culturally linked coping skills necessary to succeed in today's society.

By the way, "superstars" like Paula Abdul, Christina Aguilera, Norah Jones, and Lenny Kravitz are important for these children. These personalities receive a measure of coverage from mass media that makes them appear "valued" as singers and dancers. This has an undeniable effect (from liberating to stereotypically limiting) on the attitudes of multiracial children as well as youngsters of other backgrounds.

The school, which must be aware of these shifting cultural attitudes, must also be unswerving in its role of fostering universal respect for all students. This means that there should be no dual curricular tracks as found today in most U.S. schools. Advanced, honors, or gifted classes for the chosen few, with watered-down curricula for the many, have a research-based record of dividing schools along racial lines.

Instead of shortchanging students of mixed heritage in terms of respect and expectations, schools should consciously develop an enriched core curriculum that "looks like the students." Curriculum is at the heart of instruction. Core studies that highlight a pantheon of diverse heroes who transcend ethnic boundaries give a positive message of inclusion and acceptance to all students.

Here are some ideas for devising a service learning project in the arts for children of mixed heritage:

- Consider an art festival based on art from around the world.

- Write a curricular unit for an art class based on works of international artists.

- Invite a wide diversity of local artists to the classroom to share their art.

- Consider works that merge artistic effort and indigenous community need—for example, public murals celebrating multiethnic heritage, school murals honoring multiethnic educators, and art that changes common appliances into learning tools (e.g., old refrigerators turned into mini libraries, with creative multiethnic art on the outside of the refrigerator shell, and books and other learning materials emphasizing our common diverse heritage kept inside the unit).

- Assign art projects that use this diversity-based curricular model so students can demonstrate the new learning they have gained by sharing that knowledge with the entire community through newly created works of art.

- Inform local radio and TV stations about your project and your willingness to share your activities with their listening and viewing audiences.

You may find that projects like these change a passive, reactive learning environment into a proactive atmosphere that positively impacts not only your class but also the surrounding community. ●

Extending the School Day

Q: In addition to making what is taught more interesting and using a lot of different approaches to teach students, what more should schools and communities be doing to help youngsters?

A: They should be doing a lot, because there is a lot to be done. Remember that the percentage of time a student, kindergarten through twelfth grade, actually spends in the classroom is only 9 percent. It is that other 91 percent of a youngster's life, spent outside the classroom, which demands our attention.

One thing all students need desperately is an ongoing enrichment program. These programs provide activities that promote not only basic skills, but also higher-order critical thinking skills. There are many possible programs that can provide this kind of quality enrichment. The trick is that rather than reading or talking about a topic, the student should learn by doing:

- Playwrights club—writes and performs theatre

- Science research group—performs experiments that really "send up a rocket"

- Arts and crafts club—produces "works of art," such as gifts for sale

- Journalism class—actually publishes a newspaper

- Garden club—grows various plants

These kinds of extracurricular opportunities are common for students enrolled in schools in higher socioeconomic districts. We need such programs for all children, regardless of the geographic location of the school or the socioeconomic makeup of the student body.

Service learning can provide youngsters with experiences related to schoolwork in a wide variety of community environments. Everyone needs a sense of belonging as well as a practical belief in one's self-efficacy. Enrichment programs can provide both.

To sum up, enrichment experiences away from the classroom can provide youngsters with a wealth of opportunities to learn. That special kind of real-world learning may stimulate an interest or a career that can last a lifetime. ●

The Most Popular Class Is the One Least Taught

Q: What are the most popular classes taught to youngsters in school? Are schools making those classes available to students?

A: Science classes always rate at or near the top in popularity for students in the lower grades, yet science courses are taught less than other subjects at the elementary level. Research indicates that elementary school teachers feel unprepared in the content area, and this insecurity leads to few reading assignments in science and even fewer science experiments. As a result, little time is devoted to science at the elementary level.

Thus, many students come unprepared to high school science classes and predictably drop out of their biology, chemistry, and physics classes at an alarming rate. This dropout problem is especially prominent among minority children and girls.

Working from the premise that effort creates ability, let's outline the kind of program elementary schools should be offering all their students. Here are six positive outcomes for students that can make the most popular class the most attended class, by integrating service learning into the science curriculum:

• **Awaken student interest:** Service learning built into a school's science curriculum uses legitimate community issues to spark student awareness. It provides ground zero training for scientific issues related to public health, ecology, and urban or rural planning.

• **Emphasize experimentation:** Science is popular because it is based on research and experimentation, and it allows us to change our beliefs based on new evidence. Active research (e.g., growing a school vegetable garden and sharing the harvest with those in need) is a way to demonstrate a planned scientific activity with a positive community benefit.

• **Point out the social consequences of science:** Scientific endeavor doesn't happen in a vacuum. Discovery and implementation of scientific knowledge have social consequences that range from the preservation of clean water to use of nuclear weapons. Problems and solutions which seem "beyond the reach" of students become within the reach of the community due to the forging of bonds between schools and community organizations.

• **Encourage self-directed scientific inquiry:** When students take on the responsibility of applying a scientific approach to a problem, they develop the kind of higher-order critical thinking skills (analysis, synthesis, and evaluation) needed to make objective decisions and conclusions to help their community.

• **Use the Internet:** Here is a technology tool that literally blows the walls off the library. Wonderful interactive sites abound, and they are as close as a click of a mouse. The Internet provides a convenient and asynchronous way to extend the science curricula to the home—and then to the community by a service learning project.

• **Emphasize research:** Science is all about action—performing the experiment, using the scientific method, and communicating the knowledge gained to the community. In short, science is about learning by doing.

We know that science is initially popular with students. The challenge is not to gain the students' interest but to devise a curriculum to maintain their fascination. Here, service learning can provide a local context that is concept-based, inquiry-oriented, problem solving, and thoroughly engaging.

Learning an enriched science curriculum through active student-centered experimentation within a service learning paradigm seems to be the key to more engaged students. ●

Oral History Project: A Winner from First Question to Final Presentation

Q: Some U.S. history classes require students to put together a project that will be graded as the final examination. What is a good project that would show students how interesting and important the study of history can be?

A: Students need some intellectual stimulation to increase their involvement in the USA. An oral history project is the kind of task that will enlighten students, in a special way, about our nation's past. Specifically, it will increase their active involvement in, knowledge of, and appreciation for U.S. history.

Oral history preserves a segment of recent history by using the eyes and ears of someone who actually lived through the experience. A video camera or tape recorder is a tool that allows students to capture a person's memories electronically. Using this record of another's firsthand experience, students will begin to comprehend the value of understanding one person's memories of a specific occurrence in the overall context of U.S. history.

To the scholar, U.S. history is not a set of isolated experiences, but a collective memory from many sources—many of them from people just like you.

Here is how you can convert an oral history project into a service learning project (i.e., integrating classroom learning while meeting a community need):

- Decide to interview people from a specific historical period.
- Enhance your listening ability and discussion skills by classroom mock interviews.
- Improve your organizational skills in seeing the project through from the first question to the final presentation by making an outline of questions to be asked—always being aware that a good interview is based on building questions based on the interviewee's responses.
- Choose a specific historical event (e.g., the Great Depression, World War II, the moon landing) and an interviewee who can act as a primary source to that event.
- Increase your knowledge of the historical event by means of the interview.
- Inform local radio and TV stations about your service learning project for wider distribution of what you have learned.

- Create an Internet site with transcripts or video/audio streaming of the oral history interviews and your conclusions.

After successful completion of an oral history project, you will understand how historical events affect the lives of real people. This particular service learning project may well give you a learning experience about our nation's past that you will never forget. ●

A Child's Success Is a Joint Mission

Q: What can you advise a parent to do with a student who really isn't organized? How does a parent help a smart student who fails classes and sees the teacher as some kind of enemy?

A: Here is a goal-oriented plan called "Mission: Success" that involves three dedicated people—the child, the child's teacher, and the parent—and has five steps. As you inform the parent of each step, keep in mind the explicit goal of student achievement. One solid bit of evidence of such achievement is daily classwork. Advise the parent to do the following:

- Meet with the child's teacher. In that meeting, be very specific about the kind of cooperation outlined in the next four steps of this process. Then, get a brief summary of what material has been covered in class over the last few weeks, and what is to be covered in this and next week's classes.

- Ask the teacher for a number of concise "intermediate" projects. These might include nightly homework assignments or parts (bitable chunks) of a longer project, such as a 500-word essay or making a study outline for a quiz.

- Ask the teacher to evaluate the child's work each day. Request a written evaluation (a paragraph or so) from the teacher for each school day in the next couple of weeks.

- Work at least an hour with the child each night. Take an active role in monitoring homework. Reading textbooks aloud may be appropriate.

- Go over the teacher's evaluation each day with the child.

Explain to the child that the teacher is not the "enemy," but part of a three-member team that is on a successful mission.

Remember to always show appreciation of the child's effort, regardless of the immediate outcome. Success may come slowly at first. Learning new material and starting new study habits is a try-fail, try-fail, try-succeed process.

There is, however, one thing to count on—effort plus dedication equals eventual achievement. The "Mission: Success" plan should stay in effect until the child's grades come up to everyone's satisfaction.

Have high expectations for the child. The confidence and "can do" attitude one models are both powerful and contagious.

Parent interest and positive expectations are crucial to a child's academic success. Research tells us over and over again that the most significant factor in a child's successful learning experience is parent involvement. ●

Eliminating Drug Abuse Requires a Team Approach

Q: It is an unfortunate fact that drugs continue to be a big problem in the world, especially for young people. What can schools do to help stop kids from using drugs?

A: A team approach to drug prevention is paramount. Schools must be part of a combined effort with parents, law enforcement, religious groups, various community organizations, and the media. As a team player, the school should do what it does best—not preach, indoctrinate, or moralize, but teach prevention strategies.

There are three major elements to an effective drug-prevention program at school:

- Involve drug-prevention strategies in the coursework. Classes in health, science, social studies and parenting, among others, should teach that drug use is illegal, harmful to your health, and detrimental to your intellectual and social growth.

- Involve credible young people who care. School-organized and supervised "peer leaders" (fellow students trained

in drug-prevention strategies) can send out a singular message: Stay sober and drug-free.

- Have a clear school drug policy with consequences. Because drugs are illegal, a student using drugs will be reported to the police. Because drugs are harmful, a student using drugs must undergo mandatory counseling.

One other point should be made. Schools and communities should have attractive alternate activities to drug use.

Just "saying no" is not enough. Young people need an appealing variety of things to which they can "say yes."

The maintenance and/or expansion of after-school activities, such as team sports, dance, or just keeping the school or public library open in the evening, should not be viewed as luxuries. They should be part of a comprehensive plan to say no to drugs and yes to responsible behavior, which should go hand in hand with the fun and adventure of being young. ●

After-School Programs to Entertain Children

Q: There are so many people, from the president of the United States on down to members of the city council, calling for more community involvement in educa-

tion. These days, lots of youngsters seem to have more time on their hands than ever before. Some of these young people can make a lot of mischief right after school, especially if they are on their own with no adult in charge. What can be done to be sure these students have some kind of wholesome activities between 3 P.M. and 6 P.M.?

A: In many families, both mother and father work or a single parent holds down a full-time position. As a consequence, too many children have nowhere to go when the afternoon school bell rings.

Some public libraries are serving the needs of a growing population known as "latchkey youth." These innovative public libraries have taken on a new role to build creative strategies to meet the needs of children after the final school bell. Library staff have been reallocated to provide story hours and after-school clubs during those hours.

Other drop-in activities such as arts and crafts have been set up in the library to serve the needs of latchkey children. Some programs recruit older adult volunteers to set up 4-H Clubs to make cookies, paint T-shirts, and work on other craft projects. Still other library programs have community volunteers teach survival skills, from food preparation to traffic safety.

When public libraries view themselves as a community resource and interact with representatives from other public and private agencies, positive outcomes for the children, the volunteers, and the community at large are possible. Successful public library programs view the latchkey phenomenon as an opportunity to provide a needed public service, as well as a chance to enlist a new generation of library patrons. ●

How to Turn Students into Good Citizens

Q: It seems that people in general, and young people in particular, are really turned off to the whole idea of being a responsible citizen. How can the schools get youngsters to be better citizens when they grow up?

A: Developing the civic attitudes of children is one of the main purposes of public education. Teaching about government and politics is not just desirable in a democracy, it is imperative. Here are some ways a school can develop responsible citizens for tomorrow:

- Establish school-generated initiatives that permit students to perform community service as a regular part of the curriculum.

- Design assignments that require students to take part in political activities outside the classroom.

- Teach the U.S. Constitution in ways that highlight the freedoms that so many take for granted, of which too many others are ignorant, and for which so many have given their lives.

- Infuse lessons about freedom, human dignity, and our collective responsibility to contribute our time and talents to the common good into all subjects at all levels.

- Implement cooperative learning experiences, in which true teamwork is needed to attain standards of excellence.

- Encourage students to read about the men and women who, through their involvement with civic life, have transmitted core democratic values.

- Require every student to conduct an ongoing analysis of current events as reported by newspapers, magazines, television, and the Internet.

- Develop assignments that relate to local, state, and even national leaders, and invite these people to the campus. This gives students the opportunity to more closely evaluate those to whom power has been entrusted, the principles they espouse, and the policies they advocate.

The very health of a free society depends on knowledge of the great issues of our day, the active participation of an informed citizenry, and the preservation of our rights as citizens of a free country. Public schools must be in the forefront of enhancing students' understanding of the rights and obligations of responsible citizenship. ●

Let's Get Down to Cases

Q: Where can one find studies of everyday classroom problems?

A: Case study methods entail a descriptive report of what has taken place over time and allow us to formulate an in-depth look at a single classroom instance or event. It is a systematic way to look at reality, collect data, analyze information, and evaluate a given situation.

In an illustrative case study the researcher utilizes one or two instances to present a picture of what a situation is really like. This kind of case study presents an opportunity to give the readers an agreed-on language to understand the topic. In other words, it helps to make the unfamiliar familiar.

Another kind of case study is the exploratory case study, which is condensed investigation (as opposed to a large-scale one). This kind of study helps identify questions, select measurement constructs, and develop measurement tools. As with case studies in general, this approach works especially well for generating, rather than testing, hypotheses.

Obviously, classroom situations are highly contextualized. Case studies are made for those kinds of reality-based incidences. Fundamentally, the case study is a methodological approach to learn about a complex "happening" through a representative description leading to appropriate in-context analysis.

That brings us to a major pitfall of case studies—can they be generalized? Imagine that you inspect two square feet of freeway, situated on the road from San Diego to Los Angeles.

Within those two square feet you may describe with great accuracy the texture of the pavement, the presence or lack of potholes, the amount or lack of debris. The information may well be accurate for those two square feet, but what does it say about the rest of the 121.8 miles between San Diego and Los Angeles?

For example, how can one be sure that the two square feet selected for the study can serve as an example for the rest of the highway? Sometimes the highway turns into a ramp, passes large cities, or comes quite close to the ocean. Structural, traffic, and geographical variety affect the physical state of the highway. You can see the problem if we attempt to generalize our results.

Clearly, a limitation for our imaginary case study is the inadequate representation of diversity. Thus, case studies must adequately represent the situation under study or inappropriate conclusions may be reached.

One way to do a case study without the cost and time of embarking on many new case studies is to "mine the data" through a cumulative case study. One carefully aggregates relevant information from studies done in the past. This kind of retrospective cumulation (particular techniques in this method ensure sufficient comparability and quality) allows for more precise generalizations.

Recall that the classroom case study is a descriptive research document, often presented as a narrative and always based on a real-life situation or event.

Cases are created in order to generate active analysis and interpretation. As a teacher you may find any given case of great interest as you explore, analyze, and examine representations of actual classrooms.

A case study can frame a conversation among practitioners who approach the same narrative from different perspectives.

Here are three ways to use case studies:

1. **As exemplars:** Case studies present opportunities to affirm current theory or build new theory as you determine best practice.
2. **As opportunities to analyze or plan action:** Within the context of the classroom, problem analysis can lead to enlightened decisions, which define appropriate action.
3. **As reflection:** Personal professional knowledge and wisdom are based on introspection and higher-order critical thinking (analysis, synthesis, and evaluation)

Finally, case study evaluation presents an alternative to conventional research based on large samples, rigid guidelines, and a limited number of variables. In contrast, the case study presents the teacher-researcher with a methodology that sharpens our understanding of reality and the direction for future research and informed action. ●

3 . . . , 2 . . . , 1 . . . , Action!

Q: Teachers should be involved in decisions about what to teach and how to teach it, but what do classroom practitioners have to do to make their choices the right ones?

A: Without a doubt, teachers should be at the forefront of curricular and methodological decisions at their school. Having said that, it is crucial that the decisions made about the teaching and learning that go on in the classroom be based on informed judgments.

Informed pedagogical determinations are data-driven. Teachers must be deliberate in documenting and evaluating their practice in order to bring empirical evidence to bear on curricular and methodological choices.

One means to reach that end is action research. As a model, action research helps teachers develop policy to best meet the needs of all learners. Action research projects can identify problems, systematically collect information, and provide reflective analysis—plus implement data-driven action plans to produce positive classroom outcomes.

When a teacher "tries out a new idea" as part of an action research proposal, the results of that investigation increase knowledge about what works best for the learner. Action research centers on the daily practical challenges that arise in the classroom setting—the approach is naturalistic and uses the ethnographic research technique of participant-observation.

Moreover, teachers in an action research project can form a team. This group of educators can pool their efforts to define and act on a specific action research project. This kind of group effort can promote professional dialogue and consequently break down the kind of "four-wall" isolation so commonplace in the profession.

So how does this kind of reflective practice work? Take a look at the Ask the Teacher article entitled "Integrated Approach to Language Arts Pays Off," in Unit 8. That article mentions more than just the five approaches used to implement

a common learning experience based on the consistent use of listening, speaking, reading, and writing on a daily basis.

Significantly, the article also mentions norm-referenced pretests and posttests, which measure students in terms of reading comprehension scores before and after the intervention. In that action research project, the basic plan (pretest, intervention, posttest) provided data that could then be evaluated.

As it turned out, the results were happily impressive and led to a more informed practice on the part of the instructor.

To be engaged in this kind of reflective participation helps all educators develop the kind of problem-solving techniques and decision-making processes for designing class activities that "really work."

Action research can also focus on teacher and student attitudes that affect both academic development and social growth. By incorporating reflective analysis into evaluating what and how they teach, teachers can explore their attitudes and the implications of their classroom practices.

Using action research presents an opportunity to gain an understanding of the power of applied research and become aware of the options and alternatives teachers have in making informed decisions about the curriculum (what is taught) and methodological choices (how something is taught).

Action research has the primary benefit of providing a means to reflectively analyze the intersection of theory and practice and then to improve our knowledge of what works best in the classroom as a vital part of continuous professional growth. ●

SUGGESTED READINGS

Alloy, L. B., Abramson, L. Y., Tashman, N., Berrebbi, D. S., Hogan, M. E., Whitehouse, W. G., Crossfield, A. G., & Morocco, A. (2001). Developmental origins of cognitive vulnerability to depression: Parenting, cognitive, and inferential feedback styles of the parents of individuals at high and low cognitive risk for depression. *Cognitive Therapy and Research, 25,* 397–423.

Bos, C. S., & Vaughn, S. (2002). *Strategies for teaching students with learning and behavior problems* (5th ed.). Boston: Allyn and Bacon.

Bowman, D. H. (2001, September 19). After-school programs proliferate; funding, staffing seen as problems. *Education Week, 21*(3), 6.

Capizzano, J., Tout, K., & Adams, G. (2000). *Child care patterns for school-age children with employed mothers.* Washington, DC: The Urban Institute.

Ellis, J., Small-McGinley, J., & De Fabrizio, L. (2001). *Caring for kids in communities: Using mentorship, peer support, & student leadership programs in schools.* New York: P. Lang.

Fashola, O. S. (2002). *Building effective afterschool programs.* Thousand Oaks, CA: Corwin Press.

Field, S., & Hoffman, A. (2002). Preparing youth to exercise self-determination: Quality indicators of school environments that promote the acquisition of knowledge, skills and beliefs related to self-determination. *Journal of Disability Policy Studies, 13,* 113–118.

Grossman, J. B. (2002, October 23). Making after-school count. *Education Week, 22*(8), 31.

Markey, U. (2000). PARtnerships. *Journal of Positive Behavior Interventions, 2*(3), 188–189, 192.

McEwan, E. K. (2001). *10 traits of highly effective teachers: How to hire, coach, and mentor successful teachers.* Thousand Oaks, CA: Corwin Press.

Noam, G. G., Biancarosa, G., & Dechausay, N. (2002). *Afterschool education: Approaches to an emerging field.* Cambridge, MA: Harvard Education Press.

Pitman, M. A., & Zorn, D. (Eds.). (2000). *Caring as tenacity: Stories of urban school survival.* Crosskill, NJ: Hampton Press.

Portner, H. (2002). *Being mentored: A guide for protégés.* Thousand Oaks, CA: Corwin Press.

Reiman, A. J., & Thies-Sprinthall, L. (1998). *Mentoring and supervision for teacher development.* New York: Longman.

Ryan, R. M., & Deci, E. L. (2000). Self-determination theory and the facilitation of intrinsic motivation, social development, and well-being. *American Psychologist, 55,* 68–78.

Walker, K. E., Grossman, J. B., & Raley, R. (2000). *Extended-service schools: Putting programming in place.* Philadelphia: Public/Private Ventures.

Wehmeyer, M. (2002). Self-determination and the education of students with disabilities. *ERIC EC Digest #E632.* Arlington, VA: ERIC Clearinghouse on Disabilities and Gifted Education.

Wilgoren, J. (2000, January 24). The Bell Rings and the Students Stay. *The New York Times,* p. A1.

UNIT :10

Tools of the Trade

It's Important to Travel the Information Highway

Q: Some high schools have computers in the administration building for the secretaries and the principal, but not in the classrooms. What can students do if they don't have computers at home or at school? What would be the cost to put computers in every classroom?

A: Right now, available computers for students are not evenly spread. Some classrooms are fully equipped with a computer for every student and are wired to the Internet. Other schools are teaching as if they were still in the 1950s. We depend on computer technology more than ever. The proliferation of this technology can be gleaned in the following U.S. Department of Education factoids, which provide some ideas regarding student access to 21st century technology:

- In 2003, the ratio of students to computers in all public schools was 4.4 to 1.

- 48 states included technology standards for students in 2004–2005.

- In 2003, 8 percent of public schools lent laptop computers to students. In those schools, the median number of laptop computers available for loan was five.

- Many children depend on computer technology to accomplish their schoolwork. Research indicates that 44 percent of students use computers and 42 percent of students use the Internet for their assignments.

Teachers should advise students to keep investigating for computers they can access at school, the public library, or even a friend's house. The field of education is undergoing profound changes due to new understandings about how we learn and the application of new computer-based technologies.

Far from being a fad, computers affect curriculum (what we learn) and methodol-

ogy (how we teach). The 21st century is an information age. It's a good idea to get on the information highway, even if you have to "hitchhike" on a borrowed computer. ●

Computers' Impact on Education

Q: Everyone is talking about the impact computers are having on education. Do teachers really teach differently because they have their students work on computers?

A: Teaching and learning are undergoing profound changes due to the use of computer technology. Allan Collins, a cognitive psychologist, has indicated a number of significant changes in the classroom as a direct result of new technology:

- A shift from whole-class to small-group instruction. Teacher-centered activities are clearly decreased when computers are used.

- A shift from working with better students to working with weaker students. More time is spent with those who need it most.

- A shift from assessment based on test performance to assessment based on products, progress, and effort. In other words, the traditional "do-or-die" end-of-unit tests have reached the end of the road.

- A shift from all students learning the same things to different students learning different things. Computers are geared to the skills and interests of a particular student. Therefore, learning is more individual.

The overall duties of a teacher are much more like those of a coach than a lecturer. Computers do, indeed, change the way teachers teach and assess the learner. In other words, this is no hype. The new technology affects teaching methodology. It provides a gateway to innovative instruction. ●

Why Every Student Isn't on the Information Highway

Q: You can't turn on the radio or watch TV without being told about the wonders of the computer age. Every restaurant, department store, or gas station has at least one computer up and running. If the information highway is so important, why don't the schools get on the job and make sure every student has a computer?

A: It has been said that the information highway is a toll road. The challenge facing schools is more than just buying new computers. The issue of equitable access is critical. To a growing number of educators, access to the Internet is now viewed as a legitimate civil rights issue.

The Markle Foundation found back in 1995 the same social and racial inequities in society existed in online access. Hence, the term "digital divide" was coined to describe the haves and the have-nots of cyberspace. The U.S. Department of Education reports that only 41 percent of African American and Latino students use a computer at home compared to 77 percent of white students. Moreover, whereas 31 percent of students from families earning less than $20,000 use computers at home, 89 percent of students from families earning more than $75,000 are using computers—nearly three times as many.

Let's look at who is using computers to complete homework assignments. The majority of white students (52 percent) are finishing homework on a computer, whereas only 28 percent of African American students and 27 percent of Latino students are completing their assignments on a computer at home.

It is important to note that there is no racial or ethnic difference in computer use to complete homework—if a computer is present in the home. The reason white students are using computers at nearly twice the rate of African American and Latino students is a function of the haves and have nots—namely, access to a home computer.

Disparities during the 1990s between poor and affluent schools regarding in-school access to the Internet, according to a 2006 study by the Federal Communications Commission, seemed to have improved as a result of the government E-Rate program. The U.S. Department of Education and the Urban Institute reported that the program, funded by subsidies taken from monthly phone bills, has assisted in connecting 95 percent of the nation's schools to the Internet—up from only 65 percent back in the mid 1990s. Roadblocks to the cost of Internet access in the classroom, which once caused a digital divide, appear to be being removed. ●

Computers in the Classroom

Q: Are there some alternative ways to get computers into the classroom in schools that cannot afford them?

A: Here is a wonderful example of what a creative teacher can accomplish. This woman teaches fifth grade in the inner city. One of her friends works for a large corporation. When they upgraded their computers, the teacher convinced the corporation to donate the computers to her class as a tax write-off. She also has a friend who owns a small computer-repair shop, and he keeps her computers in working order.

It was a lot of work to get all of this done, but she keeps working for "her kids." She has spent a lot of her own money for programs and extras for her class. Because her school is in a very poor area, she has to do that or her kids would do without. She feels they need every break they can get.

This teacher's inspirational work allows all of her students to use modern technology in the classroom. One thing about inspiration: It is contagious. Inspired teachers lead to inspired students. ●

Why Computers Are Important

Q: When a student has to write an essay, does a computer have any real advantage over a ballpoint pen and composition paper?

A: When it comes to creativity and original thought, writing is writing, whether it is done

on a computer, a piece of parchment, or a clay tablet. There is, however, one great advantage the computer has for students of all ages. The ease with which one can revise work on a computer has changed the way students write essays. In the old days of pen and paper—or even typewriters—minor revisions meant doing everything over again. Besides the drudgery involved, more often than not new mistakes (spelling, grammar, diction) would occur.

Today, teachers can demand error-free essays as a performance standard after final revisions are made. With computer memory, a student changes only the errors, while other parts of the paper remain unchanged. Students can now proof and revise their papers, knowing that once the revisions are made, they have created a product that will meet performance standards.

This may sound pretty mundane, but the effect of computer-generated work is quite significant for teachers who want the final copy of any essay to be of the highest quality. ●

Getting Started on Computers

Q: We hear so much about this being a computer age. How can students become involved in getting their schools hooked up?

A: One of the great advantages of today's technology is the exciting immediate interaction between students and instructors on a worldwide scale. Computer networking is causing an information explosion. It is the kind of blast schools cannot afford to miss.

Basically, only three things are needed to get hooked up:

- Access to a computer
- A modem
- Internet access

Then you are ready to travel into cyberspace, free of the normal time constraints in school (can we ever get rid of those bells?) and those confining classroom walls. There

is a trio of resources that will allow you to network with the rest of humanity:

- Email
- File transfer
- Computer conferencing

Remember that a computer without a modem and a phone line (or even high-speed access) is like a plane that can't fly—pretty to look at, but it won't get you where you want to go.

Now it's time to make the next road you travel the information highway. I invite you to journey to www.ablongman.com.

How to Distribute Computers on Campus

Q: In a high school with 1,000 students and 400 computers, it sounds like a computer-literate student body would be a cinch. The fact is, however, that most students at the school never use the computers. The computers are spread thinly from room to room. There are three or four computers in one classroom, five or six in another.

With class loads exceeding 30 students, the entire class can't use them at one time, so only a very small number of students use computers and use is sporadic. It doesn't seem we are making the most out of our technology. Are there any solutions to this problem?

A: Teachers and schools are still figuring out operational plans to use new technology on campus. Many schools seem to be in a period of technological transition, and computers are spread thinly across the campus.

Of course, the first priority in a school's technology plan should be universal stu-

dent access to on-site computers. But until a school can fully supply the classrooms with enough computers so that students can use them when they need them, an interim solution must be found.

One approach that will permit many students routine use of computers is to set up a computer center on campus. A single room with 30 or 40 computers should be set aside, and a full-time teaching assistant should be hired. Teachers then can sign up to take their entire class for one of the six instructional hours each day.

The results of this system have been quite positive. Students who had regularly scheduled access to the computer center turned in a greater number of high-quality essays, reports, and term papers than they had before the computer center was operational. Thus, as scheduled class trips to the computer center became routine, both the quality and the quantity of work grew. With the cost of portable computers decreasing, notebook computers and other portable devices give districts the option to present students their own device. Technology rooms are becoming more and more passé as preloaded systems with wireless networking enable students to travel with their technology through time and space.

Every school has different needs. However, regular student access to the best technology available should be a common goal for all schools. ●

Are Computers Worth the Expense?

Q: Computers in the classroom are all the rage, but trends in education come and go. How much are we spending on computers for schools, and how do we know that these expensive machines make a difference?

A: These questions are of concern to every taxpayer. The United States spent an estimated $10 billion in 2006 on education technology. That sounds like a

lot of money—and it is. The fact is that computers are becoming more prolific as the technology of choice for more and more students. The U.S. Census Bureau reports that there are 14.2 million computers available for classroom use in the nation's 114,700 elementary and secondary schools in the 2005–2006 school year. For youngsters ages 3 to 17

- 83 percent use the computer
- 43 percent use the Internet
- 75 percent, whether at home, school, or elsewhere, use a computer to complete school assignments
- 66 percent use a computer at home to complete school assignments

As to whether computers are making a difference, it does appear that education technology has an impact on student performance. Recent findings indicate that students taking computer-based instruction have greater self-confidence, higher self-esteem and more motivation to learn. The most dramatic results are said to be found among students with special needs and students with a record of low academic achievement.

Computers with the Internet, multimedia curricula, and other two-way collaborative packages, are a gateway to knowledge. This technology has the potential to impact every student in the nation regardless of socioeconomic status, geographical location, or level of education. ●

Technology in Today's Schools

Q: With all the emphasis today on technology in the classroom, what has happened to the humanities, music, poetry, and being creative? Is this emphasis on technology such a good thing for students and teachers?

A: First, let us define technology. Technology seems to be, in the minds of many, a new phenomenon born in the later stages of the 20th century. In fact, technology has been a part of human history since humans shaped and used the first stone tool.

It has been said that technology is the "how" that links the "what is" to "what should be." It has been our constant companion through the ages in the form of tools, systems, and approaches to help us better manage our environment.

The word *techné* originally meant the knowledge to get the job done. In order to be truly educated, a person must be, to some degree, technologically literate.

The accelerated pace of technological change in the world must be reflected in the modern classroom. Schools today are constantly trying to catch up to technological advances and bring them into a classroom setting. This does not mean that all technology in the classroom is effective in getting the job done.

Let's review the three most common approaches found in today's schools:

- **The additive approach:** Technological tools (computer, DVD, other media) are added to regular instruction as a supplement to basic instruction.

This approach is not always effective in having a significant impact on student achievement.

- **The integrated approach:** Carefully selected tools and materials are integrated into regular instruction. With extensive planning and preparation, this approach has the potential to be effective in creating a significant increase in student achievement.

- **The independent approach:** Instruction is totally reformatted so that an active integration of individuals, materials, and machines—with the direct intervention of the teacher—brings about the desired educational outcomes. This approach has the greatest potential to increase student achievement, and it is also cost-effective.

The cost-effective nature of the independent approach stems from the notion that teachers must shift from simply dispensing knowledge to managing learning. In other words, when a computer or video can present a concept as well or better than a teacher can—use the tool!

As the computer dispenses basic information about a subject to most of the class, smaller groups can meet with the teacher for more intensive and personalized instruction. When teachers can concentrate, for example, on small-group activities in music or individualized education in poetry, creative outcomes can be anticipated. This kind of intimate rapport building between teacher and student, which educational technology can assist by being a dispenser of knowledge, is the hallmark of effective teaching. ●

Computer Age Changes Librarians' Roles

Q: In the Computer Age, who needs school libraries and librarians? With nearly everything available on the Internet, are libraries—filled with books and run by librarians—still necessary in the age of the online computer?

A: This is an insightful question. Times are changing, and librarians should be in the forefront of technological change. Although traditional ways of doing things in school appear at times impervious to new technology, it seems obvious that revolutionary changes in how we access information should significantly change the role of a school librarian.

Rather than lessening the role of a librarian, however, the addition of online technology expands the role of this information expert. The position is less one of a relatively passive manager of a warehouse and more one of an active information specialist.

With new information from a myriad of resources, the librarian actually can have a more direct impact on classroom curriculum than ever before. Collaboration with teachers and students is key. New technologies mean greater information retrieval that leads to the prospect of a greatly enhanced learning environment in the classroom.

For the librarian who has transitioned from warehouse manager to information specialist, many "new hats" must be worn. Each new hat actually extends the librarian's influence on campus, for in order to do the job, he or she must be:

- A resource consultant
- A locator and buyer of needed hardware and software materials
- A learning strategist
- A facilitator of technologies
- An instructor of teachers and students in the best ways to use the new technologies

This, of course, means that the librarians themselves must be quite knowledgeable and proficient in using all the technological "gadgets," which they must then teach to instructors and students.

Online sources are of increasing importance to librarians. Whereas "ownership" of information (books) characterized their position in the past, access to information (online, CDs, DVDs, or video) becomes the new criteria for evaluating librarians.

In many basic ways, a World Wide Web of information has replaced the walls of the library, but one thing remains constant: The knowledge of students and what they are studying remains fundamental to library service. ●

Learning on the Internet

Q: What are the educational options for two parents who equally share the responsibilities of bringing up three children under the age of five? Both parents want to spend as much time as possible at home with the youngsters, but they also want to continue their own education. Are correspondence courses a good way to go?

A: New alternatives brought about by new technology can make your home a virtual campus. The traditional correspondence course, the earliest form of distance learning, has gone through many waves of technological change. Advances such as audiotape, videotape, radio, and television and satellite transmissions have delivered education packages to the learner for decades.

More recently, desktop and notebook computers, the Internet, and the World Wide Web are making their own tremendous impact in distance learning. Just on the horizon, artificial intelligence and virtual reality may bring the next new wave of distance learning.

Of paramount significance, distance learning embodies two things that you are looking for—learner-centeredness and control. Distance learning is the use of various technologies to deliver media and connect individuals when time or distance separates teachers and learners. What this means is that anyone with a computer can be a distance learner. This indicates a profound change in the delivery of education.

The seemingly concrete barriers of time and space in teaching and learning are crumbling. Presently, there are numerous educational institutions offering online instruction and corporate training. Well-known schools such as Penn State and Indiana University are offering online degree programs.

Exactly how is this done? The following list indicates some of the ways teachers link up with learners in modern-day distance learning:

- **Email:** Delivers course materials, feedback, discussion groups
- **Informatics:** Use of online databases, library catalogs, websites
- **Bulletin boards:** Discuss particular topics
- **Downloading:** Obtain course materials or tutorials

To parents who must divide each day among many family tasks, the advantages of learning on the Internet are quite straightforward. First, the obvious flexibility of time and place of educational experience gives new options to the student. Asynchronous study (getting online at any hour of the day or night to self-direct your education) is quite popular.

Second, the possibility of reaching teachers and students worldwide from your home in the pursuit of your studies clearly expands your learning opportunities. Third, access to current information that is constantly updated (unlike the 40-volume set of encyclopedias in your bookcase) provides a virtually boundless resource of knowledge.

What is needed is a commitment to learning. After all, learner motivation, self-discipline, and responsibility are requisites to a quality formal education on campus, in class or at home online. ●

The Best Kind of School Technology Plans

Q: It is hard to go to a PTA meeting these days without seeing the subject of computers in schools on the agenda. Almost everyone thinks computers are a good idea, but how do we know if we are using these expensive machines correctly? What does effective use of computers in the classroom look like?

A: To begin, let's agree on three basic premises in building a school's technology program:

1. Computers are a tool for learning. Teachers must still teach with enthusiasm, and students must still approach learning with vigor.
2. Computers cost money. Each school must establish a realistic level of financial and human (staff development) investment that it is willing to make.

3. Computers should be an integral part of the reformatted curriculum. An active integration of individuals, materials, and machines can add up to desired educational outcomes.

Keeping these three conditions in mind, here is a list (suitable for a PTA meeting) of what to do to make your school's technology program enhance student achievement:

1. Ensure universal access to the new technology (i.e., students get computer time when they need it) for all students on an equitable basis.
2. Create an interactive online environment where relevant issues are investigated.

3. Use different computer-based technologies (e.g., word processing, asynchronous audio and video access, the World Wide Web) in order to adapt to a myriad of different learning styles.

4. Develop programs that maintain interaction between teacher and student. The computer is not a substitute teacher.

5. Begin computer-based instruction by reinforcing basic skills where necessary. Next, move towards using this technology to strengthen critical thinking skills (analysis, synthesis, and evaluation).

6. Emphasize heterogeneous groupings of students in the computer lab and on the Internet. In teaching collaborative social skills, the computer offers an opportunity for the learner to communicate with an ever more diverse group of students.

A school technology program that follows these steps will be most effective in combining the best of technology and education. ●

Technology Offers a Big Plus to the Instructional Process

Q: Schools have spent billions on computers in the last 30 years. Do people really learn more—do they really learn things faster? Is there any research to tell us if all this new technology is really worth it?

A: First, let's consider the use of technology in basic skills programs, such as computer assisted instruction (CAI). The evidence gleaned from more than a generation of using computer technology to teach basic skills has shown conclusively that students learn more, and more rapidly, in courses with CAI. The gains are across the curricula, from regular education to special education, from preschool through university.

The military, in which short and efficient training time is a high priority, presents corresponding strong indications about the efficacy of CAI. In fact, CAI can cut military training time by one-third, and can be a more potent cost-effective factor than increasing instructional time, adding tutors, or decreasing class size.

As successful as basic skill programs are, they are only very small parts of what is now offered in the ever-expanding realm of educational technology. Elaborate multimedia products and an ever more highly evolved online network technology have given millions of students the power to research subjects, complete learning tasks, and communicate messages. As students are empowered by this new technology, they now have more control over what, how, and when they learn.

It is hard to overestimate the dynamic impact of computer technology in the field of education. For example, what better library can one have than the Internet? Online capacity virtually blows away the bookroom's walls—the "shelves" of the online library are practically infinite. Even with the most basic navigating skills, students can access quality information from a practically limitless storehouse of knowledge—which is updated with every tick of the clock.

Imagine knowledge as an ever-expanding and thus ever-changing entity. Accordingly, the new educational technology has forever changed the way we learn and even the way we think.

If computer technology is integrated at the center of what is being studied, learning should never again be the mere acquisition of a defined and static body of information, but instead a never-ending quest in an ever-changing boundless universe of knowledge. ●

The Potential of Distance Education

Q: There are so many new educational opportunities, especially for adults, on the Internet. What are the advantages and disadvantages of distance education? What do teachers need to know that they don't know now to be able to teach on the Internet?

A: Distance learning solves access problems. Walking to your home computer is easier than commuting to a college campus. There is also evidence that distance learning is friendly to a student's pocketbook. In Florida, there is confirmation that certain distance learning models decrease students' time-to-degree.

On the other hand, there are real concerns over copyright and intellectual property rights issues. Since the Internet contains an ever-expanding reservoir of information, there exists a gray area over ownership of certain online materials. What are called for are explicit policy guidelines establishing ownership, fair use, or duplication of materials produced by publishers, faculty, students, or the school.

Quality control of virtual universities is another issue. Distance education simply requires a different evaluation paradigm than conventional classroom education. There needs to be a consensus among all educational entities on the indicators of successful student achievement in distance education. Furthermore, such an evaluation design must ensure consistent data collection, incorporate state goals, and fulfill national guidelines in order to qualify for federal funding.

Of course, all authentic educational change is dependent on faculty acceptance and implementation. A teacher's successful adaptation to technology is in many ways contingent on understanding how new technology affects both teaching and learning. Profound changes in the physical educational environment bring about a fundamental shift in the cognitive psychology of learning.

For instance, in distance education there is a transformation from all students learning the same things to different students learning different things. In addition, there is a change from the primacy of verbal thinking to the integration of visual, auditory, and verbal thinking. In short, the focus of the traditional educational endeavor shifts from teaching to learning.

Other factors in the successful adoption of distance education by faculty are ease of use, real educational value, and an appreciation of the revolutionary impact of distance education. On this last point, higher education faculty must come to realize that distance education at the collegiate level can provide a one-stop educational shopping center for a constituency that is truly worldwide.

Distance education must be perceived as a single wire that links the classroom, library, career placement center, workplace, and home. The immense and as yet untapped potential of distance education knows no boundaries. ●

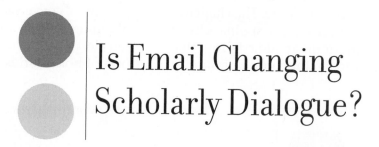

Is Email Changing Scholarly Dialogue?

Q: Many universities and even high schools have started online programs. Does the use of email messages between teachers and students change how a course is learned? Can a student really get a quality education online?

A: There is no doubt that online courses are redefining the learning environment in terms of both time and space. As the content of teacher and student interactions is altered by computer mediated communication, learning is undeniably transformed.

Researchers have referred to email as electronic written messages that take the place of voicing ideas. In an electronic message, the difference between writing and talking gets blurred because of the peculiar manner in which email messages are formed.

Although one cannot be interrupted when expressing thoughts in writing an email message, there are significant similarities between an oral dialogue and computer mediated communication. Because most users reportedly spend little if any time planning, writing, and revising email, these electronic messages can be characterized as spontaneous.

Some researchers believe that it is the spontaneity which is responsible for rampant misspelling, nonstandard punctuation, and irregular lexical usage. On the other hand, research in the United Kingdom found email was more similar to written than spoken language because of a richer use of vocabulary.

Although some aspects of email communications may resemble oral or written language, it seems clear that this kind of written talk changes the way we interact, and therefore think. In other words, how we learn and communicate determines what we learn.

As academic discussions take place in this new form of written talk, a fundamental question should be addressed. Does the informal or even conversational tone of computer mediated academic discussion affect the quality of thought and interaction?

The answer may be found in the quality of the academic prose within the electronic message. Although informal and conversational email messages have their place in demonstrating that knowledge, the use of standard grammar and a well-defined lexicon should not be dismissed as mere relics of an age gone by. Precise complex critical thought relies heavily on nuance and specificity. What is called for is not lexical density but unambiguous expression.

Accordingly, short phrases and incomplete thoughts, common in many email communications, are no substitute for the short declarative sentence. Uncorrected misspellings, prevalent in many email messages, simply get in the way of clarity. Clearly, in the age of the "spellcheck," these mistakes are easily remedied with the click of a button.

Undeniably, email discourse offers an opportunity to write more. The challenge with email is to retain the spontaneity of thought without the muddled prose that inevitably leads to miscommunication.

With this in mind, a quality education can take place online not in spite of electronic discourse, but because of it. When a learner writes, he or she is given the opportunity, through the written word, to confront and clarify personal ambiguities.

The pathway to a quality education online is to retain the spontaneity and passion of conversational language, while planning, composing, and revising written electronic communications to get the best of both worlds. ●

Online Classes Change the Concepts of Time and Space

Q: Many high schools are now putting their classes online. How are online classes different than normal classes given at a school site?

A: Classes conducted in cyberspace take place in a learning atmosphere substantially free of the traditional notions of time and place. Such a radical change in the learning environment can cause anxiety on the part of the learner.

That is why it is crucial, from a student's first encounter with the online experience, that he or she feel welcomed and supported. These two requisites fulfilled, a student should begin to feel empowered. It seems self-evident that a "can do" attitude on the part of the student is necessary in order for this mode of education to have its most potent effect.

Accordingly, among the very first communications a student might have from the online teacher, at the top of the computer screen should be something like this: "Thank you for your interest in this course. Your awareness of this powerful new technology to educate is appreci-

ated. As we explore this subject together in cyberspace, remember that I am here for your success."

A teacher's screens should create a place where students can collect significant ideas through lectures and can express themselves through the threaded discussions, assignments, and essay exams. They should also make students feel increasingly secure that they are proceeding in the right direction.

Students don't want to choose between either autonomy or affiliation. They want and need both. Therefore, the online learning modules must provide an environment that promotes both thought-provoking independent learning activities (assignments and exams) and stimulating interdependent activities (threaded discussion and, in the not too distant future, audio and video conferencing).

The combination of cognitive and psychosocial support is imperative. The primary goals of all online courses remain the same as traditional on-site classes.

An online course uses the tools of computer technology in cyberspace to enrich and extend it. Online courses, which provide Internet links, offer up-to-the-moment access to information not ordinarily available in a traditional classroom setting. In addition, learning activities in an online course inherently support the acquisition of Internet-related skills. These are skills that will benefit the learner long after the class has been completed.

One of the limitations to this approach would be an instructor's unwillingness to learn, adapt, and develop new learning activities. These initial barriers can be overcome in a relatively short period of time by preservice and in-service training of teachers. Such training equips instructors with appropriate online curricula and specific methodological approaches to mitigate student attrition while increasing learner knowledge and satisfaction. Online courses are yet another way to break through the confining dimensions of time and space in order to bring a quality education to those who wish to learn under this new dynamic format. ●

How to Teach an Online Course

Q: How does teaching an online course differ from teaching in a traditional classroom setting?

A: An online teacher has new tools with which to teach. Tools are helpful, but only when one knows how to use them. It has been said that a fool with tools is still a fool. It is essential that online learning tools be integral to and essential for the immediate task.

Like any new technology, the Internet can either perpetuate poor curricular (what is taught), methodological (how something is taught) or evaluative models, or it can transform them. The key responsibility for leadership in the creation and maintenance of an outstanding online course clearly rests with the trained instructor.

Ultimately, the curricular and methodological focus of an online course will reflect the values held by the educator in his or her relationship with the students. These values should include a commitment by the instructor to be both an expert in the field and a caring facilitator of learning.

In order to make the most of the Internet as a technology, a teacher must understand the enormous potential advantages of this particular technology. An online course taught by a competent educator has the capacity to increase learner flexibility, provide access to expertise, and facilitate communication (e.g., threaded discussion) among learners who cannot meet at the same time or place. Moreover, this technology can increase self-directed learning and promote collaborative learning.

Online education offers a unique learner-centered paradigm. Students can become actively involved in combining their existing knowledge with new learning in an interactive environment where ongoing feedback is not only requested but also required. Class participation via threaded discussions is the most essential part of the design and delivery of the courses.

So what are threaded discussions? Basically, they are asynchronous (they can be added anytime to the discussion) opinions that students send to a certain page (a predetermined screen on your computer).

In an online course, these opinions would combine with a student's authentic personal experiences to synthesize explicit connections back to the required readings, leading to further input into the threaded discussion. It is in the threaded discussions that learners are asked to constantly use their higher-order critical thinking skills (with the teacher's guidance) to stimulate shared thoughtful interaction on a variety of course topics with the entire class. ●

What Makes a Quality Educational Website Experience?

Q: What should a student look for before taking an online course from an accredited school?

A: Online education is truly an exciting prospect. In a very real sense, your computer screen serves as a chalkboard, textbook, and library without walls.

That being said, there are some pretty straightforward considerations when judging whether an educational website can really deliver the kind of quality educational experience found in academic coursework. Let's look at three nuts-and-bolts technical issues:

1. Be sure the technology you have on your home computer can capture the graphics, sound, video streams, and/or animations used in the course. It is a good idea to take an orientation course based on the same online class model. In this way you can find out, before you start the class, if you have all the installed or downloaded software you need.
2. Be sure that the site is stable. What we are talking about here is the 24-hour availability of the site. One big advantage of online education is that you can take it when you want. Therefore, it should be not just consistently but constantly accessible.
3. Make sure all links are functioning. Special features like audio or video links should not end up as a "404 Error" message.

Another issue deals with course presentation. The goal is to make the screens simple and coherent. The guiding rule is that the complexity of the course should be in curriculum and student response to interactive questions, not in the presentation or navigation of the screens. That being said, here are two fundamental content considerations:

1. Check for a site map. Whenever there is a large amount of material to be covered, such as in your course, there should be an outline of topics on a single screen that allows the student to find and access the subject matter with one click of a mouse.
2. Check for "preset" links within the course. Although you still have to buy a textbook for many online courses, the real advantage of being online is immediate access to

other informational sites. In a well-constructed course, other site links are already programmed into the course. This makes even extensive research a "push-button affair."

If you are satisfied with both the technical and content considerations, then online education may well be for you. Online education gives the learner the options of when and where to engage in the learning process, along with getting consistent feedback from an online teacher. This is an educational model that is sure to grow and flourish, extending education to a truly global audience. ●

Quality Online Learning

Q: What should a student look for when selecting an online class? What should the student expect from an online teacher?

A: With the number of online students now in the millions, this question is one that students and teachers are confronting every day. A quality online class should include:

- Clear course description
- Realistic course goals
- Specific student outcomes
- Point values for each kind of assignment
- Grading policy with accompanying scoring scale

This kind of information is vital in order to begin the course with the knowledge of what is expected and how work will be evaluated.

Once a student knows "what" to do, the question of "when is it to be done" becomes important. Look for an online program that has an asynchronous design. In other words, find a class that allows you to work at your own pace. This means you can go from unit to unit (back and forth) and have the option of getting a little behind or staying a little ahead of all the chronologically listed assignments. Think of this as becoming captain of your own ship as you glide through cyberspace. Classes that give students the control and flexibility to determine when they are to do the work fit best for a wide variety of highly personalized learning styles.

What then becomes critical is not "when" the student does the work, but "if" the student accomplishes a given assigned task. Of course, along with the freedom to determine the pace at which work is to be done, the empowered student must take on the responsibility to be sure all work is finished on or before the last day of class.

Another critical factor in choosing an online class is to be sure that the teacher responds to the students no longer than 24 hours after any student communication. Instructors must check on their class to grade papers or answer asynchronous discussion questions in a timely manner. In fact, teachers that respond to students once in the morning and again in the evening (a 12-hour response cycle) may well stimulate a more productive learning model.

Correspondingly, the complexity of an online course should not be found in figuring out convoluted messages or nonintuitive tools on the computer screen, but in the quality of interaction between student and teacher. Remember, search for online courses that give clear and concise information, straightforward assignments, and allow the learner to have control and flexibility in pursuing studies at his or her own pace. Do this and you may well be able to point and click your way to a first-class education. ●

Testing by Email

Q: How can students take examinations using email? Isn't there a security problem? Are there any advantages?

A: Email communications are part of the new electronic classroom in a school without walls. Email messages allow students who live near or far from an actual school site to have equal access to an education.

In terms of testing by email, the methodology is really quite simple. Here is an eight-step breakdown of how an email examination can occur in a secure environment:

1. A student visits a predetermined testing site on or off campus and presents appropriate identification to the test proctor.
2. The proctor at the site gives the student a previously formatted disk.
3. The student inserts that disk into a computer, and opens a file with one of a rotating group of examination questions.
4. The student answers the questions (true/false, multiple choice, short answer, or essay).
5. The student then takes the disk with the questions and answers and returns it to the proctor.
6. The proctor sends the student's answers to a predetermined email address (e.g., a school archive site

and/or an individual faculty scorer) and then stores the actual disk in an appropriate secure location.
7. The faculty scorer (a member of a group of scorers specially trained to maintain interrater reliability) then scores and grades the test, and informs the school of the results within ten working days of receiving the examination.
8. The school then informs the student of the outcome of the examination.

In terms of security, what one has is a proctored test with adequate student identification, based on a rotating examination format. That is a pretty secure design, depending on how many alternate test formats are available. It should be obvious that to avoid cheating, the more rotating alternative test formats the better.

As for the advantages of testing by email, five come to mind:

1. Students can have a variety of locations and/or times in which to take the test.
2. Students can proofread and spell-check their short answers and essays, being absolutely sure that their "writing" is legible.
3. Copies of the rotating alternative forms of the examination are not

to be copied onto paper, making it almost impossible to get a "hard copy" of the test.

4. A trained core of faculty scorers (who all use the same scoring rubric, have the same in-service training, and pass an interrater reliability test) score the examinations.

5. Students can expect to be notified within ten days of their test scores, by phone, letter, or email message.

Email exams offer convenience, speed, efficiency—and a legible exam to boot. Look for this testing method to grow in popularity from grade school to graduate school. ●

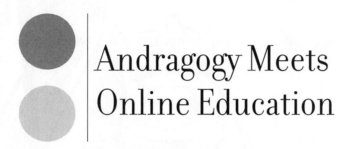

Andragogy Meets Online Education

Q: Are the courses available over the Internet of the same quality as in the classroom? With online education growing so quickly, especially at the university level, how are these online courses being developed so that real learning takes place? As a teacher candidate there is a high probability that you will either take a preservice or an in-service course or workshop online.

A: The goals and curriculum of an online course from an accredited university should be the same as in the classroom. The difference between a higher education course given online, as opposed to one taking place in a classroom, is in the methodological approach. Correspondingly, there is a need to articulate a particular educational philosophy (e.g., andragogy—"the teaching of adults") when training an online professor or in orienting an online student.

An appropriate philosophy informs a coherent methodological approach so that a professor will prepare using distinctive techniques, and the online teacher candidate will be assured that he or she will receive an enriched learning experience appropriate to an online format.

An important relationship exists between teacher development and online education based on the andragogical notion that adults are self-directed learners.

Research indicates adults are the products of authentic lifelong experiences and have the desire to gain increased knowledge to face the tasks they encounter in their studies—and in life. An online course that asks students to use their critical thinking skills (analysis, synthesis, and evaluation) by means of reflective written work is on solid ground. For example, essays that request explicit connections to required readings (new knowledge), as well as the revelation of authentic personal experience, demand that adults confront their ambiguities.

Accordingly, online program designers can implement andragogical theory to address:

- Support services
- Program content
- Delivery systems
- Target audience
- Program goals

- Faculty training
- Student orientation

Online teacher education classes at the collegiate level can be developed and put into practice as tutorial, group, or independent instructional modes. Given a background of understanding the stages and transitions of adult life, as well as paying special attention to the interrelationship of adult development and career advancement, certain kinds of instructional techniques are indicated. For instance, online approaches that include contract learning, threaded discussions, experimental learning, portfolios, and self-pacing in an asynchronous environment seem most fitting.

For a growing number of teacher candidates, a powerful new model exists online, where andragogy intersects cyberspace. ●

Online Collaborative Learning

Q: Is there a model for successfully instructing teachers online?

A: Research indicates that one of the most commonly mentioned characteristics of teacher education is that it should be collaborative in nature. Clearly, the foundations of modern teacher education have emerged out of the progressive education movement. Notwithstanding this well-known conceptual framework of participation and collaboration, there has been a dearth of empirical evidence to support collaborative learning.

Recent research in online education demonstrates that collaborative learning should become part of a formal or institutionalized teacher education methodological approach. Collaborative learning works through the online experience in four distinct ways (especially in asynchronous threaded discussions):

- Facilitators and learners become participants in an educational process that is both active and reflective.

- The usual hierarchy between the facilitators and learners is modified, as common inquiry is stressed.

- A cyberspace community is created based on scholastic interactions within a 24-hour period.

- Knowledge is both created and transferred.

The locus of control and knowledge shifts from the individual to the participating online community.

The philosophical roots for this kind of student-centered learning go back to Dewey, Piaget, and Vygotsky, all of whom wrote and lived before the invention of online education. Their notion that collaborative learning assumes that knowledge is socially, as opposed to individually, constructed by a community of learners is crucial. When learners shape and test ideas, and authority is distributed and experienced among all in the learning community, the process is inherently participatory and therefore collaborative.

Collaborative learning differs from autonomous learning in that the facilitator designs the course with appropriate rigor so that learning occurs to the greatest extent possible. The role of the facilitator determines the extent of a collaborative learning environment by shifting authority and commensurate responsibility for learning to the student.

The facilitator does not perform the traditional role of authority figure and transmitter of knowledge. Instead, a process of mutual inquiry is implemented in which students are viewed as co-learners. For the online class, a redefinition of control, power, expertise, and authority is mandated. What is called for is a judicious mix of the facilitator's sense of responsibility to cover course content and his or her unconditional commitment to enable students to learn on their own and share with the online community. ●

Collaborative Online Education

 Q: How can a teacher get students in an online class to work collaboratively rather than competitively?

 A: In order to attain that goal, a facilitator prepares learners for collaborative work through

Onsite Traditional Model versus Online Collaborative Model

Traditional Model	Online Collaborative Model
Student as listener, observer, note taker	Student as problem solver, contributor
Class spurs competition	Class spurs collaboration
Synchronous as to time and place	Asynchronous as to time and place
Independent learning	Interdependent learning
Instructor as authority	Facilitators and peers share authority
Information via text	Information via online text and multi-media resources
Instructor sets pace	Student sets pace

explicit explanations of how the shared process can work in an online class. An example of this can be found in a course information section that permits students to work in a collaborative learning situation. A rationale and a coherent framework are essential.

An online collaborative learning situation has been formulated only when the facilitator has decided the appropriate learning activities, established clear objectives, used suitable participatory techniques, developed meaningful questions, and provided a clear sense of expected outcomes.

This prepared environment provides an atmosphere in which participants feel at liberty to exchange ideas and share notions in order to create community-based knowledge. The result can be an authentic democratic setting where students have a sense of well-being and acceptance.

The seemingly dichotomous needs of affiliation and autonomy are both fulfilled through the commitment to indi-vidual growth and group development inherent in online collaborative education. This culture of online collaborative learning is constructed with the learner in mind. Well-defined shifts in learning take place.

The benefit of the online collaborative format is that it provides for an increase of democratic decision making. In addition, the participants can acquire insights into their own academic and social development as well as the potential of group-generated knowledge.

By making explicit connections back to the texts and using authentic personal experiences, learners are able to expose and resolve previously hidden biases and share their collective knowledge and wisdom.

The empirical evidence from online education strongly indicates that students' learning is enhanced by means of collaborative group work in a noncompetitive environment. ●

Online Access to High School Education

Q: How can online education help high school students have access to a quality education?

A: Perhaps one of the most socially dynamic notions about online education is the creation of an equitable learning environment. Theoretically, many students (e.g., minorities, the less affluent, persons with disabilities, those who live great distances from a campus) who have not fully experienced equal access to the learning environment in the traditional classroom can now feel connected to a community of learners. Engaging all online learners requires the following:

- Teachers must model acceptance of every student, regardless of gender, perceived ability, race, or ethnic background. It has often been stated that 80 percent of all teaching is modeling. Reaching out in cyberspace is an inclusive enterprise.

- The curriculum (subjects or topics) should reflect the needs of the group being taught. Recall that high school students come with an array of experiences and previous constructed knowledge from a variety of cultural domains. Understanding backgrounds is critical in developing partnerships. Images and examples should reflect, acknowledge, and validate the prior knowledge and diversity among these learners.

- Courses should be taught with an asynchronous design (i.e., there are no start or end times during a course of study, other than the final day of class) so that work can be accomplished when the student has the time to do reflective thought, which may lead to enhanced analysis, synthesis, and evaluation.

- The teacher must be a leader. A great leader doesn't produce followers, but other leaders. Correspondingly, teachers must be change agents, believing that change and development are possible for all.

- The teacher must realize that his or her role and the learner's role at times coincide in assisting in the learning process—as in an open-ended threaded discussion.

Online learning is now providing an educational revolution due to its extraordinary capacity to reach across the age-old barriers of time and space and provide a quality education to those who have too often been left behind. Teachers who engage students as partners in learning may well enjoy a fruitful collaborative learning process as they lead high school students to new levels of understanding and action. ●

SUGGESTED READINGS

Beare, H. (2000). *Creating the future school.* New York: RoutledgeFalmer.

Bowen, C., & Durbin, T. (2001). Convergence: Bringing together new and old technologies. *Communication: Journalism Education Today, 34*(4), 3–8. (EJ 624 609)

Dennis, E. E., Meyer, P., Shyam, S., Pryor, L., Roger, E. M., Chen, H. L., et al. (2003). Symposium Learning reconsidered: Education in the digital age. *Journalism and Mass Communication Educator, 57*(4), 292–317.

Eib, B. J., & Cox, S. (2003). Integrating technology with teacher inquiry. *Principal Leadership, 3,* 54–58.

Ellsworth, J. B. (2000). A Survey of Educational Change Models. *ERIC Digest.* (ERIC Document Reproduction Service No. ED 444 597).

Ertmer, P. (2003). Transforming teacher education: Visions and strategies. *Educational Technology Research and Development, 51*(1), 124–128.

Gunawardena, C. N., & McIssac, M. S. (2003). Distance Education. In D. H. Jonassen (Ed.), *Handbook of research in educational communications and technology.* Mahwah, NJ: Lawrence Erlbaum.

Hopkins, D. (2001). *School improvement for real.* New York: Routledge.

Huesca, R. (2000). Reinventing journalism curricula for the electronic environment. *Journalism and Mass Communication Educator, 55*(2), 4–15.

Koszalka, T., Grabowski, B., & McCarthy, M. (2003). Reflection Through the ID-PRISM: A Teacher Planning Tool to Transform Classrooms into Web-Enhanced Learning Environments. *Journal of Teacher and Technology Education, 11*(3), 349–378.

Lin, X. (2001). Reflective adaptation of a technology artifact: A case study of classroom change. *Cognition and Instruction, 19*(4), 395–440. (ERIC Document Reproduction Service No. EJ 641 752).

Nicholson, J. (2001). Curricula go hightech: Schools adapt their programs to address technological changes. *Quill, 89*(6), 14.

O'Connell Rust, F., & Freidus, H. (Eds.). (2001). *Guiding school change: The role and work of change agents.* New York: Teachers College Press.

Popo, W. (2001). Integration of educational media in higher education classes. *Educational Media International, 38*(2–3), 95–99. (ERIC Document Reproduction Service No. EJ 631 310).

Simonson, M., Smaldino, S., Albright, M., & Zvack, S. (2003). *Teaching and learning at a distance* (2nd ed.). Upper Saddle River, NJ: Merrill Prentice Hall.

Tooley, J. (2000). *Reclaiming education.* New York: Cassell.

Wood, E., & Bennett, N. (2000). Changing theories, changing practice: Exploring early childhood teachers professional learning. *Teaching and Teacher Education, 16*(5–6), 635–647.

unit :11

Education:
A Family Affair

Parents and Teachers Must Work Together

Q: Many parents have heard that their involvement in their children's education is important. Parents also know that reading is important. Is there a formula to get more parent involvement in elementary or middle school reading? Is there a program for interested parents and teachers to follow?

A: Educational research is clear: Parental involvement yields enhanced student achievement. Teachers play a critical role in parent involvement.

It is important that teachers take the time to prepare students for the literature they are about to read. Any learner has a much better chance of being fully engaged with the written word if the teacher provides relevant background knowledge and draws links to student experiences before reading is assigned.

Here is a seven-step reading program that can build a strong three-way educational partnership (student, parent, and teacher).

- Parents should accompany their children to a school library, a public library, or a bookstore with a teacher's list of 15 books.

- Every three weeks, the student selects one of the books on the list.

- Depending on the age and reading skill of the student, the student and parent read the chosen book individu-

ally, or the book is read to the child by the parent.

- Reading and discussing the book become an everyday activity at home.

- Every third week, student–parent groups (a teacher or other staff member can act as a facilitator) who have read the same book should meet at school.

- They should be seated in a circle and expect an enjoyable discussion made up of certain general questions about the reading that lead to a free-flowing discussion.

- Following these group meetings, students write letters to their parents commenting on the group discussion.

This format is powerful because it involves the parents on a day-by-day basis (reading and discussing the book at home). The model can also serve a diverse student body. Book selection and reading can be done in any language. Reading, after all, is a transferable skill. To read well in Spanish, German, or French will help a student's English reading skills.

If the program still doesn't get off the ground at school, launch the seven-step program at home. Besides improving reading skills, it will give the parent and their children hours of enjoyable time together. ●

Communicating with Parents

Q: Many students in high school spend the entire day in a state of boredom. There are youngsters who never do homework, and their behavior in class leaves much to be desired. What should a new teacher do to get everyone involved in learning?

A: To get everyone involved in learning, a teacher must first decide who "everyone" is. A wise definition of everyone includes the teacher, all the students, and their parents. However, teaching high school in the 21st century means that you may never see many of the parents of the youngsters you teach. Therefore, a way must be found for continual communication with parents to let them know what assignments are due and how well their son or daughter is doing.

Enter the telephone. When a teacher phones all parents at least once every two weeks, the calls become almost informal. The parents and the teacher simply search for solutions to little problems before they become too big. Teachers will discover that the feedback from parents is so positive, their interest so high, and the results (in terms of completed assignments and classroom behavior) so gratifying, that calling parents is well worth the effort. ●

How to Get Involved in School Reform

Q: Many school districts are going through some pretty big changes. With the 21st century underway, schools feel a need to keep up with the times. What are some ways the community can get involved in this important process?

A: Whether a school is going through a renewal reform or an overall restructuring, ongoing communication between home and school can lead to active community participation in bringing about changes in the way we educate. Here are some suggestions for community involvement:

- Ask questions. Be sure you get clear definitions of all the terms you will be discussing for the changes you are considering.

- Go to meetings with an open mind but also with ideas. A view from outside

the school walls can be both refreshing and objective.

- Be sure to obtain a clear written outline of the goals and objectives of your school's changes. The more clear the outline, the more serious the school is about making real changes.

- Real reform is a step-by-step process. Keep a checklist of what has been and is to be done.

- Make sure that students take an active role. As you invite students into the process, you will be preparing a new generation of community-service-oriented people like you. ●

Reform Movements

Q: Some parents have been notified that their schools are undergoing a "reform." What exactly is meant by school reform, what can you, as a teacher, tell parents to expect, and how can they help?

A: Reform movements in schools are considered a little less drastic than school restructuring. Restructuring means the school is ready to make major changes in the way it delivers educational services. Reform, however, is more limited in scope, and it has two major categories.

First, the school may change its subject matter and teaching methods. These reforms are concerned with what students should be learning and the best methods to bring about that learning. Examples of this kind of reform may include:

- Using computers in the classroom
- Stressing multicultural influences in history and literature

- Implementing a back-to-basics approach
- Introducing concept-based mathematics

A second type of reform has to do with school governance and administration. The major concern is the process by which decisions get made on campus. At more progressive schools, all stakeholders share real power to make site-based decisions in the best interest of the students. Stakeholders may include parents, teachers, administrators, students, interested members of the community, and non-teaching staff.

Shared leadership has the advantage of opening the process up to a diverse group so a variety of ideas from different perspectives are aired. Subsequent decisions reached by a consensus of all parties involved (for instance, a dress code) have a better chance of being successfully implemented.

How to Choose the Best Preschool

Q: How would you advise parents to rate different preschool programs? What should they look for when making their evaluations?

A: There are a number of things to tell parents to look for over and above whether the director and staff have the appropriate state credentials. On visiting the preschool site, check to see if the teachers are engaged with the children. As the teachers work with children, be sure they reflect the kind of interest, understanding, and respect a parent would want shown to a child. In short, what a parent is really looking for is student–teacher rapport.

Check class size, and see if it complies with the state's standards. At this level of education, individual instruction (one-on-one attention) is critical.

Notice certain schools seem to have an aura of friendliness. The communication skills of the staff have a lot to do with a happy, harmonious school climate. To sum up, if parent and child always feel welcome, the staff is doing its job. ●

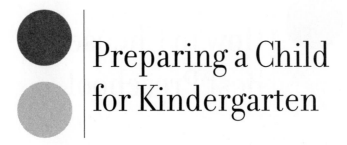

Preparing a Child for Kindergarten

Q: Are there things a five-year-old should be doing each day to make him more ready for kindergarten? What kinds of physical activities should he do to prepare for school?

There are certain physical skills that most kindergarten teachers expect students to possess. For instance, walking, running, and climbing are some of the large-muscle skills you can observe and develop with your child. In addition, skills requiring eye-hand coordination, as in using a crayon or scissors, are examples of fine motor skills. Moreover, it is also assumed that children have acquired both auditory and visual discrimination of the world around them.

Such skills will help them determine the following concepts: same and different, the names of colors, and shapes and sizes. Meaningful play with a child will present the parent an opportunity to introduce, observe, and develop many of these skills. ●

Preschool Checklist

Q: What advice would you give parents to evaluate a preschool so they can send their child to a place where he will learn and be happy? Are there written standards for preschools?

A: There are published quality standards for preschools. The following checklist adapted from the Michigan State Board of Education should be of some value to you as a parent and a consumer.

It is essential that parents visit the preschool before making their choice. After a child begins to attend the preschool, parents should be sure to visit the child there. On-site inspection during the instructional day is more valid in terms of the evaluation parents are requesting than any glossy brochure or even an open house.

One other caution: Any preschool that doesn't have an open-door policy for parent visitation should be taken off the list. Here, then, are eight standards to look for in a quality preschool:

- Safety and comfort
- Use of play to attain understanding
- Developmental (step-by-step) curriculum
- Acquisition of concepts through manipulation of objects
- Use of various methods to present concepts
- Activities that challenge and lead to success
- Individualized instruction
- Incorporation of children's interests into the learning activities ●

Appropriate Teacher Conferences

Q: What advice would you give to a parent about when it is appropriate to conference with a teacher?

A: To be truthful, it is hard to think of a time when a teacher–parent conference would be inappropriate. Perhaps such a meeting would be inappropriate at an open house, when the parents are many in number and the time is limited. However, good teachers, as a rule, are always open to conferences.

Such a meeting is always appropriate when a child isn't doing well in school. Parents should not wait for the school to email or telephone them. It is very important that parents take the initiative and call for such a meeting. A conference is a learning experience for both teacher and parent. For a parent, a successful conference will define a problem area and indicate ways to help their child at home.

Remind parents to conference with their child. An open discussion of real problems a child is having in school can lead to real solutions. When a parent goes to a conference, he or she should be looking to identify why the student is not doing well and ask the teacher to develop a plan of action that will lead the child to academic success.

One very effective tool is a learning contract. The teacher can devise a learning contract (the more specific the better) to state item by item what is required of a student in terms of homework, tests, quizzes, and papers. Once all the cards are on the table, a parent can take direct and informed action, working each day with the child to fulfill the learning contract. Remember, direct communication between parent and teacher about a student who is not doing well in school should lead to specific activities (such as a learning contract) a parent can do at home with the child.

Research tells us that the coordinated efforts of parents and teachers can improve a child's performance in school. This only stands to reason. Parents are their children's first, most frequent, and therefore most important teacher. ●

Appropriate Questions at an Open House

Q: Most schools have an annual open house, where parents spend time in the auditorium listening to the principal and then go to the classroom to meet the teacher. What kinds of parental questions are appropriate at an open house?

A: There are many kinds of questions that will help a parent form a solid partnership with the teacher in order to best instruct a child. Here is a list of questions for a parent at the next open house:

•   **Ask about the curriculum.** What exactly is being taught? How does this course logically sequence with what the student has just learned and what he or she is about to learn?

•   **Ask about methodology.** How is the material going to be covered? What percent of the class is lecture, group discussion, or laboratory work? What kind of individual instruction will be available?

•   **Ask about materials.** What are the textbooks to be used? Is there a supplementary reading list? Will the student need a computer for certain assignments? Does the student have access to computers when he or she needs them?

•   **Ask about class discipline policies.** What are the academic consequences for a child who is continually absent or tardy? What are the policies on "makeup" work?

•   **Ask how grades are determined.** What percent of the grade is earned by testing, projects, or homework? Can bonus work be part of the evaluation?

•   **Ask about expectations for the students now and at semester's end.** Specifically, what kinds of skills will be developed, and what level of knowledge will be attained?

A parent may not have time to ask all of these questions, but he or she can use the open house to set up an appointment with the teacher to satisfy laudable curiosity.

One more point should be made: A well-prepared teacher should have a course syllabus (an overview of the semester's work) to hand out at open house. A good syllabus and a handout on class rules and policies should provide straightforward answers to most of the questions listed. ●

Unhappy with Your Teacher?

Q: A child may be unhappy with a teacher—and that teacher may be you! What can you do along with the parents to resolve such a situation?

A: It is quite normal for children to like some teachers more than others, and it's not unheard of to dislike some teachers to the extent that one feels unhappy. We learn best when we are happy and feel a mutual trust and admiration for our instructors. The crucial question that must be asked is: Does this unhappiness significantly affect a child's learning? One appropriate index would be to look at the student's graded work. If a youngster's grades are the same or higher than the previous term, learning may not have been affected.

By staying in that "uncomfortable" class, a young person may learn to cope with a mildly unpleasant situation and still be successful. The virtue of perseverance is built on such experiences. Steadfastness learned in youth can pay large dividends in later life. However, if the youngster's attitude toward the teacher has affected his learning, immediate steps must be taken. As a teacher, ask the parents to do the following:

- Explain to their youngster that the teacher is not an adversary. In fact, the relationship between student and teacher is a kind of learning partnership.

- Promise the youngster that they will meet with the teacher as soon as possible so that a mediated solution might be found.

- Meet with the teacher. A face-to-face meeting is best, but a phone conversation will do.

Many teachers are unaware of a particular student's feelings about them. Most teachers will immediately try to remedy the situation, whether the student feels there is too much work or not enough work, or if there is just a clash of personalities. Once parents have met with the teacher, they should ask the youngster to go at least halfway and give the teacher's new approach a chance to work.

If all else fails, a change of teacher may be the wisest option. However, children might mature faster by remaining in the same class if the problem is recognized and a mutually agreed-on solution is reached. Sometimes, unhappy circumstances can turn into opportunities for academic as well as social development. ●

What to Expect from a Student Teacher

Q: What should parents expect when a student teacher is instructing a class? Should they be concerned about how much student teachers actually know?

A: Student teachers are interns. When an airline hires a pilot with a recent license, or a hospital employs a doctor just out of medical school, an on-the-job training period is required. Student teachers are usually directly under the guidance of both a university professor and the classroom teacher. Before entering the classroom to student-teach, these interns have had a core of education classes along with the course work required to be competent in their field.

What student teachers may find most difficult is not the material they are teaching, but class management. Whatever the problems are, they can be resolved under the guidance of both the classroom teacher and the university professor. Research indicates that a strong and collaborative relationship between teacher and student teacher leads to a successful internship.

One advantage of having a student teacher in the classroom is that it provides an "extra" instructor for the students. It is always advantageous to reduce the student-to-teacher ratio.

All parents should talk with their child's teacher from time to time. In this case, you have two instructors with whom to dialogue.

When one thinks of the big picture, there is a definite upside to having a student teacher. The teacher-to-be is getting professionally trained in a realistic setting, and students get more attention and support because they have two instructors.

In short, parents can expect classroom competence and quality instruction from the teaming of a student teacher with an experienced teacher. ●

Classroom Visit May Help Concerned Parents

Q: How might classroom visits help parents concerned with their children's education when the child claims to be stressed about going to school?

A: As a teacher it is important to advise parents, when asked, how best to help their children in school—sometimes when those children are not even in your class. Every concerned parent needs to find out what is really taking place in the classroom. The stress referred to in the question is probably not just being felt by the child, but also by the teacher. In fact, recent research indicates that teachers rank students who have serious or chronic behavioral problems as their primary cause of stress.

In order to know what is really going on, it may be a good idea for parents to visit the classroom for a day to observe not only the child, but also the teacher. Parents already know how they want their child to act. They want the child to be focused, on task, respectful, spontaneous, and have a sense of well-being in the class. Their visit can on that day confirm or deny their expectations. However, the child is only one of the persons a parent must observe. The other person is the teacher. There are four things a parent should look for when evaluating a teacher.

First, it is crucial that the teacher model prosocial behavior (acting for the common good). Modeling by the teacher is the most basic element for enhancing student socialization. In other words, it is one thing for teachers to talk the talk, but do they walk the walk?

Second, when it comes to desirable social skills and coping strategies, look for the "what" and the "when." The "what" is the teacher's ability to consistently project positive expectations to foster students' self-esteem. Are students treated as well-intentioned learners whose appropriate actions draw expressions of appreciation? A teacher's word of support and understanding go a long way in building positive reinforcement for appropriate classroom behavior.

The "when" is the teacher giving positive reinforcement at the time the appropriate behavior actually occurs. Appreciative remarks given an hour, a day, or a six-week grading period later simply will not accomplish the desired effect. It is especially important to understand that unless reinforcement is given when the acceptable behavior is occurring, the reinforcement may actually confuse the student. For example, when is the right time to reinforce a student who is struggling with a writing assignment and is easily discouraged? The time to reinforce a student is when that student is still engaged in the work—when he or she is most in need of a positive boost to stay on task.

The third thing to do in evaluating a teacher is to see if the teacher focuses on desirable behavior (what to do rather than what not to do). Let's be clear. Teachers have the right and the responsibility to exercise class control by setting well-defined boundaries of acceptable student behavior.

Fourth, teachers should model behaviors (acting focused, friendly, and flexible) that lead to student self-regulation.

A minimum number of class rules and a liberalizing of those edicts as students become more independent and responsible over time indicate that teacher's flexibility.

How well the child's teacher scores on this four-point observation list may well indicate to what degree the teacher is a positive force in the child's social growth. ●

How Parents Should Deal with Teachers

Q: Everyone knows that students need the help of both teachers and parents. But how can parents and teachers avoid getting into arguments about the best way to teach children? Maybe teachers take classes on how to deal with parents, but parents don't take classes on how to deal with teachers. What should parents know about how to deal with teachers in order to help their children?

A: It may surprise you to learn that most teachers have received very little, if any, training on fostering and maintaining a working relationship with parents. What is important for both parents and teachers to realize is that they know the child in different settings.

The school and the home can be two very different environments. The teacher and the parent may be unaware of how the child acts in each of these different settings. One way to bridge that gap is frequent communication between parent and teacher.

Teachers really should take the lead in letting parents know when they can

contact them—before school, during a class session, or after school. In addition, teachers should also indicate how a parent might contact them directly when questions arise—by telephone, a letter carried by the student, or even email.

Parents, on the other hand, need not wait for teachers to initiate regular contact. One way a parent can bring himself or herself up to speed on what is occurring in the classroom is an on-site visit. The more involved parents are in what occurs in the classroom, the more likely they are to understand the teacher's philosophy, aims, goals, and practices.

When parents see their children in a different environment, they can better form realistic learning strategies to assist their children in studies at home. As parents and teachers confer about the student, they are actively sharing the responsibility of the child's education and socialization. Parent–teacher dialogue, based on mutual respect and sincere interest in the academic and social development of the child, forms an adult "brain trust" that can only enhance student achievement. ●

Father's Involvement Is Very Significant

Q: At many Head Start programs, there are very few adult males participating with the kids. It seems that in most cases, the fathers simply aren't around. What can be done, if anything, to increase adult male involvement in preschool programs that serve low-income youngsters?

A: The idea that all fathers of children from low-income and high-risk neighborhoods are absent and don't have contact with their children is a myth. Research indicates that a majority of mothers in a preschool at-risk program reported their children had regular contact with their father or other male role model in spite of the high instance of single-parent families. Furthermore, in another study of Head Start programs serving low-income families, a man (male relative, boyfriend, or father) was present nearly 60 percent of the time.

Because of the lack of initiatives to encourage these men to take part in the children's education, the parenting strengths of these men have not been built on. In fact, when these males become involved, they can have positive impacts in many areas of children's development. This only makes sense, because we know that research studies consistently reveal that high student achievement and self-esteem are closely related to the amount of parental involvement in education.

What is needed is for educators to be specific about their goals in targeting men in parent involvement programs. Staff development is key. Since most early childhood educators receive sparse training in the area of parent involvement, in-service training will be needed to develop and implement male involvement initiatives.

In encouraging male involvement, the male who acts as a father figure, even if not the biological father, should be included. These father figures play a very significant role in the lives of these children and should be recruited for parent involvement programs. Of course, adult male involvement should in no way lessen the participation of mothers. In fact, mothers need to support such initiatives as increased adult male involvement in order for such new ideas to be successful.

Men can become wonderful resources as efforts are made to build a stronger relationship between the community and school. The ultimate goal is one that all can agree on: to help youngsters achieve happy and successful lives both at home and in the classroom. ●

The Powerful Effect of a Father's Involvement on His Children's Education

Q: Is it true that because fathers are assumed to be the breadwinners, they throw the responsibility to mothers for a child's education? At many parent conferences, open houses, and PTA meetings, moms seem to be overrepresented. If fathers were more involved, would it make any real difference?

A: In two-parent families, the participation of mothers in school activities (school meetings, events, and volunteer groups) outstrips the involvement of fathers by a 2 to 1 margin. Single-parent families have comparable levels of parental school participation whether they are headed by a mother or a father. In fact, single mothers and fathers are more similar in their parenting behavior than are the mothers and fathers of two-parent families.

As to the second part of the question, research indicates that involvement of a father in his child's education can have a significant positive effect. For example, roughly 50 percent of children in two-parent families get mostly excellent grades (A's) when their fathers are highly involved in their schools. That total falls to about one-third when fathers have a low level of school participation. Moreover, when fathers are highly involved in their children's schooling, students are only half as likely to repeat a grade or be suspended or expelled.

Perhaps even more revealing, the level of a father's involvement in his child's schooling seems to be a more powerful indicator of the youngster's success in school than the extent of the mother's involvement, father's and mother's education level, household income, or the child's race/ethnicity.

Schools would do well to welcome (and even target) fathers' involvement in a wide range of campus activities designed to let them know the positive effect they can have on their children's education. One result, enhanced student achievement, would be well worth the effort. ●

Changing Schools Requires a Community Effort

Q: If you could change one thing about how education is handled in school today, what would it be?

A: This is a very simple question, yet it is difficult to answer. To fix the inside of schools, we should utilize what is on the outside—we should initiate real community involvement in the schools. True involvement with the entire community (not just the parents who have children in school) is crucial to the long-term success of any school.

Did you realize that by the time an American child reaches age 18, he or she has spent only 9 percent of his or her life in school? It seems our expectations for what happens during that time are quite optimistic.

There is a lot of pressure, especially on teachers, to make some pretty dramatic changes in the students. There are times when even experienced teachers, faced with 30 to 40 students in a class who are from ever more diverse ethnic and linguistic backgrounds, can feel a bit overwhelmed. Many schools are crowded, and seem to lack a most important element—the time for student and instructor to sit down and talk, one on one. What is the answer?

A powerful solution lies within the community itself. There is an old African proverb: "It takes a whole village to raise a child." All adults, whether they have school-age children or not, have a great stake in public education.

Those who could volunteer their time and effort, however, historically have not been called on by schools to roll up their sleeves, come to school daily, and pitch in. Think of the possibilities of unleashing this wealth of public-service-oriented adults on the schools.

In short order, we could have individualized reading sessions in which students could read aloud to an adult. They could have that one-on-one talk about the meaning of a story and share an important idea or two. The sharing of our country's history, by those who have lived it, could give students the kind of values that don't jump off the page of a textbook.

There are many senior citizen groups and business organizations ready to help the schools—not just on a one-shot event, but as loyal members of a school community to be there on a continual basis. This is a new constituency that schools should be working night and day to build. It is a very underutilized resource.

Imagine a school with as many adult teachers and community helpers on campus as students. The school's atmosphere would change from one of accepted, student-modeled boredom (with sporadic episodes of violence and vandalism) to one of adult-modeled cooperation and mutual respect. This one change of opening the school to the adult resources that now exist in the community would bring dynamic and lasting changes to schools. ●

Summer School Approach to Learning

Q: Why do students who have trouble passing classes during the regular school year have such a higher rate of success in summer school?

A: The answer to this question can be found in what we call intensive education—one course at a time. When you take one subject at a time (as in summer school) instead of six (as in most regular schools), you can focus more readily on what needs to be done. Research indicates having just one teacher, one set of classroom rules, and one subject for homework can make life a bit simpler and help achievement rise.

Getting schools to change to a summer school schedule year-round would need the approval of all the stakeholders—the students, parents, teachers, administration, and probably the school board. However, it is well worth trying to facilitate the change, as it appears it would greatly enhance most students' school performance. ●

School-to-Work Transition

Q: For students not going on to college, it appears their high school education would not be a very big help to them. Do the schools have any plans to better suit high school kids to the real world of work?

A: Progressive schools and educators do have a plan. It is called "school-to-work transition." This school-to-work approach should be a systematic and community-wide effort to help all young people by:

- Preparing for high-skill and high-wage careers

- Offering rigorous and relevant academic instruction

- Securing the basic and critical thinking skills to pursue postsecondary educa-

tion in an ever-changing marketplace of new technologies and new jobs

Such a learning program demands that young people have active learning experiences that happen in real-world contexts. The school is not the only place to learn. The workplace, the neighborhood, and the home should all be viewed as valuable learning environments.

Because new places to learn have been discovered, a wide range of successful adults can now serve as mentors. Their efforts in "coaching" students in, for example, their "real world of work" can give students the critical help necessary for their personal success now and in the future, in school and at work. ●

Employability Skills

Q: What are the skills that students need in order to get employed? Has anyone actually asked employers to list what they are looking for when someone interviews for a job? What kinds of classes can schools offer to make students more qualified for paid work?

A: When it comes to employability, employers in a Canadian study reported looking for three critical traits:

- Candidates must be able to think and communicate and must participate in

"THE JOB HUNT"

the first interview to the end of each working day. A genuine smile, an air of quiet confidence, a sense of humor, and dedication to getting the job done are elements that can be practiced and refined.

- Candidates must be amenable to working with others. Working successfully with others on the job demands maturity, respect, tolerance, and the ability to learn from those around you.

With respect to what kinds of classes a high school could offer to better prepare students for future employment, the entire high school's educational program should be geared to the world of work. But if a student is looking for a specific course offering, he or she should consider a speech class. In a dynamic speech curriculum, students have the opportunity to engage in group discussions, join a debating team, practice interview techniques, and give speeches to inform, persuade, and even sell. All the speeches and interview opportunities are done in front of a "live" audience and are evaluated by the teacher.

In many ways, a good high school speech program gives students a direct opportunity to practice the aforementioned three most desired skills for employability. Understanding, acquiring, and practicing the skills that employers deem necessary give a prospective employee a real leg up. ●

lifelong learning. Communication is crucial because it is the main way human beings transfer information. An official from the National Aeronautics and Space Administration once stated that the most important course for prospective engineers and scientists was English. The official went on to explain that even the greatest scientific breakthrough was meaningless unless the specialist could orally explain or write down the idea so that the entire scientific community could understand it.

- Candidates must demonstrate a positive attitude, be responsible, and be willing to adapt. Attitudes that are positive and flexible are crucial from

Parents Are Their Child's First and Most Important Teachers

Q: Each summer as students exit for the long break from regular classes, interested parents may ask you, as a teacher, the following question: What should our children study over the summer, and how can a parent help out?

: Parents are a child's first and most important teachers. Let them know, as they assume the role of instructors, to keep in mind that learning activities should enhance their child's eagerness to learn. Learning activities in the summer should reinforce school lessons. This sounds simple and logical. It may, however, be a real challenge. Many schools do not make a user-friendly curriculum available to the parents during the summer (or even during the school year).

If the school does not have such a curriculum guide, then, in your role as a teacher, introduce learning guides for parents to help their youngsters explore authors, poems, films, books, and videos as a family. Construct such "what to teach" guides with meaningful activities presented in a learning sequence of warm-ups, exercises, and extensions. Such activities can develop various academic skills (math, vocabulary, spelling, reading comprehension, and critical thinking) as well as social skills (following instructions and sharing with a group).

Let's look at some of the materials available for summer learning. For example, one way to build a summer learning model is to use the hobby of collecting. Author Rita Newman points out those families can reinforce and expand a child's learning during the summer months by collecting interesting objects. Collecting encourages the development of at least three skills: classification, categorizing, and decision making.

There are any number of books at the public library to help parents teach a child to read, draw, and compute. If these books spur your child's curiosity and eagerness to learn, they can make a valuable alternative curriculum. Another idea comes from author Kris Bishop, who devised a program called "Learning Luggage," in which students can take home a selection of science, math, creative arts, or language arts tasks in a suitcase. Parents and children work together to complete all of the developmental tasks in the suitcase and then exchange it for a different piece of luggage with different activities.

Remind parents, as they work with their children through the summer, that this is something they should also be doing the other nine months of the year. By the time children in the United States reach age 18, they have spent only 9 percent of their time in school. Parents are in charge of the other 91 percent. Parents obviously have the best opportunity to make the most dramatic impact on the academic achievement of their children.

Recent research indicates that learning begins at birth. Stimulating affective cognitive and psychomotor development is inherently a parental responsibility. The summer academic activities are just a small portion of an ongoing responsibility that must begin early in the child's development and be a continuous duty of the child's first and most important teacher—the parent. ●

How to Help a Child with Homework

Q: Getting homework done has become a major issue in many households, and a lot of children aren't turning in assignments. What can parents do to help—short of doing the actual assignment for their kids?

A: Here are a few pointers you can suggest for parents to follow:

- Provide a clean, quiet, well-lighted study environment. Fewer distractions can make for better focus, and the work can be done with dispatch.

- Establish a specific homework time. A consistent time for homework to be done is especially important when starting long-range projects. It is important to consistently accomplish "bitable chunks" of those lengthy term papers or science projects that tend to be put off until the last possible moment.

- Always praise effort. Even when a student becomes frustrated, praise the effort he or she is giving.

- Help a child by asking questions that lead him or her to a solution, rather than giving the answer yourself.

- Check completed homework. It is always good to monitor the product your son or daughter is turning in to school. This shows that you value education and believe that looking at your child's effort is worth your time.

- Never hesitate to contact a child's teacher if you have any question about a specific assignment or the school's homework policy in general. ●

A Child's Self-Esteem

Q: What can a parent do to help a youngster who thinks he or she is really dumb?

A: To begin, it is important for children (and parents) to understand a very significant distinction. Just because a person does a dumb thing doesn't make him or her dumb. In fact, everyone does dumb, foolish, or silly things—but that doesn't define us as people.

As for a "bad" student, there is no such thing. There are students whose skills are strong and students whose skills are weak. "Good" and "bad" are moral, not educational, evaluations.

That being said, the child needs to make some healthy changes. One idea is to replace negative verbal statements that he has drilled into his or her brain with a new way to frame an experience. Instead of saying "I'm dumb," the child can say "I did a dumb thing"—the difference is immense. One statement labels and condemns the person. The other labels a situation. The difference is not trivial; we can change a situation far more easily than a mistaken negative belief about ourselves.

The problem with pinning a negative label like "dumb" on ourselves is that it becomes a self-fulfilling prophecy at home and at school. Parents should work with the child to label his behavior, not him. This is the first step to changing both. ●

When Children "Can't" Do Homework

Q: If a bright child says "I can't," every time he or she is told to do homework, what can you, as a teacher, advise parents to do?

A: One of the most common complaints of students who are asked to do difficult work is "I can't." Try putting this common retort to the $5 test, which generally yields good results.

First, when a student says "I can't" to an assignment, ask her to make a sincere effort. If the student repeats that she cannot do the work, put a $5 bill on the desk and say, "Won't you try?" It is a rare student who doesn't perk right up and say, "I'll do it if you really give me the $5 just for trying."

At that point (tucking the portrait of Abraham Lincoln back into your wallet), explain to her that what we have just observed is the difference between "I can't" and "I won't." Students who say "I can't" almost always mean "I won't."

Many students are simply afraid to fail, and therefore give up without trying. ●

Start Teaching a Child about Nature Now

Q: When and how do you begin to teach a child, especially a city kid, about nature?

A: Here is a message about the appreciation of the environment you can discuss with parents. The answer to the first part of this question is simple—as soon as you can. Children can develop a sense of awe, wonder, and enjoyment of nature at an early age. Imagine taking a child from Montana on her first trip to a beach with palm trees, warm tropical breezes, sand, and surf. What an ideal learning laboratory!

As to how to teach them about nature, young children learn best about the environment by having the opportunity to interact with it. Many children (and not just "city kids") spend most of their time indoors. They go to their bedroom to listen to a CD, are driven to school rather than walk, and are even taught natural science in a classroom rather than outdoors.

The problem is obvious. Their opportunities to understand and appreciate the environment by means of actual contact with the great outdoors are limited. However, even a child living in the middle of a great metropolis can become fascinated with nature and get started learning and caring about it. Here is a three-step process for parents to follow:

- Start with what is at hand. There is no immediate need to head for the Grand Canyon. Find a single ant making its way up a tree. Relate that ant to something familiar to the child, such as being a member of a family. Locate other ants (other members of the clan). Explain that they are very social insects, like bees and termites. See where they are going

and what they are carrying, and try to imagine the purpose of this activity.

- Stress interaction rather than "facts." Be a guide to your child and share in the wonder of nature instead of trying to verbalize too many abstract facts. Environmental learning is a hands-on experience. Your focus should be on what the child finds interesting.

- Model a genuine feeling of respect, interest, and wonder. Research tells us that modeling behavior has a strong effect on the learner. Children tend to emulate their parents. Your attitude toward nature can light the spark that gives your child a lifelong love of the natural world. When positive and stimulating experiences with nature start in our formative years and occur frequently, our love of exploring and understanding the environment can last a lifetime. ●

What about Homeschooling?

 Do parents have the right to decide to teach their children at home? How do homeschooled children do in comparison with children who attend regular school?

A: Homeschooling is considered a legitimate way to meet each of the 50 states' compulsory education requirements. Each state does require that you notify the state or local education agency that you wish to homeschool your child. Depending on the state in which you reside, there may be a requirement to submit proposed curricula and examinations. In addition, some states require that the parents themselves have reached a certain level of education.

In terms of how well homeschoolers do in comparison with traditional school students, there rages a hot debate. Because it is very difficult to get a representative sample of homeschooled students, there can be no definitive answer to how well they do academically. However, scores of homeschooled students who have taken state-mandated tests indicate homeschoolers, on average, have better test results.

Another important component of schooling, however, is social develop-ment. Opponents to homeschooling, including the National Parent–Teacher Association, the National Education Association, and the National Association of Elementary School Principals, have argued that home-schooling may be detrimental to students because it isolates them from other children in the community.

Again, research in this area is not clear. Each homeschooling situation should be evaluated individually. Obviously, if the child never leaves his or her home, social interaction clearly would be stunted. However, homeschooling may not indicate isolation from the community. Homeschoolers may and do join scouting groups, church groups, and other community-based organizations that can provide these children with rich opportunities for social interaction.

Homeschooling is a growth industry. Its future in the computer age may be much more than mom or dad assigning a history lesson or a math problem. As interactive technology improves, the traditional school vs. homeschool controversy may evolve into a cyberspace partnership between school and families. With a personal computer and a modem, homeschoolers have the opportunity of going online to listen to, ask questions of, and respond to teachers or other experts from the elementary level through graduate school. ●

Helping the Unsuccessful Student

Q: If a student who is starting high school has not been getting the best grades, and seems pretty shy at times, what can you advise a parent do to make the student's high school experience a good one?

A: Teenagers are known to go through phases when nothing appears to them as "going right." In a single day, they can experience continuous negative feedback from any number of people. It can be a day that includes parents nagging them about an unkempt bedroom, teachers complaining about incomplete homework assignments, and classmates ridiculing the teen's "uncool" clothes. This can make for the kind of distress that leads to a disruptive display of temper.

One of the toughest phases for a teen is the transition from middle school to high school. It is a time when too many adolescents fall into the "at-risk" category. Some indicators of students who are "at-risk" are:

- Poor grades
- High absence rate (missing a week or more of class a semester)
- Discipline problems (multiple trips to the counselor to solve in-class problems)

Inform parents that if they notice these indicators, there are certain things they can do. Of course, listening to their son or daughter to understand his or her concerns is critical. However, listening may not be enough. Given the long-range importance of a successful educational experience in the life of a teen, a direct plan of action may be needed in order for the parent to have the quality and kind of information needed to provide real help to their youngster.

Here is a plan parents can put into action:

- Spend a day at school and shadow your student. This may be inconvenient for the parent and cause some embarrassment for the student, but that day will provide important firsthand information about the challenges an "at-risk" student faces.

- Keep continual contact with the school and teachers by using the phone to receive meaningful updates concerning class attendance, grades, and behavior.

- Maintain a clean, quiet, well-lighted place for study. Have a routine time for homework every afternoon or evening.

- Introduce the idea of long-range plans, that is, have the teen start thinking about a career. This may bring added relevance to the youngster's studies.

Remember, the teen years are a time of awkward and sometimes painful adjustment. Expect a few emotional hills and valleys on a child's journey through adolescence to adulthood. ●

How to Help a Child Overcome Social Inhibitions

Q: What kind of school activities should a shy student become involved in to overcome his inhibitions?

A: Making certain that children form social relationships with other youngsters is important for their cognitive and social development. Whether we are talking about a "shy" student or a "social" student, they both need to have friendships. It is these very friendships that help develop a more group-centered perspective on life, rather than the egocentric view common to very young children.

All students benefit from peer relationships because such interactions inherently present them with the opportunity to build crucial interpersonal skills. Remember, the more isolated a child is, the less time he has to learn the give-and-take of social interaction skills.

It is important to find out what kind of cooperative learning activities are available at school. Look for learning activities that are centered around a "buddy system" or small groups that enhance student-to-student relationships.

Research has indicated these peer relationships have real value. Children who learn to work well with other youngsters achieve more because they tend to learn more. One student teaching another is a win–win situation.

This model permits both students to learn social skills while they exchange academic content. The student doing the learning can grasp a concept or a study skill from a peer in an anxiety-free situation, while the child who is doing the instructing is reinforcing what he or she already knows.

All children need to feel that they belong, are accepted, and are valued by parents, teachers, and other students. Everyone benefits socially and academically when the school allots instructional time for students to actively engage in working relationships with their classmates. ●

Parents' Role in the Education of Their Children

Q: What exactly is the role of parents in the education of their children? Many parents claim they do not have the time or energy to do what the teacher herself is supposed to be doing each day in class.

A: The role of parents in education is crucial to the success of their children. The research is clear on this question. Parental involvement makes a positive difference in student achievement and self-esteem. Such involvement also improves the parent–child relationship at home.

With all of these obvious advantages, the issue of what a parent should do to get involved is most important. Suggest these ideas to parents:

- Exercise their choices. Parents have choices in recommending coursework, selecting programs, and even choosing the schools their children attend. They should become informed on the alternatives and take an active role in these critical decisions.

- Visit the campus. A parent's periodic physical presence on campus is important because it indicates to the student and the teachers that they care enough to make an on-site inspection of the learning process.

- Open the lines of communication. Far more important than reading the school's newsletter is direct communication with a child's teacher. Use email or the phone. Although under-utilized, the phone provides an up-to-the-minute "report card" of a child's daily challenges and successes.

- Read aloud to children. Research has shown that reading aloud increases both a child's ability to read and his or her interest in reading. Also encourage a child to read to their parents.

Inform the parents of the importance in being proactive. Parents need not wait for the school to contact them. They can and should make the effort to get involved. The time and energy they spend may well add up to their child's receiving better grades, having an improved attitude toward school, and demonstrating appropriate behavior in class. Let parents know that getting involved is worth the time and energy. The positive results of their efforts will be experienced and enjoyed with their children. ●

How Parents Can Help with Homework

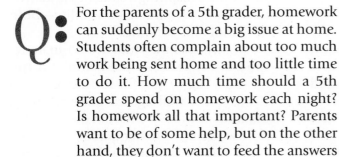

Q: For the parents of a 5th grader, homework can suddenly become a big issue at home. Students often complain about too much work being sent home and too little time to do it. How much time should a 5th grader spend on homework each night? Is homework all that important? Parents want to be of some help, but on the other hand, they don't want to feed the answers to their children.

A: Learning is about time and content. When the amount of time is extended and the content is augmented, the opportunity to learn is increased. Homework is one way of extending time and expanding content.

How much time to spend on homework is the matter of some debate. Some researchers indicate that from 4th to 6th grade, 20 to 40 minutes a day is just about right. Other educators say about 10 minutes per grade level is appropriate. Under this approach, a 1st grader should spend 10 minutes a day and a 7th grader 70 minutes per day. For your 5th grader, we can split the difference at about 45 minutes for each after-school session.

As to the importance of home assignments, let's return to the factors of time and content. Obviously, homework allows more curricular material to be covered, supplemented, and reviewed than on a regular school day. Homework simply expands the clock and the learning experience in a way that asks the student to take on added initiative and responsibility. The student's extra drive and expanded obligation at home should add up, over the long haul, to greater academic achievement.

Never forget that homework demands teamwork. There is a definite shared responsibility in order to offer this greater opportunity for student learning. It should be an axiom of education that teachers, parents, and students form a learning partnership when it comes to homework.

The teacher's role is pretty straightforward. There are three common types of homework a teacher will assign:

• **Preparation:** For example, reading about the life of Thomas Paine may help students prepare for a unit on the American Revolution.

• **Reinforcement:** The idea is to bolster newly acquired skills. Learning longitude and latitude may include finding major cities or mountain ranges using the degree values of a handy geographical grid.

• **Continuation:** Homework may well be an extended program of study. The science project or the term paper that expands on material already covered in class brings depth to learning. Just as it is the teacher's responsibility to make homework relevant, it is equally important for the assignment to be understood by the students. Teachers should consider having students begin certain assignments in class in order to get everyone off on the right foot.

Understanding the "how" of an assignment can be every bit as significant as knowing the "what." Of course, it is the teacher who assigns and explains the homework.

In doing this, the teacher sets everything in motion—as a runner on the first leg of a relay race. Next, the baton is passed to the parent. The involved parent is the second member of our three-way partnership in the educational enterprise known as homework.

Parents can do a number of things to help their child do his or her assignment successfully at home. There are some simple things a parent can do, such as encouraging a child to write down the homework assignments in class, limiting after-school activities to make time for homework, and establishing a specific homework time.

In addition, there are specific ways parents can assist in their child's homework by dialoguing and acting as a resource to the learner. First, the parent can ask the youngster to explain the homework assignment in his or her own words. Second, a parent can suggest and help find sources of information (a trip to the bookstore, a ride to the library, the use of the Internet).

Third, once the information has been gathered, a parent can ask the youngster to summarize the material, once again in the learner's own words. Fourth, it is always important to praise the child's efforts. A parent's endorsement goes a long way toward inspiring a student's initiative, independence, and responsibility—both in school and at home.

Finally, it is the student's ultimate responsibility to snare the baton and run the final leg to the finish line. Given a clean, quiet, well-lighted place to study, the student will benefit from the extended time in terms of better grades, improved study habits, and a healthier, "can do" attitude about learning. ●

Parent Involvement That Pays Off

Q: How do parents go about being actively involved in the education of their children so it really pays off?

A: Indicate to the mother and father of a child that if they are looking for a pay-off, parental participation is the winning ticket. Study after study has shown that parental involvement in a child's education is a highly effective way to increase student achievement while building strong family ties.

The combination of student, parent, and teacher is a powerful learning force that keeps everyone informed, involved, and actively participating in the ultimate goal—a student who builds success on success. Here are ways they can become actively involved with their child's education:

- Have a consistent reading and/or homework time each evening. For preschoolers, this can be a story time when the parent gets to use oral interpretive skills. For older children, this time could be spent reading a high-interest, appropriate-level book.

- Visit one's child while class is in session. This is the best way to have an idea of what a child does at school all day, what a child is learning, and how he or she interacts with the other students and the teacher.

- Ask the teacher for supplementary materials. These materials can be used at home in order to expand on what is being learned in the classroom.

- Reward effort. It is important to reward children while they are in the process of doing good work. The reward lets the child know to keep up with the desired behavior.

- Display a child's work at home. A painting, a salt and flour map, a composition about Christmas, or a successful spelling test can be hung "with honor" with a metal magnet on the refrigerator.

- Keep work doable. When appropriate, help a child divide "tons" of homework into smaller tasks. We learn best in "bitable chunks."

- Ask questions each day about school, homework, or a book the child is reading. Be prepared to have an interesting conversation about what has been learned each day.

The time and effort parents spend becoming involved in their child's education will pay the most rewarding dividends of all. Parents will earn the love and respect of their son or daughter for the help, the encouragement, and the interest they demonstrate for their youngster's constant improvement as a student and as a person. ●

Review a Child's Work to Improve Performance

Q: Parents may well ask you about having their child become successful in a class that you are not teaching. They may well tell you that they do not know how poorly their child is doing until it's "too late." Teachers give homework, assign readings, and administer tests, but they seem to keep problems a big secret from these parents. What can you tell a parent of a child who is not achieving as he or she should?

A: Be straightforward and relate that parents should not wait for report cards, but should instead initiate telephone calls to the teacher, schedule visits to view instruction in the classroom, and make appointments with the teacher. However, even these steps may not be enough to let both the student and the parent in on the "secret" of how well a child is doing in school.

What is needed is a way to expose the work a student is doing, and thus dispose of the secretive nature of grades. As we know, in an effective school the teacher doesn't give grades—the student earns them. Therefore, what is called for is evidence of achievement. A very common bit of evidence is the student's work: essays, projects, homework assignments, quizzes, and examinations. This kind of student work can be found in a portfolio. If this child's teacher is not keeping a portfolio of the typical work the students are accomplishing, request that all work be sent home to the parents so that they can develop a portfolio.

Every week or two, parents should spend 30 minutes reviewing the work with their child. Researchers conclude that a lot of good things can come from such meetings:

- Parents encourage their child to take responsibility for scholastic performances.

- Parents teach their child the process of self-evaluation.

- Parents provide a context in which to improve their child's communication and organizational skills.

- Parents promote an open and honest dialogue with their child concerning the child's number one vocation in this stage of life—that of being a student.

As the child exhibits and explains the work to the parents on a continual basis, their knowledge of *what* the child is doing as well as *how* the child does his or her work will increase. Moreover, the child's understanding of what it takes to be successful in school should become clearer.

As the child comes closer and closer to desired academic goals, a child's self-confidence should grow. As a result, over time the parents should notice their child's continual cognitive development and emotional growth.

Parents are a child's first and most important teachers. When the situation calls for it they should obtain or create a portfolio of the child's work immediately and set up "parent–student conferences" at home on a consistent basis. No more secrets. ●

Families Involved in Classroom Learning Experiences

Q: Could you suggest some ways that families with diverse cultural backgrounds can get involved with the schools so that they can contribute in a concrete way to the education of their children?

A: No one now doubts that parents powerfully influence their children's notions about themselves, their own families, and other groups in a society becoming ever more diverse. Therefore, it would be foolish for any school to ignore the first and most important teachers in a child's life: his or her parents.

Schools should suggest meaningful goals and activities that incorporate the parents' assistance and support directly into the school's curriculum. For instance, a school with a wide diversity of cultures should view the parents as resources in increasing multicultural awareness. Regularly scheduled parental presence in the learning process at school offers the opportunity for all students to see their classmates' parents (as well as their own) interact positively with students and staff.

Parents might also help plan and implement field trips to locations where specific moms and dads have expertise (e.g., museums, natural habitats, and laboratories). Classroom question and answer sessions with various parents from different cultural backgrounds might elicit significant information about cultural beliefs, dress, food, and customs about which a student may have no information, or worse yet—be misinformed. Parents have the power to bring authentic diverse voices into a classroom, which can build bridges of knowledge to other students by means of direct human interaction.

When a school assignment features the families of students, such wonderful coursework as oral history projects (interviewing relatives) or creating original books (photographs and documents of relatives) depends on the contributions of family members. These kinds of family oriented oral history projects and family photo and document albums can become an important part of the curriculum. When students find out about the folkways, customs, and traditions of their own families, they find out more about themselves. Knowledge of this kind can be an essential building block to a child's enhanced self-esteem.

Correspondingly, knowledge about other cultures represented by a diverse group of parents can lead to more than just tolerance. It could well show the way to respect and love others. Parents and teachers working together to build a curriculum in which diverse knowledge is shared by the active participation of the students' family members is a strong learning model. Family involvement in education is all about implementing a plan to use our greatest learning resource, family members. ●

Specific Kinds of Family Involvement Really Work

Q: Everyone assumes parent involvement helps the child become a better student in school. Specifically, what kinds of parent involvement in a child's education really make a difference?

A: To begin, we should focus more on "family" involvement rather than just "parent" involvement. Many times, the contact person in charge of child's education isn't necessarily the mother or father, but perhaps a grandmother or grandfather, or even an older sister or older brother.

The point is, whoever that extended family member may be, that person should enter into a kind of compact with the school that the education of a child is a shared responsibility. Due to the mutual nature of this agreement, it is important to delineate those practices that research has shown to be truly effective.

The following five types of family-involvement endeavors constitute specific components which can lead to a child's academic success and social development.

1. High expectations: Attitude affects efficacy. Those family members who translate their expectations to a child will reap what they sow. Lofty expectations point the way to towering results. By the way, this is a double-edged sword. A family's low expectations for the child can be just as powerful a self-fulfilling prophecy.

2. Controlled environment: A clean, well-lighted, quiet place to study is critical. Combining an appropriate learning space with a routine time and with the television turned off can lead to focused academic pursuit (homework) which extends the learning day.

3. Joint learning activities: Taking time to learn as a family places a value on education. When the family decides to read together, take a trip together, or simply to discuss a book or a movie together, higher-order critical thinking skills may be stirred and future academic success can clearly be facilitated.

4. A stimulating home environment: Quite simply, the home should be a place full of opportunities to improve literacy (i.e., the immediate availability of appropriate reading materials) and social skills. Learning is all about opportunity. What a child learns is directly tied to the environment in which he or she is raised.

5. Emphasis on effort: Creating ability, like life itself, is a try–fail, try–fail, try–succeed endeavor. A family who teaches the child the value of effort in learning and respect for others will stimulate the ultimate goals of enhanced academic achievement and social growth.

The productive nurturing of a child is a collective endeavor implemented by caring human beings. Accordingly, the day-to-day formal instruction of a youngster is largely dependent on a special agreement among the parents (and/or extended family members) and the school to assume a mutual responsibility for the child's education. ●

Parents' Role in Science and Math Education

Q: What are some things that parents can do to make sure that their youngsters receive high-quality science and math classes?

A: The key is for parents to insist that their children are presented with the most enriched science and math curriculum. In this way their youngsters will be challenged intellectually as they prepare for a life of self-directed learning. In addition, competent and caring instruction by enthusiastic teachers is vital in order to set an environment in which student effort is appreciated and the intrinsic fascination of math and science is experienced daily through hands-on experiences.

Students learn science and math best by hands-on activities. Here are some ideas about getting the most out of science and math courses that you can directly communicate to parents:

- Investigate which local colleges offer summer math and science programs for children kindergarten through 12th grade.
- Visit museums that emphasize science exhibits and offer programs for school-age children.

- Visit a local library for books and entertaining science- or math-related projects.
- Click on the TV and watch *NOVA*, Bill Nye—The Science Guy, *National Geographic* Specials—and be sure and watch them (thank goodness for the VCR!) with your youngsters.
- Visit bookstores or even toy stores and look for books with math puzzles and science activities done with everyday home items.

Knowledge of math and science is an important factor in the intellectual and social growth of all children. Parents, as the first and most important teachers in a child's life, have a particularly important role to play.

The future is being dictated by science and mathematics as demonstrated by new technologies. With a knowledge and appreciation of science and math, today's children will be able to shape their future. They will become adults able to make decisions in a technological society as informed citizens. ●

How to Tell Youngsters about the World of Work

Q: What is the best way to tell youngsters about the real world of work around them? Some schools have a career day and others may even have apprenticeship programs, but aren't there better ways? These career days and apprenticeship programs seem to be either a one-shot deal or only apply to a small minority of students. Should careers be mentioned more often in school?

A: There is an approach in which teachers introduce career concepts into their daily teaching activities. It is called the infusion approach, which means that career concepts are integrated into the curriculum across all grade levels and in all subjects. Teachers connect activities in the classroom with the changing labor market.

The regular classroom teachers plan career development concepts and strate-gies into their everyday teaching activities. The goal is to have informed students who transfer specific job information, knowledge, and skills into various career opportunities.

Of course, there are a number of steps for the student to take on the path to a career choice. Students are encouraged to examine and judge their school performance. They then can identify in which areas they feel most competent.

Accordingly, students can observe the world of work through job shadowing (following a professional at a job site). The idea is for the student to move away from the one-day, one-time, or one-unit curriculum career course.

In a dynamic and ever-changing world economy, a school-to-work career emphasis in every subject, every day, seems like quite a sensible notion. ●

SUGGESTED READINGS

Brown, L. J. (2001). Networking with the community. *School Business Affairs, 67*(5), 23–26. (EJ 629 307)

Carroll, D. J. (2001). Respecting the grapevine. *Principal Leadership, 2*(1), 21–23.

Christenson, S. L., & Sheridan, S. M. (2001). *Schools and families: Creating essential connections for learning.* New York: Guilford Press.

Comer, J. (Ed.). (1999). *Child by child: The Comer process for change in education.* New York: Teachers College Press.

Cutler, W. W. (2000). *Parents and schools: The 150-year struggle for control in American education.* Chicago: University of Chicago Press.

Deily, M.-E. P. (2001, March 28). Poll: Words, actions fail to match on public engagement. *Education Week, 20*(28), 12.

Dodd, A. W., & Konzal, J. L. (2002). *How communities build stronger schools: Stories, strategies, and promising practices for educating every child.* New York: Palgrave Macmillan.

Epstein, J. L. (2001). *School, family and community partnerships: Preparing educators and improving schools.* Boulder, CO: Westview Press.

Fichtman Dana, N. F., & Yendol-Hoppey, D. (2003). *The reflective educator's guide to classroom research: Learning to teach and teaching to learn through practitioner inquiry.* Thousand Oaks, CA: Corwin Press.

Hiatt-Michael, D. (Ed.). (2001). *Promising practices for family involvement in school.* Greenwich, CT: Information Age.

Hornby, G. (2000). *Improving parental involvement.* New York: Cassell.

Kralovec, E., & Buell, J. (2000). *The end of homework: How homework disrupts families, overburdens children, and limits learning.* Boston: Beacon Press.

Lopez, G. R., Scribner, J. D., & Mahitivanichcha, K. (2001). Redefining parental involvement: Lessons from high-performing migrant-impacted schools. *American Educational Research Journal, 38*(2), 253–88.

Power, B., & Bagley, M. (Eds.). (1999). *Parent power: Energizing home-school communication.* Portsmouth, NH: Heinemann.

Stipek, D., & Seal, K. (2001). *Motivated minds: Raising children to love learning.* New York: H. Holt.

Vincent, C. (2000). *Including parents?: Education, citizenship, and parental agency.* Philadelphia: Open University.

Whitley, M. D. (2001). *Bright minds, poor grades.* New York: Perigee.

Glossary

acculturation the process of learning another's language and culture in order to successfully function socially in more than one society; the desired outcome of bilingual education.

ADD attention deficit disorder.

ADHD attention deficit hyperactivity disorder.

andragogy a theory and methodological approach geared specifically to teaching adults.

at-risk the state of being in danger of failing, and/or of dropping out; most children are at-risk at some time or another.

bilingual education a curricular approach for any student engaged in learning a second language in which both the first (native) language and second (target) language are used for instruction. The goal for all students is to become biliterate and bicultural.

charter schools learning institutions that reflect their originators' varied philosophies and curricular and methodological approaches. Charter schools can be exempt from various state and district rules and regulations.

cooperative learning a particular teaching strategy that involves learners' participation by promoting positive interaction in small groups.

critical thinking skills one's ability as expressed by analysis, synthesis, and evaluation to collect, judge, and ultimately use information in an effective manner.

culture of the classroom the learned behavior and the psychological processes through which students in the classroom conceptualize their role as learners. The classroom culture emanates from the teacher as model.

de-tracking to transform a traditional homogenous grouping of students (based on perceived ability) to a heterogeneous model in order to present all students the most enriched curriculum.

diversity a central characteristic of the U.S. educational experience in which the combinations of gender, ethnicity, race, socioeconomic condition, and culture in students create great variety.

dyslexia a reading disorder evidenced by persons of otherwise normal intellect who have not learned to read even though they have been exposed to sufficient instruction.

ebonics a form of nonstandard English having roots in the languages of West Africa. "Ebonics" literally means "black sounds."

gender bias inequality in educational opportunity due to sexual categorization that promotes subsequent unequal treatment and ultimately results in unequal educational outcomes.

gifted student a learner with specific abilities and traits who demonstrates high ability. A multidimensional view of intelligence is indicated to create an inclusive learning environment for all learners.

historically underrepresented students those societal groups with a traditionally disproportionately low number of students at the collegiate level, namely African American and Latino learners.

integrated language arts approach a curriculum that cultivates students' experiences across the subject areas of language, science, social studies, fine arts, and mathematics. Multiple forms of curricular representation create an atmosphere in which the world is presented and understood through various activities (e.g., speaking, writing, listening, reading, drawing, computing, dancing). These links among language-based activities enable learners to learn about and through language.

motivation a student's desire to participate in the learning process. Teachers are responsible to set a scholastic and caring environment through modeling and communication of expectations to set the conditions for the student's conscious decision to learn.

multicultural education a psychodynamic, behavioral, and humanistic learning experience emanating from distinct racial/ethnic groups within a culture.

multiple intelligences Howard Gardner's proposed way of thinking of intelligence under eight different categories, each demonstrating a certain kind of learning (linguistic, logical/mathematical, visual/spatial, musical, bodily/kinesthetic, naturalist, interpersonal, and intrapersonal).

oral history a social science project that preserves a segment of the recent past by using the eyes and ears of those who actually lived through the experiences. Accounts of these experiences are given to the student who records and reports the voices of primary sources.

parent and/or family involvement the child's first and most important teachers (i.e., parents) supporting their children. This may include direct instruction in the home (e.g., helping with homework), while staying within the school's "information loop" to best assist their children's academic development and social growth.

performance assessment an approach that evaluates a learner's activities by requiring the student to create an answer or product that demonstrates skill or knowledge.

retention the practice of having a student repeat a grade due to lack of academic achievement. A poor educational practice because there is a serious risk that retained students will be harmed—with no consistent evidence of long-term benefits. Swift remediation for students who are falling behind by means of a wide variety of methodological approaches is recommended.

scaffolds support mechanisms (modeling, synthesizing, etc.) to help students better understand what is being taught.

SDAIE (specially designed academic instruction in English) teaching the language of instruction in a content course through scaffolding.

service learning learning activities that involve students in community service projects, which emanate from the class curriculum. It functions as a philosophy of education by demonstrating the belief that education should develop students who become involved in their community in a socially responsible way. Moreover, it performs as an instructional methodology, creating a blend of service projects, based on indigenous community needs, with the academic curriculum through active engagement.

sexual harassment a specific kind of verbal or physical conduct, sexual in nature, which subjects a person to unfair treatment.

social promotion the practice of promoting a student based on age, regardless of academic achievement. As with retention, it is a poor educational practice.

standardized tests examinations that are designed to give a common measure of students' performance. This common "yardstick" reveals to evaluators the degree to which school programs are successful, while providing information concerning the skills and abilities of today's students.

standards a framework for curriculum development based on a sequenced set of identified topics of study, in order to judge curricula and evaluate the quality of student achievement.

test bias unfairness that is present when a question on an exam is answered differently by individuals of the same ability who come from different cultural, ethnic, class, gender, or religious groups.

tracked schools schools that offer different curricular tracks (one academically superior, the other academically inferior) based on a student's perceived ability.

Index